GW01149557

BEACH HOLIDAYS

FROM PORTUGAL TO ISRAEL

BEACH HOLIDAYS

~~~~~~~~~~~~~~~~~~~~~~~~~~~~~~~~~~~

FROM PORTUGAL TO ISRAEL

by Melvin and Anita Benarde

ILLUSTRATED

DODD, MEAD & COMPANY

NEW YORK

Maps and drawings are by Anita Benarde.
Photographs are reproduced through the courtesy of:
British Airways, pages 10, 62, 163, 222; Heyward Associates, Inc., page 11.

Copyright © 1974 by Melvin and Anita Benarde

All rights reserved

No part of this book may be reproduced in any form without permission in writing from the publisher

ISBN: 0-396-06891-X
Library of Congress Catalog Card Number: 73-17867
PRINTED IN THE UNITED STATES OF AMERICA

Gather a shell from the strown beach
    And listen at its lips: they sigh
    The same desire and mystery,
The echo of the whole sea's speech.
            The Sea-Limits
            D. G. Rossetti

Foreword

Over the past three years we have basked, swum, combed and poked around on beaches from Portugal to Israel. They are numerous and they are different: sandy, rocky, stony, golden, tan, brown, black, barren, tree-shaded and more. They offer a range of accommodations from camping sites to luxury villas, and they are excellent bases from which to explore a country.

To get the data needed, we traveled with our three teenagers—Scott, (University of Massachusetts, Amherst), Andi (University of Delaware), and Dana (Princeton High). From our collective research, we know that beaches are not equally suitable for families, young marrieds, older couples, singles and teenagers. We know which are and we have tried to tell it all.

As there was a world to cover, we often parted. Scott and a photographer friend, Craig Wolfe went off to investigate the new Riviera in France, as well as some of the resorts in Turkey. Dana and Andi usually traveled with us. Without the girls our horizons would have been severely restricted. It's amazing what two teen-age lovelies can do by way of gathering information in a hotel, restaurant, disco, or just lying on the sand in the sun. It was obvious that a beach could not be adequately described by one person. As a "working party" we were able to learn what a place has or doesn't have.

Although a family cannot write a book, everything I wrote was submitted for approval, suggestions and corrections. We also agreed on the beaches to include and exclude. And our decisions were by no means capricious. We used three criteria. The first, was meant to make the book less than encyclopedic. Consequently, the North African coast was an early casualty. Secondly, a beach was not simply sand with water lapping its shore. It had to have adequate accommodations as well as places of interest within a reasonable distance. Finally, we wanted to bring new and uncrowded beaches to the attention of American vacationers. This will explain our choice of the French and Italian beaches. As to the Greek islands, they are so numerous that we intend to write a separate book on them.

Part of the romance of the Mediterranean and travel abroad will be planes and trains that are late, shortcuts over roads that can dismantle a car, and toilets that do not work. The list of minor aggravations is long and events difficult to anticipate. The idea is to see other ways of life without drawing harsh comparisons—at least not until you've returned home, and thought it over.

With these few caveats, we wish you "bon voyage," and ask you to write us about the places we've recommended.

—MELVIN A. BENARDE
Princeton, New Jersey

Contents

PORTUGAL: THE ALGARVE 1

  Climate; Transportation; Accommodations; Beaches: Lagos, Praia da Rocha, Praia dos Tres Irmaos, Carvoeiro, Armação de Pêra, Albufeira, Quarteira; Places of Interest; Shopping; Food and Drink

SPAIN 34

  Transportation; Accommodations; Beaches: Costa de la Luz, Costa del Sol, Costa Blanca, Costa del Azahar, Costa Dorada, Costa Brava; Shopping; Food and Drink

FRANCE: THE NEW RIVIERA 82

  Climate; Transportation; Beaches: Leucate-Barcarès, Cap d'Agde, Saint-Cyprien Plage, Collioure, La Grande Motte; Places of Interest

THE ITALIAN ISLANDS: SARDINIA AND ELBA 96

  SARDINIA — Climate; Transportation; Beaches: Costa Smeralda, The Southern Coast; Places of Interest; Shopping; Food and Drink

ELBA — Climate; Transportation; Beaches: Portoferraio-Biodola, Procchio, Marina di Campo, Cavoli, Capoliveri and Porto Azzurro; Places of Interest; Food and Drink

MALTA   131

Climate; Transportation; Beaches: Malta, Gozo; Places of Interest; Food and Drink

YUGOSLAVIA   151

Climate; Transportation; Camping; Beaches: Dubrovnik, Montenegro and South, Ulcinj; Places of Interest; Food and Drink

TURKEY   181

Climate; Transportation; Camping; Izmir; Beaches: Foça, Çeşme, Kuşadasi, Bodrum and Marmaris, Antalya, Alanya, and Mersin; Food and Drink

CYPRUS   217

Climate; Transportation; Beaches: Famagusta, Kyrenia, Paphos, Limassol, Larnaca, Cape Andreas; Places of Interest; Shopping; Food and Drink

ISRAEL   237

Climate; Transportation; Beaches: Ashkelon to Tel Aviv, The Sharon, Caesarea, The Carmel; Shopping; Food and Drink

GOVERNMENT TOURIST OFFICES   263

INDEX   265

BEACH HOLIDAYS

FROM PORTUGAL TO ISRAEL

Prices quoted in this book are given so that readers can judge comparative costs of accommodations and traveling expenses. With inflation and fluctuations in international currency rates, prices will probably change in coming seasons.

THE ALGARVE

ONE HUNDRED EIGHTY-FIVE MILES due south of Lisbon, some four to five hours by car or thirty minutes by plane is the Algarve coast. Called Al Gharb by the Moors who occupied the area for hundreds of years, this "garden of Portugal," with its seemingly endless ribbon of golden beaches and secluded coves, stretches away to the Spanish border.

In the hundred miles from Cabo de São Vicente (Cape St. Vincent) in the west—the most southwesterly point in Europe—to Monte Gordo in the east are scores of fishing villages and small towns whose exquisite beaches beckon the traveler seeking relaxation in sun and surf.

Climate. From January to December, the air temperature in the Algarve varies from a low of 50° F. to a high of 82° F. Through the winter, December through March, the temperature averages 56° F., and the balmy climate brings the almond trees into snow-white blossom in January. During June, July, and August, the heat is tempered by off-shore breezes.

In winter, although the water temperature rarely falls below 56° F., it is a little too chilly for most Americans. The Swedes apparently think this is marvelous, as they flock here during February, March, and April. In summer, the temperature of the sea averages a delightful 68° F.

Transportation. The southern coast of Portugal has inherited its angular whitewashed buildings, orange groves, and distinctive filigreed chimneys from north Africa.

The Moors, who conquered Portugal early in the eighth century, were not expelled until 1249. This five-hundred-year occupation left an imprint that can still be seen today in the facial structure and sharp penetrating eyes of the Algarvians, as well as in their culture and architecture. Their dark clothing is in stark contrast to the brightness and color of their homes and other buildings.

The Algarve is actually two quite distinct areas; to the west, the Barlavento consists of rocky crags carved out by the waves, sandy beaches studded with giant rocks, and half-hidden caves. To the east, the Sotavento, the coastline, backed by aromatic pine woods, is an endless series of golden beaches, with abundant shellfish.

It's easy to get there. From New York, TAP (Transportes Aereos Portugueses) has daily flights to Lisbon with connections for the thirty-minute flight to Faro, capital of the Algarve. TWA and Pan-American fly into Lisbon on a regular weekly schedule. From London, BEA (British European Airways) has several daily two-hour flights to Lisbon, as well as daily flights to Faro, the capital of the Algarve. In the spring of 1974, BEA and BOAC will merge to form the super airline, BA—British Airways.

Lisbon is a major port-of-call for any number of major and minor steamship lines; and it is connected to the main capitals of Europe by comfortable express trains. Unfortunately, if you like trains as much as Anita does, it is an iffy six or seven hour all too often sweltering trip from Lisbon to Lagos or Faro. Again, unfortunately, the train schedules were not planned with the vacationer in mind—at least not the one who prefers to sleep in the morning. Trains leave daily at about 8 A.M. For those who require speed, BEA (BA) and TAP have daily jet flights that whisk you off to

Mini ferry between Portugal and Spain.

Faro in about thirty-one minutes; twenty-nine, if the wind is right. But for us, the way to go is by car.

Plan on a five to six hour drive (including at least one rest stop for lunch) through the slow, winding section of Portugal's extensive cork-tree belt and rice fields.

If you are coming from Spain by car, don't expect a fast trip to the Algarve. Although Spanish roads are fair to good for the most part, much of the driving will be over mountains or along the coast and therefore fairly slow. Expect hairpin turns and narrow roads winding around mountains and sides of cliffs.

You may drive inland from Badajoz, Spain, to Évora in Portugal, then south to Beja, and from there pick up the N2 into Faro, but the more direct approach is from Seville and Ayamonte. At Ayamonte drive directly through the town to the ferry pier. Here, you'll be in for a passport check and will need to purchase a ticket for the ten minute crossing on the tiny ferry. Because the ferries can take only three, six, or eight cars at a time, and crossways at that, you may have a short wait.

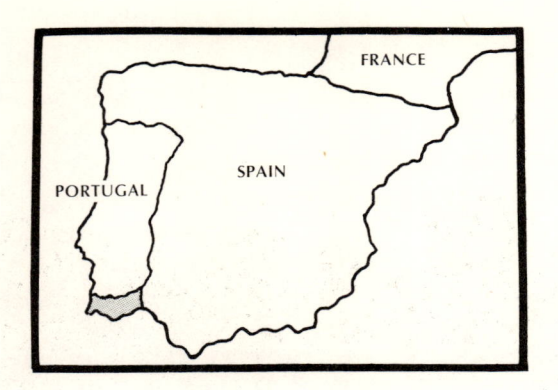

PORTUGAL

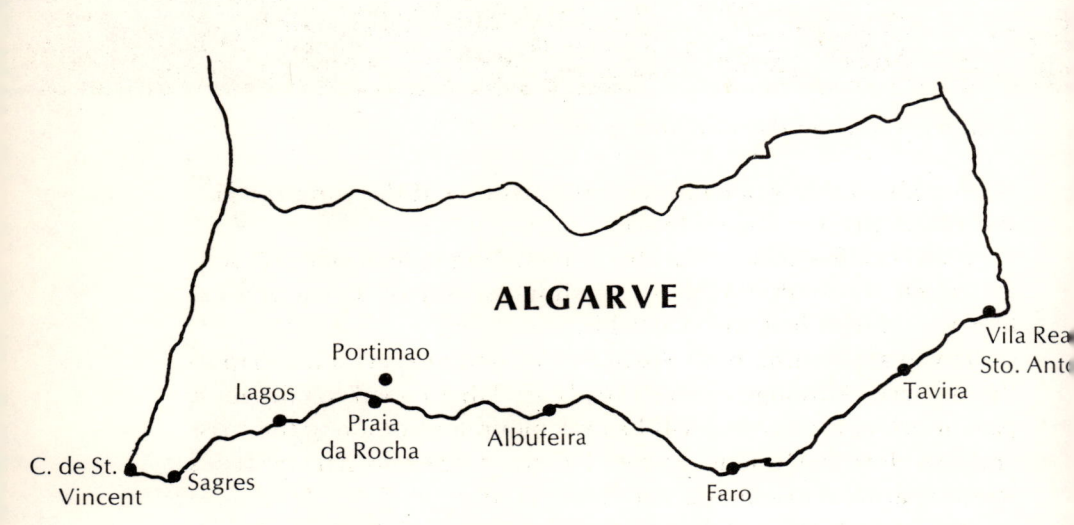

SPAIN

FRANCE

ALGARVE

C. de St. Vincent
Sagres
Lagos
Portimao
Praia da Rocha
Albufeira
Faro
Tavira
Vila Real Sto. Anto

Accommodations. Throughout Portugal, the Director-General of Tourism has established standards for various levels and types of service in the accommodations offered to tourists. There are no less than thirteen types of accommodation available in the country, ranging from luxury hotels with a four-star designation to second-class pensions. Below hotel accommodations—in price—are the estalagems, state-certified but privately owned inns, in two classes, luxury and standard.

One special group of hotels is referred to as the "Five Sisters." They are hardly quintuplets; rather, their kinship is one of class. The Sisters—Hotel Algarve in Praia da Rocha, Penina Golf Hotel in Montes de Alvor, Hotel Dona Filipa in Vale de Lobo, Hotel Da Balaia in Albufeira, and Hotel Alvor Praia in Alvor—are all five-star deluxe hotels. They are scattered the length of the Algarve, and although they bear little resemblance to one another, they are an agreeable quintet.

When you are a guest at one of these hotels, any of the others will be delighted to serve your full-pension luncheon or dinner. All you need do is ask for an exchange voucher at the reception desk of your hotel. This arrangement allows you to roam the Algarve without the limitation of the sound of the lunch or dinner bell. And you can be sure that each of the Sisters is eminently capable of setting an august table.

By the way, in all types of accommodation, full board or full pension means room, lunch, dinner, and breakfast, while half pension includes room, breakfast, and one main meal—lunch or dinner, whichever you specify in advance.

In trying to upgrade its standard of accommodation, the government has itself become a hosteler. The pousadas (the word comes from repose or rest places) are inns run by the state. However, the word inn must be used loosely. The recently opened pousada in Estremoz, although only twenty-three rooms, is nothing short of pure luxury. Each pousada is as representative as possible of the region in which it is located. The pousada at Sagres, for example, is perched on a cliff overlooking the sea, while the pousada of São Brás de Alportel sits amid the Algarve's almond orchards. In addition, the inns serve the regional food specialties.

Because these inns are so inexpensive, and are such desirable places to stay, they are in great demand. Visits are restricted to not more than five days at any one time. Of course, this means making reservations a good bit in advance of your planned visit.

To round out the full complement of accommodations, Residências (private homes) can usually be rented for at least a month; some can be had by the week.

Three levels of pensions—luxury, first-, and second-class—are generally available in most areas. Lists of these can be obtained from the Portuguese Tourist Office in New York City, or at the tourist office in Lisbon or Portimão, if you prefer to wait until you get to the Algarve. Even though we have met a number of people who dote on traveling without prior reservations, we strongly recommend that in this area, especially between June and September, reservations be made well in advance. Demand is far greater than the number of rooms available.

Finally, a relatively new type of accommodation has become available. These are the high-rise, fully equipped apartments, whose weekly or monthly price includes electricity, water, and gas as well as maid service and laundry (for apartment linen). The Aquazul, with 73 apartments in Praia de Rocha and 102 in Lagos, is an example of this type of accommodation.

We found the apartments attractively furnished in contemporary design. We all liked the idea of having a refrigerator so we could chill the succulent peaches and other local fruits and eat them cold any time we pleased. Although many Portuguese hotels do not provide a radio or TV in rooms, even in the most expensive hotels, these apartments have a television room as well as game rooms, cocktail and lunch bars, and an elegant dining room. It goes without saying that both food and service were excellent, but then one comes to expect this throughout Portugal.

Because these apartments are so well set up for families and because of their relatively low cost (about $70 per week for two people), at the height of the July-September season they are in great demand. Reservations for these apartments can be made by writing directly to Edificio Aquazul or Edificio Intercal, Praia da

Rocha. However, you can also do as we did; allow TAP airlines to make all the arrangements for you.

BEACHES

The Algarve beaches—some curve for miles along the margin of a bay, others are miniature in size—win accolades not just for their beauty, but for their setting. Small fishing villages, melon-green water, flower-scented hills, fine hotels, and the Algarvian way of life. Carved by the sea in curious shapes, the soaring, honey-colored cliffs that ring many of the beaches are unsurpassed anywhere.

Most beaches of the Algarve, quiet and relaxed, are pleasantly different from the bustling cosmopolitan atmosphere of Cascais and Estoril. Many tiny, secluded coves offer almost total isolation, and there are grottos and caves for those interested in exploration. The surf is calm and safe throughout the year, ideal for youngsters as well as those who really want to swim. No undercurrents here.

Although there are several beaches along the Algarvian coast that stretch for a quarter mile, even a mile of golden, almost powdery fine sand, many measure only a few hundred yards between tree-topped cliffs. Few are ever crowded; in fact, you may often be alone. More often than not, a 200-yard miniature beach will be shared by no more than a dozen people.

Lagos. South from Lisbon, the N120 ends at Lagos. For most people Lagos seems to be a landmark because of the traffic circle where the N120 is exchanged for the N125 and the final leg of the trip to Praia da Rocha and Portimão. But Lagos shouldn't be just a place to drive through. It has a number of first-rate beaches.

At least a dozen miniature beaches grace the five to six miles of coast around the town. By most standards, Dona Ana, Camilo, Leixdo da Cruz, Barranco Martinho, Canarial, Estudantes, and Pinhão are small. Few are more than three hundred yards long and thirty to forty yards wide. But all are fascinating in their location and character.

One of the most extraordinary is Praia da Camilo. Honey-colored cliffs, two-hundred-feet high, form a backdrop to it and give the beach privacy. Only those who really care will follow the trail down to bask, bathe, and boat here.

A bit easier of access and not as isolated is the picturesque Dona Ana beach. In the same general vicinity around another bend are Estudantes and Pinhão, both the result of the sea's relentless biting away of the surrounding cliffs.

A large stretch of sandy beach that is away from the others and lacks the Algarve's characteristic cliffs is Meia Praia. Just east of Lagos, a well-marked side road leads off to the left. Meia Praia, less than a mile down this road, is a quiet, undeveloped half-mile expanse of fine beige-colored sand, fringing the Bay of Lagos. This is a great place to perfect water-skiing techniques. If you're a snorkeler, there's lots to see.

Luckily, hotels have not yet been built on these beaches. Most require a fairly good walk or hitch. Several hotels in town provide transportation to and from the beaches.

Lagos has an old center and a new periphery. These are first-class apartments such as the Aquazul for those who prefer to set up housekeeping, and there are several good second-class hotels such as the Golfinho, on a cliff above Dona Ana beach, and the sixty-six-room Meia Praia, directly across and facing a flat sandy beach that bears its name. This is a quiet, family-type hotel that caters to young children. The moderately priced fifty-six-room Hotel São Cristôvão on the Rossio de São João, offers glorious views of the wide bay.

A number of first-class A and B residências can be found close to the beaches. For example, Pensão Residência Sol e Praia is only a short walk from the cement steps leading down to the beach at Dona Ana.

Although Lagos has not become a watering place for students, many do come here to get away from such centers. Relatively inexpensive lodgings can be found in the old town near open-air cafés and within easy walking or hitching distance from the beaches.

Because Lagos is an important fishing port, it is a particularly good place to watch the comings and goings of the colorful fleet, as well as a good place to buy and eat fresh fin and shell fish.

Between Portimão and Albufeira, a distance of some eighteen miles, there are twenty-eight beaches. Each has its own character. Just take any turn off to the right, when heading east out of Portimão (left when heading west from Albufeira) on the N125, and you'll come to a beach, with or without a village. Three considerations may influence your decision as to which is for you: do you prefer lots of people, a handful, or none at all? Do you want accommodations on the site, or are you only interested in a particular beach on a particular day? There is a beach for every mood, so take your choice.

Praia da Rocha. Although Praia da Rocha could be considered an example of a fairly large beach that is both public and private and uncrowded, except on Sundays, it's too unusual to be an example of anything.

The beach is perhaps a mile long, the full length of the Avenida Marginal, Praia's main street. Praia da Rocha means, loosely, Rocky Beach. But rocks are nowhere in sight. The "rocks" are in fact the scattered remains of the cliffs that escaped being completely nibbled away by an unceasing sea. These irregularly shaped golden rocks are from ten to fifty feet high. They make an incredible spectacle studded on the sand and in the water. Not only do their shadows offer shade in the heat of the day, but they are great fun to dive off, swim around, or just sit on for the view.

A wall of golden, weatherbeaten cliff forms a gently curving margin around the beach. From the Avenida Marginal at the top of the cliffs, a series of steps winds down to the sandy beach. The water at its edge is a shimmering golden green.

Although Praia da Rocha must be numbered among the world's great beaches, it is not great for surfing. And this is true of all the Algarve beaches, generally. Water skiing and boating, yes, but surfing, emphatically no. The water is just too calm. Of course, the swimming is nothing short of great.

The scene is greatly enhanced by the many nations represented. In the next beach chair you may hear French, Swedish, Dutch, German, or Italian. And you'll certainly hear "*Raja Fruta*," the cry of the Portuguese ice cream vendor walking the beach. Most of

Praia da Rocha's golden beach.

these people are friendly and anxious to meet Americans. They often speak English, and the beach offers ready-made opportunities for conversation.

Unless you're familiar with the back roads around Alvor, you'll come into Praia da Rocha through Portimão, the center of the canned fish industry, as well as its entertainment capital. If you drive in to Praia da Rocha, just as the town's only policeman is directing weekend traffic, you'll have a good opportunity to view the beach and almost the full length of the main street.

Although there are a number of hotels in town, two are outstanding. Hotel Júpiter, a four-star accommodation, has 144 rooms. The most expensive, with full pension during the high season, is less than $20 a day for two. In addition, state law requires that children up to eight receive a 50 percent rate reduction when occupying their parents' room. By the way, all hotels in Portugal add on a service charge of 10 percent and a tax of 3.1 percent in tourist areas.

The Júpiter, because of its central location, and because it has a bowling alley, sells foreign newspapers, has a Guerin car rental agency as well as a *cambio* (money exchange), is a bustling place. Teenagers have found this one of the best spots to congregate, especially from seven to ten P.M.

Hotel Algarve, one of the "Five Sisters," is a short walk from the Júpiter. The entrance to the hotel is right on the Avenida Marginal. Walk into the lobby and through several large, well-appointed common rooms to its terrace. From this vantage point you can appreciate its strategic setting on the cliff side. Its two hundred rooms, each with a recessed balcony, face the sea, and the view of the beach is panoramic and breathtaking.

The area of beach directly below the hotel is reserved solely for its guests. This is just about the only place on the entire beach that chairs, lounges, and sunshades are not available to the public. For a hotel guest on a crowded Sunday in August, this can be most convenient. Hotel Algarve has it all: elegant service, excellent food, fine accommodations, and beautiful location.

It may be well to reiterate that along the mile of beach are a

Hotel Algarve is on a curving cliff overlooking the beach at Praia da Rocha.

number of sunshade sites that are open to everyone. If you find a spot you particularly like, you may reserve it for a week or two at a time—and no one will take your place should you leave for an extended lunch. All you need do is look for the men with *Salvador* written on their T-shirts. *Salvador* is not only the lifeguard, but also the concessionaire. And speaking of lifeguards, take note of the tall bamboo flagpoles staked out at intervals along the beach. Although you'll see the green flag flying on most days from June through the end of September, watch for the red flag which means danger—no swimming until the flag comes down.

During the weeks we spent on the beaches, we saw only the green (swim freely) flag draped limply around the pole or flapping in the breeze. One afternoon, however, I noticed a chart near the *Salvador*'s stand that showed three flags: green, white, and red. On inquiry, I learned that the white means no swimming; the red, no bathing at all. Apparently, they differentiate between bathing, going in the water to cool off, and swimming, going out beyond where you can stand.

Because I couldn't understand how water in this area could be dangerous at any time, I sought answers. A few questions in the right places produced the information that a formidable warm wind, the Levanter (akin to a sirocco or mistral), blows in every so often for two, four, or seven days at a time, producing high waves and fast, rough water. People who don't believe the color signals can get tumbled and hurt. When we were there, however, the swimming was nothing short of great. As in the rest of the Algarve, the sea bottom is firm, smooth sand.

Praia da Rocha is a quiet resort; its main activity, besides swimming and sunning, is strolling. The nightly promenade up and down the Avenida Marginal, with window shopping and talking, is about as much excitement as the town offers.

Swingers will find discotheques in Albufeira or Faro—twenty and forty minutes away, respectively. It isn't even necessary to have your own car or motor bike; buses for both towns regularly leave from Praia or Portimão. Don't forget taxis—they are inexpensive and easily available. One woman told us she traveled the entire Algarve by taxi, to and fro, even stopping in rental offices for information on apartments. The entire day's fee, including a generous tip, was less than twenty-five dollars.

In addition to the deluxe hotels, there are three four-star estalagems and several pensãos, whose prices are moderate to low—well below the hotels. For example, Estalagem Mira Sol has thirty-eight rooms, all with private bath facilities. These are available, if you reserve early. Since the rooms cost about $15 per night for two, with full board, they don't go begging. Estalagem De São Jose across the street, with its terrace dining room above street level, is just a short walk from the beach. It has a bar, tobacco shop (which sells a number of other items), *cambio*, and twenty-five guest rooms, twenty-four of which have private bath. You have the option in these estalagems of having meals there or not.

Pensão Solar Pinguim on the Avenida Marginal, owned by an English family, offers magnificent sea views from its clifftop location. Eight of its sixteen rooms have private bath facilities, and unlike most pensãos, it has food service and a bar.

Praia dos Três Irmãos. While walking the beach at Praia da Rocha we met an American couple of Portuguese extraction who suggested we see the Hotel Alvor Praia. One afternoon while in Portimão, we decided to drive over. It is located two miles from Portimão, on the Beach of the Three Brothers (Praia dos Três Irmãos). This 215-room hotel, another of the "Five Sisters," must rank with the most handsome. The grounds are spacious and well tended, flowers are everywhere, and the grass is all but manicured. The view of the beach from the pool high above, is remarkable. Because of its design and location, this beach is quite private. A bend in the cliffs separates it from the remaining ten miles of Three Brothers Beach, which skirts the coastline from Alvor almost to Lagos.

An even more agreeable surprise came when we entered the hotel. We thought we had seen beautiful hotels—but we did not expect to find one such as this tucked away on a corner of the Portuguese coast. I knew also I had found a great swimming hole when, walking out into the surf up to my armpits, I could look down and see my toes.

Perched as it is on a promontory above the beach, the Alvor has a commanding view in all directions. Until two years ago, the only view was the blue-green sea and the uninterrupted sands stretching as far as the eye can see. With the erection of the Torralta complex there's been a major change. The Torralta is a series of five high-rise apartment buildings, a number of one- and two-bedroom villas, Hotel Don João Secundo, several restaurants, a cafeteria, bars, shops, a discotheque, and a large pool. We all agreed this is a great place for teenagers. Families can come here knowing that their children will have enough company to keep them happily occupied.

The Torralta complex is not simply a lot of buildings thoughtlessly thrown together. The grounds are well landscaped, and all facilities are integrated within a master plan, which calls for an additional twenty-five high-rises and hotels spread along five miles of beach. Because the beach is so long and wide, and because care has gone into the planning, I have no fears that this will deteriorate into a Coney Island or a Torremolinos in the next ten years.

The beach is one of the few in the Algarve that doesn't require a walk down from a cliff. This one is level, with dunes breaking the line of sight. On the most crowded Sunday in August, you can find at least three miles of beach to yourself by walking two to three hundred yards past the farthest building.

For rental information on the Torralta Apartments write directly to Torralta Club International de Ferias Conjunto Turistico, Praia de Alvor, Algarve. Reservations for Hotel Don João II can be made by writing directly, or by working through the Portuguese Tourist Office or a local travel agency.

Carvoeiro. If Praia da Rocha and Alvor are too crowded for you, or you prefer an even smaller village, drive into Portimão and take the harbor road over the bridge and out of town in the direction of Albufeira. Pick up the N125 and stay on it for the 8 kilometers (4.8 miles) to Lagoa. Don't make the mistake of asking for, or going in the opposite directon toward Lagoa. At Lagoa, follow the signs to Praia da Carvoeiro off to the right and along a walled dirt road for a mile and a half. You'll be accompanied by old women

Praia da Carvoeiro's vest-pocket beach.

riding burros sidesaddle and men and women in colorful horse-drawn carts.

Driving through the pastel-colored village of Carvoeiro itself, you come directly to a car park at the plaza. At this point, all you need do is step out of your car, and you're on a mini beach, fifty feet from the water's edge. This stretch of sand is about a hundred yards long, really just a cove between cliffs. The water is clear and inviting and the cavelike dugouts in the side of the cliffs offer shade from the sun. If you're looking for a typical village, this could be it. But you'll have to do your own house hunting. On the other hand, splendid villas are available in the surrounding hills. These can be negotiated for with local estate agents or the Commission of Tourism in Portimão.

At the rear of the square is a road leading up into the hills. Smiler's Bar is in the first building at the head of the road. If you're just spending part of the day, and want a drink and a bite to eat, try Smiler's. It serves a good variety of tapas (the Portuguese hors d'oeuvres), local wines, and excellent sangria.

A few yards along the same road is the Papagaio Branco, (White Parrot) where John Gorman-Watson holds forth. John is a young Scottish expatriate who emigrated to Praia da Carvoeiro several years ago. He is a hair stylist by profession, and according to the comments we heard about him, he is the best in the entire Algarve. In addition to hair styling, John runs a boutique of unusually high style.

Having looked around, continue along this road, which leads up into the hills. Over the rise you'll come upon the brand-new 200-room five-star Hotel Almanzor, set high on a cliff and built in a V facing out to sea. What a dreamy setting. Even if you're not a guest here, you will be able to use the dining room.

Farther along this road you'll come upon a huge bowllike area off to the right and a small sign—*Vale do Centianes*. You can see the sea out there, but not the beach, and that's the best part. Here is a real hideaway.

The first phase requires walking down 150 steps (which implies walking back up again, too). The second phase is picking your way along a trail that hugs the face of a cliff. It's quite a chore and you've got to watch your step, but people of all ages do it, and the reward for those who do is the glorious long, empty golden beach.

Back in Carvoeiro, take a look at two restaurants and consider returning one night for dinner. From the car park on the main square, O Barco is to the right and across the road from Smiler's Bar. It is an old fishing boat that has been converted into a snack bar, and because its dark, weathered wood blends in with the surrounding area, you might miss it. The other, O Patio, a smartly decorated restaurant at the left of the square right down at the beach, specializes in fish and steak á Patio. They're both easy to recommend.

If you're looking for a swinging evening out, try Sobe E Desce, an English-owned and operated disco. It opens at 10 P.M. and goes until the early morning hours. Carvoeiro is very quiet by day, but it picks up considerably when the sun goes down.

Armação de Pêra. About halfway between Praia da Rocha and Albufeira—some nineteen beaches and fifteen miles east of Praia dos Três Irmãos—is a charming town with beach to match. Although Armação de Pêra is a small town off the main highway, it is larger than Carvoeiro and offers more accommodations along its golden beach. The Hotel do Garbe dominates the beach at the western end of town. Built on a cliff with direct access to the sea, the brilliantly white hotel is encircled by flowers and trees. Its wide V shape provides all its rooms with an unrestricted view of the spectacular seascape.

This family-type hotel has its own fleet of boats for coastal excursions and water skiing, and an eighteen-hole golf course as well as horseback riding facilities are within easy reach. The rooms are greedily snapped up, making it difficult to get reservations. Bookings are currently running eight to twelve months in advance. Why not, when you consider that rooms for two with full board, even in high season, are modestly priced.

Armaçáo is actually a series of beaches, of which the largest, with the Hotel do Garbe, is at the western edge of town. At the eastern edge, the Albufeira side, is Fisherman's Beach, Residência CMAR, the EVA bus station and, as Anita puts it, a completely opposite way of life. In between these two extremes are gradations of moderate to low-cost accommodations. Although Armação can cater to a variety of tastes, it is generally a quiet beach and village. For the disco and night-life set, Albufeira is just six miles down the road.

The Algar, a four-star estalagem on the Avenida Beira Mar, Armação's main street, is directly across the street from a mini beach. Three jumps out the door and you're at the cement steps leading down to it. Not only does the Algar have its own restaurant, but down the street and around the corner to the left is the Cottage, a small, quaint Swedish restaurant and steakhouse. The Algar is well located and its prices are reasonable.

Several blocks farther on, Beira Mar narrows considerably. Beyond this point, the town takes on another aspect. Past the few shops next door to the Hani is the beginning of Fisherman's Beach and the older part of town. Follow the Rua das Redes and you'll pass a sidewalk café and small restaurant, Cervejaria Miramar; the twenty-one room four-star Residência CMAR is the large building directly ahead. Fisherman's Beach is another one of the few that can be approached directly from street level; no cliffs here.

Armação has a few restaurants that should not be overlooked. On the east side of town overlooking the beach is Fernando's Hideaway. The decor is unusually colorful and beautiful seaward views accompany the international fare.

For strictly Portuguese food, try the rustic A Grelha, on the Rua do Alentejo, near the beach. This is a good bet for seafood. You'll need directions for both of these restaurants, as they are not on the main street. Finding some of these places is part of the fun.

Beyond the Hotel do Garbe, a mile or so outside of town, is an unusual and totally unexpected development. If you're not looking carefully, you could miss the tan-and-white sign at the crossroad, and you'd miss Vilalara, one of the most posh residential estates in the entire Mediterranean basin.

Vilalara, built by a Portuguese architect but owned by a Swiss development company, is situated amid spectacular gardens overlooking a secluded and altogether private sandy beach known locally as Praia das Gaivotas—the Beach of the Seagulls. But you'll not find it on any maps. Because of its tucked-awayness, this can be considered a private all-to-yourself beach.

Currently Vilalara consists of thirty-two luxurious villa apartments and a restaurant. By the summer of 1974, Vilalara will have a total of 140 one- and two-bedroom apartments and villas. Even with that order of increase, I can't foresee overcrowding, since the area is sufficiently large to handle the additional growth.

The club and all the guest houses, ingeniously designed to blend into the surrounding cliffs, are faced with golden-toned concrete. The walls are thick enough and the design is so open that the apartments are cool during the warmest part of the day. Curiously, the architect designed these units so that there are no sharp edges, even on the steps or around the windows. All are smoothly rounded.

Each of the apartments is fully and charmingly furnished and has a superb view of the gardens and the sea. Each has a separate

Gull's-eye view of Vilalara, a luxurious secluded resort.

entrance, a kitchen with refrigerator and stove, one to three bedrooms, a living room, and covered veranda. Several have a roof-terrace for sunbathing. All have large living rooms.

Although a number of apartments have been privately purchased, most are available for rental. In high season (July 31 to Sept. 15), two people can rent a Type C apartment for about $100 per person per week. This price obtains for rentals of one to three weeks. Should you want to rent for a month or more the same apartment would rent for $600 for two. There is no charge for children under two, and for children two to eight, there is a 50 percent discount on the weekly rate.

You can either cook your own meals, which means shopping at the micro-supermarket on the estate or in Armação or Portimão, or you may eat in Vilalara's restaurant. In the restaurant, a continental breakfast and two meals will run $45 per person per week. Here too, a 50 percent discount applies for children.

While there is no charge for using either the tennis courts or the putting green, there is a water-skiing fee of about $10 per hour. And an eight-passenger cabin cruiser can be rented for $7 per hour. But remember, Vilalara is only for those who want luxury, privacy, and tranquillity. A break in this regimen can be taken by simply driving into Armação, Albufeira, or Portimão. But on the estate, which is strictly off limits to sightseers, it's "no jumping" allowed.

If you prefer the "jumping" atmosphere, Hotel do Levante, a relatively small but first-class hostelry tucked away on its own beach, between Hotel do Garbe and Vilalara, may be just for you.

About a quarter of a mile beyond the Garbe turn left at the sign indicating Hotel do Levante, and take the narrow dirt road into the Levante's parking lot. This is a modern, moderately priced hotel, and it prides itself on its typically Portuguese food. Here too, because of its unique location, the beach is sparsely populated and private. The long, wide expanse of golden sand slips gently down into the quiet water, and is a safe place for toddlers.

Albufeira. Albufeira, the Algarve's second largest town, is no more than twenty minutes east of Armação. In Roman times, Albufeira bore the name Baltum. When the Arabs occupied it in 716, they renamed it Al-buhera. By the time the Portuguese conquered the area 534 years later, the name was well set.

The Arab influence can be seen in the architecture, local customs, and the people generally, giving the area a special attraction. It also has the animation and excitement of a busy county seat. It has a bevy of shops, markets (open-air and closed, including a supermarket), bistros, cafés, and a wide variety of accommodations. And it has an excellent, long, bustling beach.

We can recommend without reservation the Estalagem do Cêrro, an English-owned hostelry. Although estalagems are for the most part privately owned, don't conjure visions of an eighteenth-century coach stop. Most of these are modern buildings. Although privately owned, they are controlled by the Ministry of Tourism as to standards of decor, sanitation, (every room must have bath facilities), menu, and price. If the owners want to increase their prices, they must apply to the Ministry. This requirement is instituted in order to prevent prices rising above a level that would vitiate the concept of the estalagem. Although prices at estalagems vary, they do not go above a set level. Hotel prices are always higher.

Estalagems are also limited as to size; the largest has seventy rooms, while the smallest has only seven. Estalagem do Cêrro has fifty-one rooms, which should suggest to you the need for early booking. Reservations for July should be made in February or March. A number of hotel managers were quick to tell us that although they welcome Americans, who at present are few in number compared to the English, French, Swedes, and Germans, they would not be surprised if hotels and estalagems refuse one-night reservations. This type of accommodation causes too many booking dislocations.

Pousadas, the next lower type of accommodation, are government owned; they are designed, built, furnished, and controlled by the government, but run by individuals on a 10-percent profit basis. All but one are run by Portuguese. Prices in pousadas are, of course, lower than in estalagems, which means great value for the money.

In contrast is the Hotel Sol e Mar, the largest hotel in Albufeira, owned by the Rank Organization of London. It is in the heart of town and dominates the main beach. As this is a moderately priced hotel and popular with our British cousins, the demand for rooms is brisk, so early reservations are required.

Albufeira has a number of hotels, pensãos, estalagems, and residências. But it also has the five-star, 138-room Hotel de Balaia, some three miles east of Albufeira. The hotel is located in a secluded forty-acre clifftop setting, overlooking its own undeveloped golden beach. This beach would be hard to equal; it's private, with no way to approach it except by sea or through the hotel grounds, and it is a long way down. About eight hundred yards of tawny sand lies between weather-beaten terra-cotta cliffs. The clearest pale green water breaks on its smooth shore. The umbrella pines that dot the cliff tops and the Spanish blade guarding the flanks make the picture an incredibly lovely one.

One need not leave its vast grounds to find just about everything a vacationer might want: tennis courts, mini-golf, pool, bar, grill room, disco, night club, lounges, card room, and excellent food with service to match. This hotel is another of the "Five

Albufeira has a bustling public beach.

View of the private beach from the grounds of the Hotel de Balaia.

Sisters," which means you'll pay the price.

On Albufeira's main beach, a fine sandy one about a half mile long in the center of town, the water is sparkling clear, pleasantly inviting, and never too cold. Here you will see fishermen cleaning and mending their nets. If you're a collector, the shells they discard are yours for the taking.

Curiously, at this beach "rooms" (that's hardly the proper description) have been built directly into the cliffs; the doors are flush with the cliff face. Here one can change into a bathing suit.

The larger public beaches also have snack bars where juice, ice cream, soda, and sandwiches can be purchased. Every so often you'll see a woman carrying on one arm an esparto grass basket filed with fruit for sale, while balancing a good sized box on her head. These clever units contain pull-out trays with an assortment of pastries. Don't pass them by.

By the way, even if you are not a guest at the Sol e Mar, you can rent a beach chair for about 30 cents a day, and water skiing is available at $4 per half hour.

A broad spectrum of evening activities is available in Albufeira. Teenagers generally congregate in or around the plaza in the center of town, then move off to any number of discos. O'Giva (the Shield) just off the square has no admittance fee and, according to Scott and Andi, has great atmosphere, "but they push the drinks a little too hard." Music is usually American or English records, played very loud. Silvia's has an admission charge of about 40 escudos ($1.40), which includes one drink. The Pescador, located in the Sol e Mar, attracts all ages and has a similar admission fee. Both of these open at 10 P.M. and close at 4 A.M. For a less cacophonous evening, both Sir Harry's Bar and Go-Go's, just off the main square, are warm, friendly places for drinking and talking.

Quarteira. Quarteira, ten miles or so east of Albufeira, has long been overlooked by developers. Only recently has it begun to attract attention. If Quarteira doesn't give up its old-world charm to land developers, it could become the best public beach of the Sotavento. Fortunately, all the buildings are across the road from the beach. The long neglected area around Faro should emerge within the next five years as a major vacation attraction, as the developments at Quinto do Lago, Vale de Lobo, and Vilamoura are completed.

Quarteira's long beach—no cliffs to descend here—is uncrowded, but if you go away from the center of the village, about a quarter of a mile out toward Amadeu Moreira's Residência Elegante, the beach is completely empty. Shell fanciers will find that this beach has not been picked over and has a variety of interesting species. If the sea hasn't cast up anything you like, stroll over to the edge of the central market, where the fisherwomen clean and sell all manner of seafood. Not only will you find shells, but if you're eating in, this is the place to buy fresh fish. The variety and low price of the fresh fruit and vegetables inside the central market make meals a delight. Part of the fun is just walking around the stalls watching the action.

Thus far the largest hotel in town is the fifty-room Beira-Mar on the Avenida Infante de Sagres, the main street. At the opposite end of the spectrum is Residência Elegante with six rooms above its lovely restaurant and bar. Considering that a room for two is less than $8 per night, you would do well to write Senhor Moreira directly and plead with him to reserve a room for a few nights. He opened the Elegante in June of 1972 and is currently wearing several hats: bartender, maitre d', manager, and host. Even if you are unable to reserve a room, both the out and indoor restaurants are open to the public, and the food is fine. His bar is already a favorite gathering spot for many nationalities.

Quarteira is well located, just a few minutes' drive from Vilamoura and Vale de Lobo, so golfers and equestrians need not go far afield for a day on Vilamoura's greens or trails. And for elegant dining, Casa Velha at Quinto do Lago is fifteen minutes away.

Quinto do Lago, well on its way to completion, is the carefully planned development of 1600 heavily wooded acres between Almancil and Quarteira. This exclusive world will include three relatively small luxury hotels, a twenty-seven-hole golf course, riding club, tennis courts, several restaurants, night club, discotheque, shops, hairdresser, and supermarket. In addition, Club

All by myself at Vale de Lobo, Almancil.

da Quinta has 260 rentable apartments bordering a 250-acre tidal lagoon. The mile of private beach extends from Vale de Lobo to the estate, with three access roads from the lagoon.

Sales and rental of villas in Quinto do Lago can be made only through direct contact. For information, write Senhor Gastao Horta e Costa, Quinto do Lago, Almancil, The Algarve, Portugal.

A short drive from Quinto do Lago and nine miles from the international airport at Faro is Vale de Lobo, another luxury estate. This one, built by a British company with an eye to decent planning, is dominated by a remarkable eighteen-hole golf course that actually overlooks the beach and sea. The view from several of the greens is breathtaking. Unless you're a hardened golfer it's easy to drop your clubs and run for the beach.

The estate has many villas that are privately owned and rentable, but activity centers around the five-star 130-room Hotel Dona Filipa (another of the "Sisters"). For us, this proved to be a formal, rather stiff place, where dressing for dinner is *de rigueur*. I was even sent back for a tie. And although we weren't smitten by

Guests of the Hotel Dona Filipa have their own cabanas.

the food, we were by the beach. Oh, what a gorgeous one it is!

To get to the beach, it is necessary to walk to the tiled and stone plaza, with its mini *mercado* (small supermarket), book and newspaper shop, bar, and restaurant. From here, steps lead down to the beach, where Dona Filipa's guests have their own cabanas. Of course, there are cliffs for a backdrop, and the beach itself is long, wide, and virtually empty. Marvelous for strolling, shell hunting, sleeping, and swimming.

On this beach the cliffs gradually taper down to meet the sand and woods. If you want to be alone, take a walk toward the point where cliff and woods meet. Consider also horseback riding along the shore and on woodsy trails. If you're not a golfer, you can try your skill on the mini-golf course, next to the tennis courts.

East of Quarteira, some fifteen miles from Faro, still another huge residential estate is being built. This one, Vilamoura, will have the Algarve's first marina as well as its first gambling casino. Here too, golf is the order of the day; a championship eighteen-hole course has been laid out among the umbrella trees. I understand that Henry Cotten and Frank Pennick laid out this course and its facilities. However, it isn't necessary to be a guest at Vilamoura to use the clubhouse or the course. They are open to the public.

Between Faro and Vila Real de Santo António, the crossing point into Spain, are several good beach areas worth visiting. About a mile and a half from Tavira is Praia de Cabanos, with available villas, an estalagem, tennis courts, riding stables, and an excellent uncrowded beach. With Tavira so close, restaurants, cafés, and shops are within easy reach. Taviro is well known for its tuna and sardine fishing fleet.

In this part of the Algarve, being so far east and so close to Spain, the cliffs of the Barlavento have given way to flat sandy terrain. A beach town to visit in this area is Monte Gordo, with its relatively uncrowded public beach. Reigning over the beach is the 166-room four-star Hotel Vasco da Gama, on the Avenida Infante Dom Henrique.

Because of the Algarve's location, and because it is less than 100 miles long from east to west, excursions and side trips are readily made. Buses to historic cities such as Évora, Elvas, Lisbon, and Seville leave daily. Flights from Faro to Lisbon take only thirty minutes, so a weekend in Portugal's capital can be managed easily.

Places of Interest. The Algarve is not a round of cathedrals and museums. Although the people are highly religious, their lives as fisherfolk left little time for building large monuments. For the vacationer, the real places of interest are the villages, the landscape, and the activities. For example, this is one of the few places in the world that affords a grand view of land's end.

At Cabo de São Vicente, the primordial nature of the ocean can be seen in its all threatening countenance. To get there, pick up the N125 and follow it all the way west through Lagos, on to Raposeira and Vila do Bispo. As you approach these towns, the wind picks up and the landscape becomes rocky, with few trees. From Vila do Bispo the road (N268) turns sharply south, and the sparsely populated countryside is bleak and unkempt, treeless and windswept. At several places along the road the drive is close to the sea. The surf dashing at the sheer rock cliffs lets you know just where you are.

At the traffic circle, take the road leading into Sagres and follow the signs to the parking lot of the fifteen-room Pousada do Infante, located at the edge of the cliffs facing the sea. On the warmest days you can expect a stiff sea breeze here. You can join the village fishermen sitting on the edge of the cliffs and drop a line into the dark brooding sea below. You can also have lunch at the pousada or one of the beach cafés, then try the sandy beach and the surf.

Built into the walls surrounding the pousada are seats for those who prefer to sit and watch nature in all her furious glory. Many do.

Cabo de São Vicente is three and a half miles from Sagres—six kilometers of the most desolate and somber landscape. If you recall that less than half an hour's drive back you were in glorious sunshine, this change is all the more remarkable; and it's surely worth the trip.

At land's end, the most southwesterly point in Europe, you see the lighthouse and fortress built on the solid rock crags, some 250 feet above the battering sea.

A warmer and perhaps more exciting experience is found at the other end of the Algarve. Tavira is well known for its tuna and sardine fishing fleet. It is no trouble at all to arrange for a day out on a fishing boat, and watching the colorful boats bring in the day's catch is well worth while. If you've never seen a man jump into a school of tuna and wrestle one aboard, you should mark Tavira down as a place to stop. The large red cross on the white sails is the emblem under which all Portuguese ships sail. This tradition goes all the way back to the time of Prince Henry the Navigator (1394–1460), Grand Master of the Order of Christ, whose ships sailed under the same emblem.

Of course, Tavira is the place to eat lobster, tuna, charcoal-grilled sardines, and a wide variety of both shell and fin fish. So, give it a double check.

A colorful and impressive religious spectacle, the festival of

Santa Catarina at Praia da Rocha during the first week of August, is particularly compelling. The best place to watch the blessing of the fleet is in the fortress at the east end of the Avenida Marginal. From this high perch overlooking the golden beach and azure-tinted sea, you can see the gaily colored fishing boats pass around the point, each being blessed in the name of Santa Catarina, patron saint of fishermen.

On any weekday, particularly between eight and eleven A.M., the docks of Olhão are the heartbeat of the Algarve. Appproximately five miles east of Faro, Olhão is a bustling fishing center. From the Praça da Restauracão—the main plaza—follow the *Doca* signs to the piers where the boats are moored. This is where the action is: fishing boats are being unloaded, fish is being sold, sardines are being grilled, women are cleaning and filleting fish. It's a beehive of colorful activity. Bring your camera and color film.

Spend at least a little time in Silves, Loulé, and São Brás de Alportel, which will surely give you the real flavor of the Algarve. From Faro, the N2 heads directly north the twelve miles to S. Brás. One of the most delightful places to visit there is the pousada, perched like a windmill in the middle of orange and almond groves. A leisurely walk around the town will give you a feel for the region.

If you've never seen a large red sandstone castle—and I suspect few exist outside this ancient Moorish stronghold—a visit to Silves is in order. Silves is due north of Lagoa. Be sure to drive through the town and pick up the road to São Bartolomeu de Messines; a short way up the road is an unusual national monument; the sixteenth-century carved stone cross of Portugal. Don't miss it.

Loulé, one of the larger hill towns, is primarily a market town, and it is *the* place to go for fruit and vegetables. Loulé is six miles directly west of São Brás on N270, and five miles north of Quarteira on N396. Here you can get a good look at the filigreed Algarvian chimney.

A rule of thumb for most visits is that you can go just about anywhere from the N125. Stop at any gas station for directions.

Shopping. Portimão, Faro, and Vila Real de Santo António are just about evenly spaced the length of the Algarve, and each has a main shopping street that is closed to traffic. In Portimão, it is Rua do Comércio; in Faro, Rua do Santo Antónia, and in Vila Real, Rua Téofilo Braga. With no traffic to worry about, shopping can be an unhurried, pleasurable, and salutary experience.

Browsing, touching, picking up, putting down, walking out— none of these will produce raised eyebrows, inaudible muttering, or a tirade of invective. If you don't like this Madeira tablecloth, look at a dozen others. Invariably the sales people, old and young alike, are pleasant and helpful.

Porcelain, tile, and pottery are attractive and inexpensive. Vista Alegre porcelain is among the world's best. In addition to the shops in Portimão and Faro, try those in the Hotel Algarve and Hotel Alvor Praia.

Of course, the Iberian Peninsula is a natural for mats, bags, and baskets made of plaited esparto grass. These are found inexpensively everywhere, and no two shops have the same prices. As a general rule, expect to find prices varying from shop to shop for the same item. It's part of the fun.

As most of the world's cork comes from Portuguese trees, cork items of every size and description can be found throughout the province.

Plan to lunch in Caldas and then go on to Monchique. When you do, take a look at the furniture workshops, where eucalyptus-wood chairs and wooden furniture painted with the typical patterns of the Alentejo district are sold.

Shopping can be fun in the Algarve, but remember, buy it now! *Boa Viagem!*

Food and Drink. Good food and drink with typically Algarvian flavor—snacks and light lunches as well as dinner—can be obtained in many villages between Cabo de São Vicente and Vila Real de Santo António. Eating places range from the tiny out-of-the-way café-bar frequented by local fishermen to the dining rooms of deluxe hotels. Most important, however, is the excellent, friendly service that will almost invariably accompany the food and drink. It's always a pleasure to dine out in Portugal.

For us the Algarve means fish—*peixe*—and heading the long list is tuna. Until you've had a tuna salad, *salada atum,* as a main course or an appetizer, you don't know how delicious tuna can be. Sardines are another Portuguese specialty, especially when charcoal grilled—don't hesitate to stop at a street vendor's grill and have a half dozen *sardinhas assadas fresca.* There's nothing like it in the States. From here the list broadens to include *linguado,* sole, made just a little differently in each village but always titillating; *Pescada,* hake; *bacalhau,* salt cod, the national dish eaten in every village and hamlet; *Pescadinha,* whiting; and a variety of shellfish: *ostras, lagostinas, gambas, camarõa,* and *lula*—oysters, crayfish, large prawns, small prawns, shrimp, and squid, respectively. The prawns, crayfish, and shrimp vary in length from an inch to eight inches and are so plentiful you can buy them like french fries. In restaurants you will often notice SP on the menu in place of the price. This means that the shellfish are sold *segundo o peso*—by weight.

We never found out what they feed the chickens, but we do know that eggs and egg dishes are surprisingly delicious. *Ovos mexidos* are not just scrambled eggs; seasonings of some type must be added to make them taste so good. Do not overlook *óvos escaldados* (boiled), for they take on a new dimension when eaten in a seaside café.

For me, no lunch or dinner can be complete without soup. With *caldo verde,* another national dish, whose contents vary with the locality, soup rises to new gustatory heights. *Caldo verde* is a pureed vegetable soup that contains a mixture usually of cabbage, potatoes, carrots, and beans. Its color varies according to the ingredients.

Two piquant semihard cheeses, Serra and Monchique go well with most meals or with tapas, Portugal's own collection of hors d'oeuvres. Cheese and tomato on a roll at a sidewalk café, topped off with a bottle of the local red or white wine, makes an excellent light snack.

For a special treat, ask for *vinho verde.* Although the literal translation means green wine, vinho verde is really a white with a touch of sparkle. A product of the Oporto region far to the north, it is an inexpensive and lovely way to finish a meal. Three names to remember are Casteloes, Aniversaro, and Valverde.

There are several extraordinary restaurants in the Algarve. You must sample at least one or two of these.

No one should leave the Algarve without dining at Casa Velha on the grounds of Quinto do Lago in the Almancil area. An old farmhouse has been transformed into the elegant Casa Velha restaurant, serving Portuguese and international food. The colorful but subdued decor in white, orange, and yellow suntones, as well as the matchless service, would be enough to recommend it. Add to this the prepared-to-order food and the scintillating piano playing of a virtuoso. This skillful combination has made Casa Velha one of the most popuar restaurants in the Algarve. Seek out Senhor Gastao Horto e Costa and ask him to describe the plans for Club da Quinta as well as for the total development of Quinto do Lago. You just might become a permanent guest.

At the informally elegant wood-paneled Monchique Grill in the Penina Golf Hotel, you can get the best oysters in all Portugal—if you're willing to pay the price. You eat by candlelight and the glow of the charcoal grill, and the food is the highest quality. Fish and a variety of grills are their specialty.

Should you prefer a strictly formal atmosphere, try the dining room of Hotel Dona Filipa at Vale de Lobo. Senhor Charbert, the *maître d'hôtel*, is a one-man show. His greeting and seating of guests is pure theater. Watching him may even be an aid to digestion. The food is just fair, but the service is impeccable.

Fortunately good food and drink is not limited to expensive restaurants. Alfredo's in Portimão, although half the price of the Monchique Grill, is a lovely place to dine in a relaxed atmosphere, and you can always depend on a variety of fresh fin and shellfish.

Before entering Lagos from the east, take the road off to the left in the direction of Meia Praia. Several hundred yards before Hotel Da Meia Praia is Beach Club Duna. This is a dandy place to stop for a substantial buffet-type lunch. For the price of the meal you can use the pool and the section of the beach normally reserved for guests of Hotel Meia Praia and Hotel Lagos.

If you're in the vicinity of Quartiera, drop in at Residencial

Elegante's Restaurant and Bar. Amadeu Moraira, the owner of this brand new addition to the Algarve, is a Portuguese who has spent many years in London in the hotel business. He serves excellent linguado. The Bar, a meeting and drinking place for all nationalities, is open until 4 A.M.

Along N125, on your way to or from Sagres or Cabo de São Vincente, you'll see the signs for Almadena and Burgau. Two kilometers (just over a mile) on you'll be close to the sea and an attractive little restaurant. Ancora is the type of fishing village restaurant you should eat in at least once while in the Algarve. Its menu isn't large, and of course fish dishes are the specialty. For me the choice is sole, for you it may be squid (*lula*) or lobster (*lavagante*). Whatever your choice, you can depend on it being good.

SPAIN

SPAIN IS BIG. So big in fact, that there are marked differences in climate and topography around its extensive Mediterranean coastline, from Ayamonte at the border of Portugal in the far southwest to Port-Bou on the French frontier in the northeast.

In between are hundreds of miles of fascinating variations in scenery and a succession of magnificent beaches, each with its own special characteristics. The Spanish coastline divides itself quite naturally into six areas. From northeast to southwest these are Costa Brava, Costa Dorada, Costa del Azahar, Costa Blanca, Costa del Sol, and Costa de la Luz. Each coast is distinctive.

The Costa Brava, the smallest of the coasts, is totally within the province of Gerona, extending north from the village of Blanes to Port-Bou, where Spain fades into the French countryside. This coast is part of the Catalan district, which has its own dialect and customs. Literally translated, *brava* means "wild." In this instance it refers not to wilderness but to the savage beauty of the coast. Coves, bays, and inlets, each with at least a mini beach, are sheltered by cliffs and promontories of variously colored granite. The shore is dotted with small islands that mark the retreat of the coast under the incessant erosion of the sea. The inlets have such names as San Felíu de Guixols, Bagur, Aiguablava, and Cadaqués; these may be tiny but are lovely, secluded beach resorts—a fishing village fronting on brilliant blue-green water. Two swimming choices are available: sandy beach or in and out among the rock outcroppings.

The pines and cork trees stretching down from the cliffs to the warm sands, the coves forming havens almost the full length of the coast, the crystal water among the dark furrowed rocks, all combine to create a region of transcendent beauty. With its few rainy days and low humidity, the Catalonian coast is one of the more attractive resort areas in Spain.

The Costa Dorada, including both Barcelona and Tarragona, extends south to the hamlet of Alcanar, with its Barrio Maritimo and world-renowned Dublin Bay prawns. This coast is an abrupt change from the Costa Brava, especially El Maresme, that portion from Malgrat de Mar to Badalona, just outside of Barcelona.

South from Malgrat to Barcelona, the craggy, elevated coast begins to soften. From Barcelona to San Carlos de la Rápita, the Golden Coast has a variety of large and small beaches that are primarily flat, sandy stretches. Some, such as Sitges, just south of Barcelona, are "action stations" while others such as Cubellas, midway between Tarragona and Barcelona, are tiny villages of less than a thousand people; but all have fine sandy beaches.

Some call it the Fragrant Coast, others the Orange Blossom Coast, and still others, the Coast of Flowers. Whichever you prefer, the Costa del Azahar (a typically Moorish name, with the *za* in the middle of a word) is one of Spain's less crowded areas. Stretching from Benicarló to Grao de Gandía and including Valencia and Castellón de la Plana, this long, narrow stretch of low-lying coastal shelf forms a wide, curving gulf. All along this Levantine coast, orange groves are a constant companion. When not heavily laden with fruit, the trees are clad in white blossoms whose delicate fragrance pervades the countryside, giving this coast its unique quality. The beaches in this area vary from the fine sand of Benicarló to the pebbles of Chilches.

The longest of the beach coasts is the Costa Blanca, the Brilliant or Bright Coast, running along the provinces of Alicante,

Murcia, and Almería. As you move from Valencia south to Alicante, vineyards, olive groves, palms, and almond trees take the place of citrus groves. This lush greenery alternates with arid stretches and naked mountains rising around the whiteness of the towns. The sunlight bouncing off the white-washed buildings and reflected off the fine sand and clear water give the luminous Costa Blanca its name.

At Almería, the Hollywood of Spain, the coast makes a westward turn, and the Andalusian sun burns down on the beaches of the Costa del Sol. From Cabo de Gata at the tip of Almería to Tarifa, the point of land on the Strait of Gibraltar closest to Morrocco, the Sun Coast offers a number of attractive beaches and cosmopolitan resorts. Because the Costa del Sol faces directly south, it gets the greatest amount of sun all year around. It also benefits from the Sierra Nevada mountain range, which runs east to west forming an impenetrable barrier to the chilly northern winds from the hinterlands.

The province of Málaga, with 110 miles of flat tree-studded coastline, includes dozens of beaches between Maro, with a population of 800, to mightily growing Estepona, with more than 15,000.

The main feature of the Costa del Sol is the surprising mildness of its winters, with a mean January temperature of 56° F. August is its hottest month, but even with the *terral* blowing in from Africa, temperatures rarely exceed 85° F. For the most part, the prevailing winds are cooling sea breezes.

The least known and least traveled of Spain's coastal areas is the Costa de la Luz. It stretches from Tarifa on the Strait of Gibraltar to the mouth of the Río Guadiana, which forms the frontier with Portugal. Midway down the coast is Spain's most ancient city of Cádiz, now a bustling seaport. In both directions, white sandy beaches stretch for miles, and most are undeveloped and empty. The Costa de la Luz is the place to escape to for a quiet, relaxing vacation far from the crowds, noise, and tourist attractions.

Transportation. Spain's beaches are within easy reach. From the States, Pan-American has daily flights to Barcelona, right on the

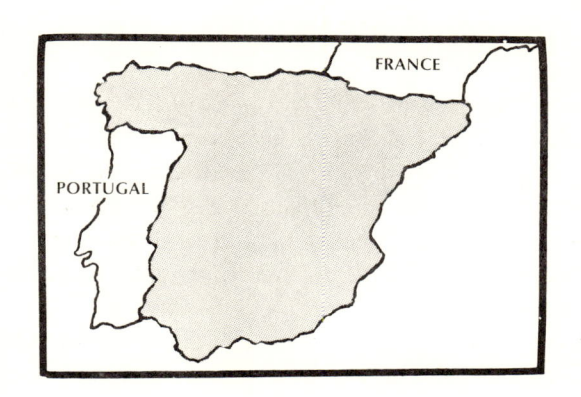

PORTUGAL

FRANCE

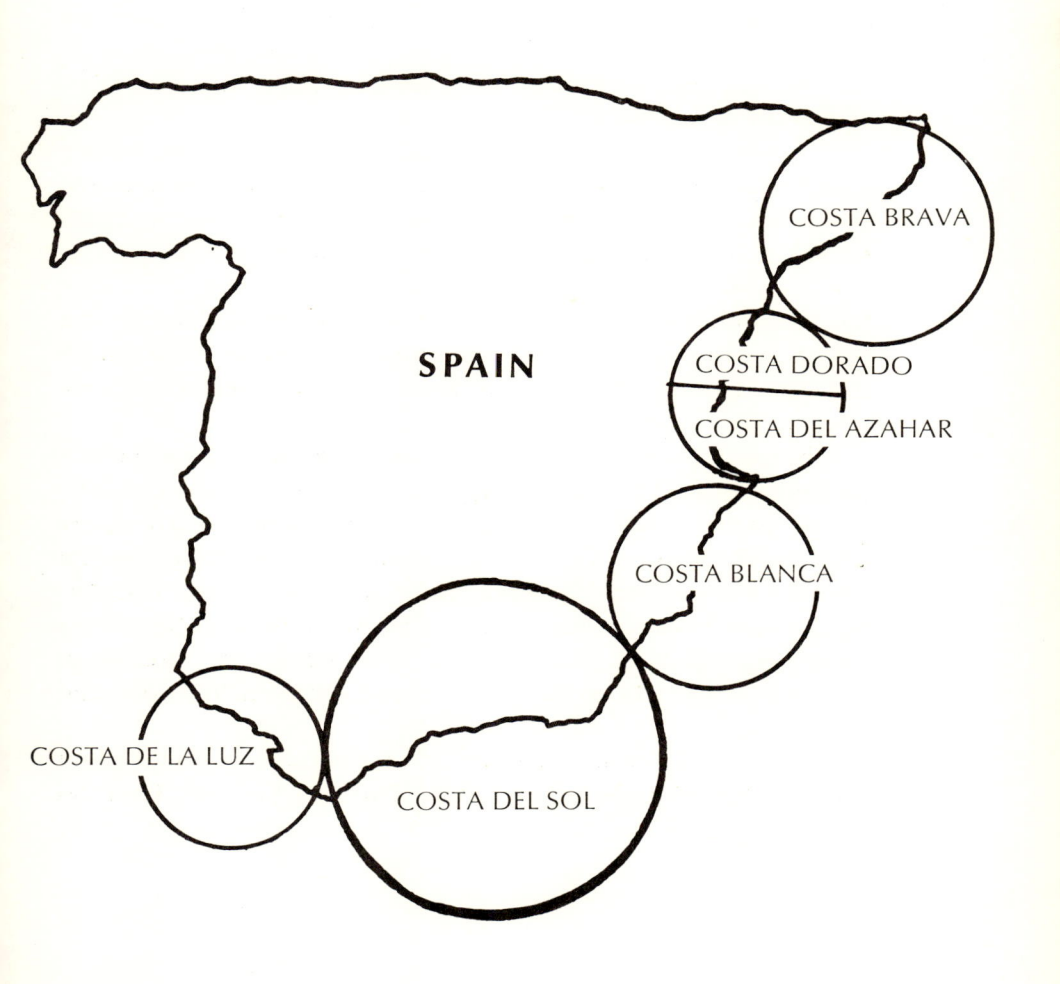

SPAIN

COSTA BRAVA

COSTA DORADO

COSTA DEL AZAHAR

COSTA BLANCA

COSTA DE LA LUZ

COSTA DEL SOL

Costa Dorada and a short ride to the Costa Brava. TWA flies to Madrid every day. From here, daily air service is available to Málaga on the Costa del Sol, Seville and Cádiz on the Costa de la Luz, and Alicante and Valencia serving the Costa del Azahar. Spain's Iberia airlines has regular service between New York, Madrid, Barcelona and Málaga; and from London, BEA (BA), has nonstop flights to Málaga.

One of the best ways to arrive in Spain is by sea. The Italian Line offers regular crossings between New York and Spain's Mediterranean ports. Another great sea voyage is available on DFDS Seaways' sister ships—*Dana Corona* or *Dana Sirena,* both of which make the two-day trip from Genoa to Málaga. They also make the short runs from Tangier and from Palma to Málaga. These are modern vessels (they came off the ways in 1969) and are a pure joy to travel on. If you're traveling by car, all you need do is drive on and park. Because they carry so many cars, these ships are often referred to as the "auto highway of the Mediterranean."

Of course, national (RENFE) and international train service is available to all parts of Spain and its beaches. Information and schedules can be obtained from many travel agents and the Spanish National Tourist Office, 589 Fifth Avenue, New York.

Accommodations. All countries have private hotels that are just so-so and others that are elegant and pure joy. Among its hundreds of hotels, Spain has a number of both. But Spain has another dimension, the paradores.

Throughout the country, the Ministerio de Información y Turismo has established a network of lodgings—paradores, albergues de carretera, refugios, hosterías, and one hotel. Nearly all are located in what most of us would consider the least frequented, at times least accessible, and most picturesque areas. For instance, the Parador Nacional Aiguablava is in Aiguablava on the Costa Brava. Secluded in a piney wood, it looks deceptively precarious on its clifftop perch overlooking a quiet sun-drenched cove and mini beach.

At Arcos de la Frontera, a short drive inland from the beach at Rota on the Costa de la Luz, is the Parador Nacional Casa del

Corregidor. It can be reached only by a narrow, one-*small*-car road, with at least a 45-degree incline and a number of "S" curves. From the balconies at the rear, you look out and down at the lush green countryside some two thousand feet below. The sight by day, dusk, or dark is incomparable.

Rather than demolish ancient castles, palaces and convents, the Ministry of Tourism embarked on a masterful program of restoration with impeccable respect for the Spanish tradition, but fitted with the most modern conveniences. These became the original paradores. In addition to the refurbished castles, a number of contemporary buildings were erected. All were planned as low-cost accommodations for the Spanish people, not as competitors with privately owned hotels. However, the charm of the paradores won them an international reputation, which has sharpened the demand for rooms. Most have twenty or thirty rooms, but would you believe a hotel with six rooms? Parador Nacional Molino Viejo at Gijón on the Cantabrican coast has only six rooms. But each parador exudes the charm you expect of Spain.

Of the fifty-five paradores, nine are on the Mediterranean coasts; two on the Costa de la Luz and Costa Blanca; three on the Costa del Sol, and one each on the Costa del Azahar and Costa Brava. None are available through travel agents; should you want to reserve a room in a parador, you must write directly to the manager, or work through an office of the Ministry of Tourism.

I might add that managers of paradores must have years of experience, and the competition for these prestigious positions is keen. Some managers are outstanding, and their paradores show it. Señor Juan Antonio Fernandez Aladro, administrador (manager) of the Parador Nacional Reyes Católicos in Mojácar, Almería Province, can't do enough for his guests. He is everywhere, inquiring into service, food, and accommodations, a warm, outgoing *caballero*. On the other hand, there can be a snobbery that is reflected in a cold atmosphere. Parador Nacional del Golf in Málaga on the Costa del Sol is just such a place—and altogether without reason.

In addition to paradors, the albergues de carretera—lodgings on the main highways—offer rooms, good food, activities ranging from swimming pool to bull ring, and telephone and postal services. Here too, accommodations are desirable but limited. Most albergues have ten to fifteen rooms. The smallest, at Zamora, has only five double rooms, while the largest, Albergue Nacional de Carretera at Benicarló on the Costa del Azahar, has forty-three doubles and five singles. The albergue at Albacete in Murcia is a great place to stop if you are visiting the castle at Almansa. But all the albergues have a forty-eight hour limit in order to give as many people as possible a chance to stay there.

Of the sixteen, four are within short drives from the Coasts. The albergue at Antequera, thirty-five miles up into the mountains from Málaga, is a perfect place to stop for lunch on your way to Seville or Córdoba. In July or August that mountain road, although high, breezy, and sensationally panoramic, is incredibly hot. Curiously enough, it is the hot breeze that thoroughly dries you out. So be prepared to stop although you've only covered thirty-five miles.

At Puerto de Lumbreras, twenty-five minutes from the lovely white hillside town of Mojácar on the Costa Blanca, is a thirteen-room, two-star albergue. (Other albergues are at Benicarló and Albacete.) Here, too, prices are exceptionally low. A night's lodging is about $7 for two.

There are only two refugios (actually refugios de montaña or mountain shelters), and neither is near a beach area.

The four hosterías are regional restaurants, delightfully decorated in the traditional style of the province and serving excellent regional food. Unfortunately none are located near any of the beaches. The closest one is at Artés, on the French border, northwest of Gerona, too far to go for lunch or dinner.

The hotel that somehow managed to get caught up in this small but elegant network is the Hotel Atlántico, an unmistakably Moorish six-story palm-fronted building overlooking the Gulf of Cádiz on the Costa de la Luz. Although run by the Ministry, it is privately owned, which may account for the fact that they allow pets. If the thought of leaving Rover home distresses you, but the thought of missing a beach vacation in Spain is too much to bear, the Atlantico could be your answer.

A final note. The Spanish government has instituted an effective and highly original wrinkle. Few countries seem to have the self-confidence required for an Official Complaints Book. Used judiciously, it can accomplish wonders.

All officially certified establishments that offer lodging must have a Complaints Book on the premises. You can be sure it's not advertised, nor is it on display. The book is available for entering complaints, comments, or claims, as guests see fit, and it also contains the established prices for every room, as well as prices for all services.

If you believe you have been done in, ask for the Complaints Book. You'll be pleasantly surprised at the salutary effect of simply asking for it. But, like all such devices, don't overdo it, or you've lost a source of strength.

Headquarters for complaints is the General Directorate of Touristic Enterprises and Activities—Direccion General de Empresas y Actividadas Turisticas, Sección de Inspección y Reclamaciónes at 39, Avenida del Generalísimo, Madrid 16. Should you have a real injustice to report, write or go in person. You'll get action.

BEACHES

Costa de la Luz. The Spanish Government may not be ready to talk about the Costa de la Luz, but we are. It may well be that now—and the next five years—is the time to come to this coast of brilliant, white-washed communities and golden beaches. Now, while it still retains its peaceful, fishing-village character, with beaches following one another in uninterrupted succession for the whole curving length of the tranquil coastline. Now, before developers turn from the south to find open space that has not yet felt their corroding touch; now, while they are still concentrating on cementing every inch of the Costa del Sol.

The Costa de la Luz, in fact, of all the Spanish coasts, has the oldest pedigree, as well as the least known beaches. Cádiz, the main city of the coast, is probably the oldest in Spain; the Phoenicians established a trading center there around 1100 B.C. And although few textbooks mention it, each of Columbus's voyages to the New World left from village-seaports along this coast. In 1492, on his first voyage, the caravels *Pinta, Niña,* and *Santa María* left from Palos de la Frontera, about halfway between Huelva and Mazagón. His second voyage fitted out and sailed from Cádiz, and the third sailed at first light from Sanlúcar de Barrameda.

The Costa de la Luz is the least developed of all the coasts, but it has some of the longest, widest, cleanest, and least crowded beaches of the entire country. If you really want to get away, the Costa de la Luz may be for you.

Between Huelva and Mazagón, flat-topped pines dot the landscape. Except for these lollipop trees, reminiscent of the African veldt, the twenty-five-mile drive is unremarkable. Huelva is a bustling port city and provincial capital. Mazagón, to the south, at the edge of the salt marshes (which force you to drive to Cádiz via Seville), is a tiny manorial village with a most dazzling peopleless beach. Playa de Castilla is seemingly endless. As far as the eye can see, the backdrop to the beach is a line of ocher cliffs interrupted by crooked lollipop trees, as if planted by some capricious gardener.

The light golden sands are flat and speckled with multi-colored sea shells. The sky is a limpid, cloudless blue all summer long, in exquisite contrast to the darker blue sea. And to top it off, you're virtually alone. There are no restaurants, cafés, snack bars, or dressing rooms on this big beach; no concessions, no vendors, no sailing, scuba or skiing lessons. Just you, the surf, and the sand. Because of the size of the beach and its distance from Huelva, it is almost empty even on the hottest Sunday in August.

There are several ways to enjoy the beach at Mazagón. The best is as a guest at Parador Nacional Cristóbal Colón, which is one of the newly built paradores. The twenty guest rooms are spacious and well designed, and the decor throughout is matchless Spanish. The common rooms in leather, wood, and brick are quietly elegant. You'll want to ship everything home that isn't nailed down.

The drive to Mazagón from Huelva seems interminable. Finally, a turn into the trees and a narrow zigzagging road brings

Above: *Saturday afternoon at Mazagón. Dana and Andi are gathering shells.*

Right: *The path from the beach at Mazagón to the parador on the cliff is a photographer's delight.*

you to the white brick parador. But the trip is well worth it. The attractive grounds, pool, walkways, and sunshades extend to the edge of the cliffs, but the building cannot be seen from the beach below.

You'll have to scramble for a reservation. At the incredible bargain of less than $10 a night for two (without food but including service charge and taxes), these twenty rooms are snapped up well in advance.

A word of caution; paradores are not "teen scenes," they are not action places. If you're a teenager craving excitement, paradores are not for you, except perhaps as a stop-over for a meal or a view.

One of the most inviting characteristics of all the paradores is their cleanliness. In fact, their bathrooms have an order of cleanliness rarely found anywhere.

However, the parador is not the only way to enjoy Mazagón. A number of pensions, hostels, and residence hotels are available. These, I must add, are not for people requiring three- or four-star hotel accommodations. Again, none of these can be reserved through regular tourist agencies; arrangements must be made through the Spanish Tourist Ministry. And bear in mind we are talking about accommodations that may run as high as $7 per night for two with private bath. Not all hostels and pensions have dining rooms, so make it a point to inquire about this.

Punta Umbria, at the mouth of the Río Odiel ten miles from Huelva, is another immense beach, surrounded by a pine woods. Here also you may rent an apartment, bungalow, or pension. In 1971 a 120-room, three-star apartment complex, Urbanización Everluz (of the Patotel chain) was opened. Probably the most expensive in the area, its rooms are less than $10 per night for two. The twelve-room hostel, La Florida, on Avenida Oceano has a dining room but no private bath facilities.

At Punta del Sebo, down river from Huelva, the beach is golden, palm dotted, and dominated by a huge statue of Columbus. There are a whole string of villages and beaches in the general vicinity of Huelva: Playa de Nueva Umbria, El Rompido, Playa de Perdigón, and Las Antillas, for example. All are authen-

Punta Umbria, at the mouth of the Odiel River, is another long beach.

This beach at Las Antillas is one of many in the vicinity of Huelva.

tic, undeveloped Spain. A knowledge of Spanish is of considerable value in these out-of-the-way beaches, and there is little in the way of shopping or nightclubbing.

Places of interest, yes. Moguer, northeast of Huelva, is the home of the poet and Nobel Laureate Juan Ramón Jiménez, whose house has been converted into a museum. An outstanding tower in the town is the sixteenth-century church of La Virgin de Granada, reminiscent of the Giralda in Seville.

In Palos de la Frontera, in front of the fifteenth-century church of San Jorge, the men who sailed with Columbus were enrolled. The church is a national monument. Nearby is La Fontanilla, a Roman spring where his ships took on water prior to the voyage.

La Rábida Monastery, where Columbus met and discussed his plans with the priests who gained Isabella's support, is only three miles away. Hostería de la Rábida is a privately owned and run deluxe pension in front of the monastery. With only five rooms, it is a pure delight.

What this area of the Costa de la Luz lacks in entertainment it makes up for in great food. Excellent fresh fish and seafood are available at bargain prices. *Pez espada en Amarilla,* swordfish in wine sauce, and *Pargo encebollado,* porgy in oil and onion, are rare treats.

To get to the beaches of Cádiz, Rota, El Puerto de Santa María, Chipiona, Sancti Petri, and La Barrosa, as well as the seemingly inexhaustible wine cellars of Jerez de la Frontera, all of which are southeast of Huelva, you must drive to Seville. On any map of Spain you will see a large roadless area between Huelva and Cádiz; it's no mistake, there simply are no roads through the marshes. But there is an excellent four-lane express highway south from Seville that spans the seventy miles to Cádiz in little over an hour. From there you can strike out and explore the beaches to the north and south and the undiscovered towns inland to the west. There are many "undiscovered" towns such as Medina Sidonia in Spain, and the Costa de la Luz has more than its share.

South of Jerez de la Frontera, at the head of the Bay of Cádiz, are Puerto Santa María and La Puntilla Beach. A short distance away on the main road to Cádiz is Valdilagrana Beach, surrounded by an immense pine forest. The firm white sand of this long beach serves as a course for an annual horse race, a beach sport that seems to be unique to the Costa de la Luz. At Sanlúcar de Barrameda, the port from which both Columbus and Magellan sailed, horse racing on the beach has become an important social event, drawing people from near and far. Such an event is an opportunity to see all classes of Spaniards at their gayest.

Remember too, that Jerez de la Frontera, Sanlúcar de Barrameda, and Puerto de Santa María form a wine triangle, where most of the world's famous sherry is made. Don't be surprised at the aroma of wine in the air! The festival celebrating the grape harvest at Jerez during September is just one more reason to plan on being there.

A particularly good place to stay is the four-star ninety-room Hotel Fuentebravia on the beach at Fuentebravia, between El Puerto De Santa María and Rota. It's an excellent location from which to visit the shopping centers and wine cellars of Jerez; Arcos de la Frontera, one of the few towns in Spain to be declared a national monument; and cosmopolitan Rota and Cádiz. For devotees of bullfights, let it be known that El Puerto de Santa María has one of the largest bull rings in Spain. Just remember that the bulls are fought from the end of March to the middle of October, and then only on Thursdays and Sundays.

Rota, at the edge of the bay, just across from Cádiz, is the home of American naval and air bases, which means that American-style English is spoken here. On the long, long beach of La Costilla it's no trick at all to spot American servicemen. The beach at Rota is a bustling place with crowds almost any day of the week, and it is a great action station for teenagers and singles.

At least half a dozen modern multistory hotels and hotel apartments line the beach, with steps or entrances on the beach side. Hotel Playa de la Luz, a two-star 190-room hotel, is on the beach about two miles from the center of Rota. This has the advantage of the very long beach, yet it is away from the crowds in town.

Thirty-five miles north of Rota, quite close to Sanlúcar, is Chipiona, a tiny seaside town with a spacious and picturesque beach, presided over by the shrine of Nuestra Señora de Regla. Nearby is a large park, the lush Garden of Eden, Coto Doñana, to the fisherfolk. The two-star Hotel del Sur is right on the beach and has fifty-four brand-new rooms. The hotel opened in 1970 and is still not widely known, so rooms are available without reservations far in advance. However, it's open only from May through October. A hostel, the Chipiona, with only twenty-four rooms and with central heating, is open all year, should you be in the area before May or after October.

On the south side of Cádiz are several small villages whose open, undeveloped beaches are just waiting for you. Sancti Petri is five miles from Chiclana de la Frontera, an old Moorish town with a quaint gypsy quarter and sulfurous medicinal baths. Sancti Petri is one of the least visited beaches; however, at last count there were four hostels and one two-star hotel. If you're camping, just park your car and set up housekeeping.

In addition to its ancient vineyards, this entire area produces many of Spain's great fighting bulls. Consequently, a tour of the bull ranches should be planned at anytime of the year. However, in the early spring the ranches of Jerez, Medina Sidonia, Alcalá de los Gazules, and Los Barrios are the most exciting.

If you are any where on the Costa de la Luz, you must not miss Vejer de la Frontera, a town steeped in Moorish atmosphere. It is perched high on a crag, commanding a stupendous view of the sea and surrounding beaches.

Heading south on the N340 you'll catch glimpses of the sea and long stretches of empty beach. Watch for the signs indicating Tarifa, about sixty miles south of Cádiz. Before you get there you should see the sign of Hotel dos Mares. This fourteen-room bungalow hotel, only five years old, is open from May through October. But stop here if only for a sandwich or cold drink, and take a walk out back to the water's edge. The empty, white sand stretches for miles in both directions, and the dos Mares is the only habitation in sight. Unfortunately, this can't last forever, so take advantage of it now. The water here is clean, cool, and perfectly clear.

From here you clearly see the North African coast, and eighteen miles away at Algeciras, car-ferries and hydrofoils make regular crossings to Tangier, Casablanca, and Ceuta.

As you round the coast at Tarifa you enter the Costa del Sol, a wholly different world from the quiet, unadvertised Costa de la Luz.

Costa del Sol. Once beyond Tarifa, Algeciras, and Gibraltar, the most southerly point in Spain, the coast of Andalusia stretches away east to Cabo de Gata in Almería. Along this two-hundred-mile coastline, the main provincial highway, the N340, connects a string of sun-drenched cities, towns, and villages: San Roque, Estepona, San Pedro de Alcántara, Marbella, Fuengirola, Torremolinos, Málaga, Nerja, Motril, Almuñécar, Aguadulce, and Almería. These dozen, with their large and small beaches, as well as a half dozen more hamlets with secluded coves and clear deep water, forms Spain's most talked-about, advertised, and popular sun coast—the Costa del Sol.

With more than three hundred days of sunshine per year, less than thirty days of rain, and an average year-round temperature of 65° F., the Costa del Sol is the target for more than two million visitors a year. Fortunately they do not all congregate in one town or on one beach—although in two or three places, it seems that way.

The Costa del Sol is Spain's action spot. Along with the long hours of sunshine and the beaches, it offers long hours of night life. The array of bars and night clubs has to be one of the most fantastic in the world. It's been estimated, by people who estimate such things, that in Torremolinos alone there are more than three hundred night spots. And in Málaga, just down the road from Torremolinos, there are probably double that number, if you include all the tiny attractive *bodegas*. Up and down the coast, there are night clubs, swinging discotheques, and scores of beach bars, where the action continues from sunset to dawn.

Between Estepona and Málaga, currently the most "in" area, the beaches and towns are crowded. Beyond Málaga, to Almería, the Hollywood of Spain, the cities and towns are smaller, the fishing villages and hamlets once more take on the look and atmosphere of Spain, and the beaches are undeveloped and uncrowded. Here there is little difficulty in getting accommodations. But for people who want to live it up, who thrive on the bustle of crowded towns, the Costa del Sol from Estepona to Málaga is the place to crowd into.

The beach at Estepona is long, wide, and public. As at many of the Costa del Sol beaches, the sand is not pretty. A number of hotels have tried to rectify this oversight of nature by bringing in white sand, but more often than not the effort is unrewarding. This is one of the more popular beach towns for the Spanish themselves, and it is also a teenager's paradise.

Although rentable high-rise apartments form a continuous backdrop to the beach, the hard lines are softened by a beautifully landscaped paved promenade paralleling the water. The promenade has become a throbbing meeting place, especially at night, when the lights go on and music suddenly emerges from any number of places.

Estepona has at least two dozen hostel residences that are agreeably inexpensive, located on the side streets and a short walk from the main thoroughfare and beach. Most are relatively small, from nine to twenty rooms. Detailed information on these is best obtained from the Spanish Tourist Ministry.

A few miles east of Estepona is the five-star deluxe Atalya Park Hotel; its 250 rooms have everything. Of course you'll pay the price—about $25 a day for two without food, and about $45 with. Although it has several splendid pools surrounded by lush tropical gardens, the hotel's attempt at making a mini beach has been less than successful. Not so the golf course, which is one of the finest.

The Santa Marta, a first-class "B" hotel (three-star) is right on its own private beach, just a few miles from Estepona. Unfortunately it has only twenty-nine rooms, which means you'll have to scramble to get a reservation.

If you're "on the beach" or sightseeing in the area, an attraction not to be missed is *El Mercado de los Artesanos*, the Artisans' Market, up in the hills in the village of Casares. This lovely Andalusian pueblo gained its name and fame from Julius Caesar, who came here to bathe in the medicinal waters. Today, pack mules and burros bring unique handicrafts to Casares from remote mountain villages. To get there, take the road off to the right, six miles southwest of Estepona. The nine-mile drive into the hills is one of the hairiest, but it's worth the effort. Just make sure the brakes are working.

Down the highway east of Estepona are the five towns and cities that bear the brunt of the holiday traffic along the Costa del Sol. Thirty-five miles separates San Pedro from Málaga. In between are Marbella, Fuengirola, and Torremolinos. If you want a bustling, small town with sidewalk cafés, shops, public as well as private beaches, consider Marbella. If you prefer a smaller town, quiet and picturesque, but with a well-deserved reputation for good food and ample shopping, think of San Pedro. On the other hand, if it's noise, traffic jams, high-rise apartments shoulder to shoulder, and streets filled with shoppers, you want Torremolinos.

Two and a half miles from Marbella and about half that distance from San Pedro is the resplendent new Andalucia Plaza, opened in 1972. From the size and decor of its many public rooms, it seems that no expense was spared. The hotel is built in two curving wings linked by a reception area around a circular plaza. What an imposing structure! All 424 rooms overlook the Mediterranean. The dazzling flowered promenade leading to the beach and pools shows the hand of a master. A guest walkway crosses under the main highway to the tennis courts and La Siesta Beach Club. For those who want elegant accommodations, near enough to the centers of activity, yet far enough away not to be overcome by it, consider the Andalucia Plaza.

No more than a walk away, on either side of the highway, are several pensions and rentable apartments. In San Pedro itself, just a half mile west, are a dozen quite suitable hostels and pensions.

On the sea side, to the left of the beach and across from the Andalucia, not visible from the highway, is the Puerto. This should not be translated literally; it's more than a port, it's a combination promenade, marina, and shopping area. There are a variety of out and indoor cafés and restaurants, where you can choose to sit and leisurely sip a cold glass of wine or order a sumptuous meal in an expensive menu-less restaurant. Don't over-

The Hilton Hotel is eight miles east of Marbella, in fashionable Elviria.

look the Puerto.

If there could be a major American-type hotel that did not act the part, it would probably be the Marbella Hilton. Officially opened in 1969, the Hilton is located in the fashionable residential district of Elviria, eight miles east of Marbella. Few hotels can boast its sixteen-acre tropical gardens, including blooming banana trees that extend almost to the edge of the sea. And few hotels on the Costa del Sol have anything but black-brown sandy beaches with rock outcroppings. Not so the Hilton; this site must have been selected and prepared with care, even to importing white sand. But best of all, this large hotel is a warm and friendly place.

The beach is well equipped; a variety of paddle boats, water skiing, motor, and sail boats are all available. The sand bottom is firm and smooth, and the breakwater makes for calm seas, good for swimming.

The Hilton provides regular bus service into Marbella, but the provincial buses also stop here, so it isn't necessary to hire a car unless you want to go sightseeing on your own.

There are a number of four and five-star hotels up and down the coast, and Marbella has its share. Los Monteros, with its private clublike atmosphere at the edge of the beach, is outstanding; the Marbella Club lures the jet set to its private beach and apartments; El Fuerte, directly on the beach in the heart of town, is luxurious.

Only six hotels in all of Spain have met the strict requirements that place them in the enviable category of *Gran Lujo* or Grand Deluxe. Two are on the beaches, one on the Costa del Sol, one on the Costa Brava. Just outside of Marbella, the Melia Don Pepe carries this cognomen. It has everything: private beach, service and more service, large rooms, and elegant decor. Interestingly enough, *Gran Lujo* does not imply most expensive. In fact a half dozen hotels within hailing distance are more expensive.

Whether or not you are an *aficionado* of the bull ring, a trip to Ronda in the Sierra de Ronda mountains thirty miles north of Marbella is worth every minute and mile. Ronda is steeped in Roman, Moorish, and Christian tradition. In addition to its many ancient houses, arches, gates, and buildings, the bull ring is the oldest in Spain and reflects the Neoclassic wood and brick circular construction of the earliest type. You can't be in Marbella or vicinity without a side trip to Ronda.

For a few years it looked as though Fuengirola, halfway between Marbella and Torremolinos, had escaped the blighted touch of the developer. Unfortunately the Costa del Sol's advertising campaign has been so successful that high-rise apartments are mushrooming all along Fuengirola's beach front. Nevertheless Fuengirola has much to offer. Still retaining its old charm as a busy fishing port, it may offer the best of both worlds—neither as small as Marbella, nor as overwhelming as Torremolinos.

Three large, almost continuous beaches border the sea, and none is more than a five-minute walk from any point along the main street. The Paseo Maritimo, a long promenade, follows the waterfront from beach to beach.

Rather than seek out hotel accommodations, you might do well to consider the high-rise apartments Perla One, Two, Three, Four, and Five, Sofico's "string of pearls" strung out along the Paseo in back of Playa de Santa Amalia. Perla Six is near Playa de San Francisco. All are rentable from the Sofico Organization (their yellow sea horse signs are all over the coast) and are completely equipped, with services including linen, daily cleaning, and utilities. Two-bedroom apartments for four people rent for approximately $25 per day on a weekly basis. The management suggests that reservations be made at least two, if not three months in advance to ensure a suite. For reservations, write or call Sofico, 261 Madison Ave., New York 10016 (212 TN-7-5090). At these prices, you might want to think about their other apartments in Estepona, Marbella, and Torremolinos.

Within walking distance of anywhere in Fuengirola is Pueblo Lopez on the Mijas road, a new version of an old Andalusian village. Bryan Hindson, the owner-manager, wisely decided to build horizontally rather than vertically. He built a series of two- and three-bedroom apartments (to rent or buy) just far enough from the center of activity. Although these are not on the beach, the walk is no more than fifteen minutes, even if you stop to browse along the way. No matter where you are staying, their lovely dining room, done in authentic Spanish decor, is open to you.

Many people walk beyond Pueblo Lopez to Campo de Tenis, although it is two miles from the center of town. Campo de Tenis is a *Finca* or estate devoted to the increasing interest in tennis. Lew Hoad, former Australian Davis Cup Champion and currently coach of the Spanish Davis Cup Team, not only has a half dozen all-weather Tenis Quick courts, a pool, a pro shop, dressing rooms, and boutique, but he personally gives lessons or will make a fourth for doubles. He also has under construction a development of rentable villas and apartments. For information on tennis or the apartments write or call, Campo de Tenis, Apartado 111, Fuengirola, Spain.

Even if you're only interested in watching, go out there. There's no charge. And they have the loveliest little dining area where an excellent lunch is served from one to four P.M.

Continuing up the Mijas road by car, bus, donkey, or even on foot as some hardy ones do, you wind your way round and round ever upward, around a mountain top to the pretty little town of Mijas, which seems to exist only as a tourist attraction. But it is a delightful trip for food, shopping, and view. Standing near the bull ring you can photograph the entire countryside more than a thousand feet below. A recently completed amphitheater for music festivals and theatrical productions will be bringing more visitors up to Mijas. At the moment my only thought is the traffic on that narrow winding road!

Torremolinos, which now is Spanish in name only, is the personification of the extraordinary generative powers of advertising and its handmaiden, development. Eight years ago, it was still a simple fishing village. Today, Torremolinos is the sun-and-fun capital of the Costa del Sol having become, in a few frenetic years, a year-round resort for over a million visitors. Consequently we cannot recommend it as a vacation resort for families, singles or even teenagers.

Beyond Málaga, the Costa del Sol is vast and mostly undeveloped. The province of Granada has at least a half dozen excellent beaches both large and small; all are uncrowded but with quite adequate accommodations for those who want more of a touch of Spain.

Nerja, with its famous sea views from the Balcón de Europa and its prehistoric caves, is well worth a half day outing. Between Nerja and Almuñécar is a stretch of highway that must be one of the slowest, most ticklish, and certainly chancy forty miles anywhere. Weaving along the coast at times, high above the Mediterranean at other times, and up around narrow trails through the Sierra Almijara. This extension of the N340 is not to be traveled at night, if there are any possible alternatives. Even Scott and Craig agreed with that.

Playa de Herradura, sixty miles south of Granada, sits in the arm of a small bay. It is one of the secluded beaches not only because of its location, but its lack of accommodations. There is a total of three hostels and three pensions. If you're camping, drop anchor for a day or two, the views are extraordinary. The beach is sand and gravel, flanked by sheer rock cliffs.

Punta de la Mona is a new bungalow-villa development on a

hillside looking out to sea. One of the beauties of this spot is its colorful gardens and walkways. Information on rentals and purchases should be sought at the Spanish Tourist Ministry.

A few short but tortuous miles away at Almuñécar are three good beaches amid subtropical vegetation. The sand at Playa de San Cristóbal is coarse, but it doesn't affect lounging. Playa Puerta del Mar has fine sand, and Berenguel has some of both. Try a different one each day.

Almuñécar, a fair-sized town of about 14,000, sits white and picturesque at the foot of mountain cliffs, separated from the San Cristóbal beach and sea by the main highway that skirts the sea wall. You can go to the beach in the heart of town, or have long stretches to yourself at the flanks, several hundred yards east and west.

If you prefer to sit on huge rocks gazing out to sea, the sea wall in the center of town has steps leading right down to the rocks. They're yours for the basking.

The Goya, a Hotel-Residence on the beach at Avenido Galindo, is a cozy fourteen-room affair, but without its own dining room. When considering a place to stay, keep in mind that SC, *Sin Comedor*, means without dining room. If you don't mind eating all meals out, this will be of no consequence. If you do mind, don't get caught.

A two-star hostel, the Mediterráneo on Calle José Antonio has twenty-eight comfortable rooms that are suitable for year-round use. It too has the beach directly in front. Although built in 1934, it has a higher rating than the brand-new twelve-room Villa Mar on the beach at Avenida de Andalucia. Newness notwithstanding, Villa Mar has no dining room; the Mediterráneo does.

Don't fail to take a walk through the twisting, typically Moorish alleys of the old section of Almuñécar—Moorish Spain at its small-town best.

Past Almuñécar to the east, N340 undergoes a welcome metamorphosis; at Salobreña it straightens out to become a normal highway. Salobreña itself, situated on a great rock, was a castle and walled district preserved from the fifteenth century. It is also one of the less traveled areas of Spain. Salobreña's clean, wide beach stretches for two sun-warmed miles. This is the beginning of an area of excellent scuba diving. That's what the signs *"Zona de Pesca Submarina"* are saying—"Underwater fishing zone." The rocky underwater shoreline makes it an excellent fish breeding and schooling area.

Although the beaches in Granada and Almería are sandy, they are beginning to show a mixture of coarse sand and rock. As the Costa del Sol merges into the Costa Blanca and turns northward, the shore becomes less flat, more primeval.

In Salobreña, the eight-room three-star Hotel Salobreña, built in 1968, offers a wide range of services and facilities at less than $7 per night for two. A short walk from the beach are several relatively new pensions that offer rooms without bath for $2 per night.

Motril's atmosphere is that of a busy port—a good place to stop and shop on your way. Beyond it is the tiny fishing village of Calahonda, which at last count did not have 1500 people. But it does have its own bay and a lovely, clear blue, deep-water cove with coarse sandy beach. Here's a place to be alone, peaceful, forgotten. Playa de Calahonda doesn't expect too many visitors. It has one thirty-room pension on the beach, Las Palmeras, which opens June 15 and closes September 15. It can offer a double room with private bath for less than $5 per night, and has suitable dining facilities. Arrangements for accommodations in their privately owned guest houses or apartments can be made through the Tourist Ministry.

The coarse sandy beach at Castell de Ferro is wide and at least a mile long. The water is aquamarine and clear to its sandy bottom. Not the least of its attraction is the setting: the beach fringed with greenery and the mountains sloping gently down, with whitewashed apartments and houses clustered at one end. So different, and very Spanish.

The largest hotel in the area, right on the beach, is the fifty-nine-room Méson Castell that opens in April and closes at the end of September. However, there are at least five year-round hostels and pensions on the beach.

With only twenty miles of N340 separating Castell de Ferro from Motril, any feelings of loneliness can easily be dispelled by a trip to the "big city."

The Cabo de Gata, in the province of Almería, marks the end of the Costa del Sol. However, before making the turn northward, two beaches deserve mention. One, Adra, is in the foothills of the Sierra Nevada; the other, Aguadulce, and its companion town, Roquetas de Mar.

Adra, thirty miles from Almería, takes its name from the Río Adra that flows to the sea through the town. To the east and west are long but narrow, undeveloped sandy beaches. If your interests run to fishing, this place has both the reputation and the fish. From September 6 to 10, fiestas are in full swing in honor of Our Lady of the Sea, and St. Nicholas of Tolentino. This is a good time to sample the flavor of Spain.

Aguadulce, with less than 500 people, is really just a spot on the map, about seven miles from Almería. It has a series of excellent beaches with palm groves, à la North Africa, stretching from Playa del Palmer to Punta Sabinar, around the Gulf of Almería.

This is a naturally sheltered and lovely area, and the government has thought so highly of it that it has been set aside as a center of tourism, which means no runaway developments. Farther south on the gulf coast is the port of Roquetas de Mar, with a harbor set up for yachts and other small craft. Roquetas has a fabulous large beach with just about every type of facility, underwater fishing, and of course bigger crowds.

On the beach at Aguadulce is the eighty-room four-star Hotel Aguadulce, one of the Melia chain and only six years old. Because it has all the amenities, we suggest you write for a reservation at least a month or two in advance.

Almería, Portus Magnus to the Romans and Mirror of the Sea to the Arabs, is large as coastal cities go—over 100,000. It has an Oriental flavor, quite different from Madrid and Barcelona. There's so much to see—don't pass it by.

Costa Blanca. Beyond Cabo de Gata, the character of the coast alters markedly; promontories, rocks, sandy beaches, and small, mostly undeveloped towns are hallmarks of the Costa Blanca. The "white coast" is actually two wide arcs that meet in a point at

Cabo de Palos. Along the southern arc, from Mojácar to Cabo de Palos, and along the northern arc, from Cabo de Palos to Jávea, sun-drenched beaches form a pale golden line of sand, with rocky outcroppings sharply etched against the shimmering blue-green sea.

Try to arrive in Mojácar during the day; you will long remember and cherish that first sight. The traditional flat-roofed houses of this Moorish town huddle together, looking like whitewashed cubes marching up the hillside. There's much of interest to see here; you could even think of it as one huge flea market, so much frippery is for sale in its profusion of tiny shops tucked away along the narrow, winding streets.

And although the town originated with the Arab Moors, Mojácar's symbol is the Indala—a stick figure interpreted as a man holding a rainbow. Everyone seems to wear silver or gold Indalas. Large iron Indalas are used as door knockers. Anthropologists have found a relationship between the Indala of Mojácar and an ancient South American culture, but no one seems to know more than that.

Mojácar has two excellent large beaches, one at Puerto Rey, down the road a short piece, and the other across the road from Parador Nacional Reyes Católicos. Here, the beach is still in a primitive state, just as it must have been hundreds of years ago. The colorful stones are smooth to the touch from centuries of washing by the incessant sea. I'll never forget the incredulous look on the custom agent's face when we opened the heavy bag he suspected was filled with taxable goodies, only to find the collection of stones we dragged around the Mediterranean and finally home. They're beautiful and nontaxable.

The water, cool and inviting with its dancing blue and green highlights, is a bit more brave than the placid sea of the Costa del Sol. For those who enjoy swimming as opposed to bathing, this area is one of the best along the entire Spanish coast.

The only change taking place near the coast is Vista de los Angeles, an English development of fairly high-priced individual villas, near the parador. Every villa will be within walking distance of the beach. The yacht club at Garrucha, three miles away, is an added inducement to settle here, if you're looking for a remote and relaxing bit of old Spain.

The parador itself is a thing of beauty, with unlimited views out to sea. The rooms are elegant, and the food a delight—as are the women and young girls who serve. You'll have to put in a reservation at least six months in advance to get a room, but it's worth it. This is not set up for overnight visitors; most people come here for six to eight days (the Ministry now allows a ten-day stay at all paradores).

The next best place to stay is the three-star ninety-eight room Hotel Mojácar in town and right on the side of the mountain. The views from its terraces are magnificent, but you'll need a car to get to and from the beaches—or anywhere else. Walking up and down may be a great way to surrender calories, but it can be awfully tiring.

Looking for particularly inexpensive pensions, hostels, and residences in the general area? Try Garrucha. The Delfin is open year round; the Costa Blanca, Los Arcos, and Villa Sorrento, all on the beach, are open only from April through October and without dining rooms. These places have a fair number of rooms, but here too it would be well to get your bid in early.

Unless the Ministry of Tourism gives in to pressure, Mojácar could remain an ideal vacationland for years to come. It has decreed that no building, including the parador, may be more than two floors high, and most comforting, all buildings must be at least sixty feet from the edge of the beach. Time will tell whether these regulations will succeed.

We have always felt that a beach in close proximity to an old fort is an uncommonly compelling site. Águilas, in the province of Murcia, has just this happy combination. Built during the reign of Carlos III (seventeenth century), the castle-fortress of San Juan de los Águilas and Torre de Cope dominate what has become a modern little town with a fine harbor and two good beaches.

Two relatively small year-round residential hotels, La Calica on the beach at Paseo Peral and the Madrid at Plaza de Robles Vives, are available. Unfortunately, you'll have to seek dinner elsewhere; neither have dining rooms. I should note that although a working knowledge of Spanish isn't necessary in Mojácar, it does help in some of the areas less frequented by British and Americans. Águilas is one such place, and Puerto de Mazarrón is another.

Mazarrón and its harbor, Puerto de Mazarrón, are situated in a sheltered bay, which is bordered by four good out-of-the-way beaches: La Isla, El Castellar, La Reya, and Bahía. The three-star Hotel Bahía is almost at the water's edge on Playa de la Reya. It's open all year round and its best rooms are less than $8 per day for two, without food. This quiet, picturesque place way out on a finger of land is well known to northern Europeans who want sun, sea, solitude, and stretchable dollars. In the Puerto, the four-star Dos Playas Hotel offers a little more—for a little more.

Farther up the coast is Mar Menor, the Lesser Sea, actually a large salt-water lagoon. The lagoon effect is created by La Manga, a narrow sleeve of land extending some fifteen miles from Cabo de Palos to the reef at San Pedro del Pinatar. Tides flow in and out of Mar Menor through *encañizadas,* opening to the Mediterranean. At the apex of the triangular lagoon is Los Alcázares with its own beach and boat club. (La Manga forms the base of the triangle.)

Mar Menor and La Manga are no hideaways. Both have become well known to a wide number of Europeans. Hotels, high-rise apartments, and residential areas have sprung up to take advantage of the unique topography that permits year-round sunning and swimming in the warm, calm water.

La Manga's miles of beaches on both the lagoon and the sea are among the best in Spain. The villa developments and two yacht clubs testify to its popularity. Quite unexpected are the Gabia, a five-star hotel with all the amenities in the Cabo de Palos area, and the four-star Entremares on the beach of La Manga. Perhaps because of the unusual location, both are surprisingly moderate in price. This is an excellent spot for skin diving, water skiing, and sailing.

Almansa and its castle in the province of Albacete, recall the all but real Knight of La Mancha, Don Quixote. A few days or more in the area of Murcia or Alicante should include a side trip to explore the castle and walk the streets of the ancient plaza. After all, this is where the knight of the "woeful countenance" tilted with windmills.

Along the northern arc of the Costa Blanca in the province of Alicante, a number of beach resorts have been gaining prominence. Among these are Benidorm, Calpe, Jávea, and Denia.

Benidorm's indigenous population of 10,000 rises to 100,000 between June and September. I suspect half the population of the British Isles passes through Benidorm during the summer. Heavens, it's not the British, but the density that would recommend avoiding this place. Another Torremolinos is in the making. At last count, there were 161 officially approved accommodations ranging from the five-star Gran Hotel Delfín to the one-star nine-room Pension Estela. For those who like the crowds à la Coney Island, come, come by all means; Levante Beach, beginning to look like Chicago's lakeshore, can manage a few more people.

A most unusual and dramatic geological formation rises straight out of the sea at the beach of Calpe. Not only the sight, but the feeling engendered by swimming around the Peñón de Ifach is awesome. The mightiness of nature measured against the

A thousand-foot-high crag rises out of the sea at Calpe.

size of man is starkly presented by this thousand-foot-high bare crag. A tunnel bored in the rock makes it possible to get to the peak, where there are astonishing views of the coast.

Calpe is a small town, but it too is growing. Hotels are rising around the rock, but being so dwarfed by the Peñón, they don't seem to intrude. Calpe's hotels and hostels are small; only one of its dozen has more than fifty rooms. The eight-story, two-star Los Hipocampos is directly on the beach, with the Peñón off to its left. Walk toward that end, and you have the beach just about to yourself.

If you're camping along the coast, this is a good area. Between Alicante and La Granadella (a few miles beyond Calpe), with its lovely little beach and some marvelous underwater caves, there are ten campsites along main highway N332. The names of the camps, with a detailed listing of their facilities and charges, can be obtained from any of the Ministry of Tourism's many offices.

A short distance beyond La Granadella are Jávea and Cape San Antonio. Jávea has the parador nonpareil, Costa Blanca, one of the larger ones and also one of the newest, with an unfettered view of the entire beach area, which has lots of room. Only a few high-rise apartments break the line of sight to the mountains.

Because of the ruggedness of the coast there are a number of coves, grottos, and inlets, in addition to the major beach. These inlets and coves are great for sailing, underwater fishing, and snorkeling. Along the edge of Jávea's beach, facing the green lawns and luxuriant palms of the parador, is a long concrete walkway, which is a good spot for fishing. Just sit with your legs dangling in the water and cast a line, or bring a chair along and stay a while.

Jávea is a good place to spend the day. Although it is highly unlikely that a room at the parador would be available for one night, it is still a pleasant place to stop for lunch and a swim.

Denia, at the end of the Costa Blanca, derives its name from the goddess Diana, whose temple once adorned this city. Perched on the slope of Mount Mongó, the city seems to run down to the edge of the sea, and is surrounded by beaches in all directions. Although Denia is a fair-sized resort town, it is only beginning to awaken to the fact that it has sun, sea, and sand to offer. For the next five years at least, it should remain quiet and off the beaten track.

A second-class coastal road skirts the sea between Jávea and Denia. If you're at one, take the time to see the other; only six miles separates them.

Costa del Azahar. Within its wide sweeping arc, the Gulf of Valencia includes both the provinces of Valencia and Castellón. For countless years exuding the fragrance of orange and lemon blossoms, this area has come to be known as the Costa del Azahar, "the fragrant coast."

The long beach at El Saler can be a great base of operations for exploring Valencia and environs, if you can manage a reservation at the Parador Nacional Luis Vives. Few paradores or hotels can boast a championship eighteen-hole golf course in its front yard and a beach in its backyard. Between the beach and the parador is a miniature golf course for those who prefer smaller doses.

El Saler is only six short miles from the heart of Valencia, which means you can go back and forth any time of the day or night. Where the parador is quiet and relaxing, Valencia is gay and festive with lots of people, shops, museums, cathedrals. You get the best of both worlds.

The El Saler public beach, probably the best in this part of Spain, is long, wide, and puffy. It's not unusual to see tents pitched and campers parked at the edge of the sand. On weekends the Valencianos are out in force. However, this is not a teenagers' watering place. For the most part, the Costa del Azahar is a family place, a place for young marrieds, not too great for singles.

Farther north in the province of Castellón, Castellón de la Plana, the provincial capital, is a modern city with wide streets and well-kept plazas. At the coast, two miles away, in El Grao de Castellón, the spacious streets, white houses of the fishermen, and Piñar Beach combine to make this an authentic bit of Spain, off the beaten tourist track.

On the left side of the port is the Paseo Maritimo, a long promenade paralleling the beach and sea. If you're here for the day or passing through, there is a parking lot in front of a building that serves as café, luncheonette, and bath house.

In response to the recent influx of European vacationers, always quick to find new and uncluttered beaches, rentable apartments have been built just across the road from Piñar Beach.

Apartmentos Los Piños for example, at 37 Grao, very close to the beach, are available for a week to a month. These brand-new, well appointed units are moderately priced at about $75 per week or $290 per month. However, if you prefer a hotel on the beach, the four-star Del Golf in the same price range is relatively small and friendly, though not as bright and shiny.

Castellón itself is a bustling town. Since it is so close to Piñar, you can easily find an inexpensive pension in the heart of the city that will place little strain on your pocketbook, and still allow you to spend lots of time at the beach—bicycling to and fro if you wish.

Peñíscola is a small town sitting on a tiny peninsula, presided over by a fifteenth-century castle. The castle and the excellent beach have made it a much-visited tourist center, although not for Americans, so far. Nevertheless, the welcome mat is out for you and knowledge of Spanish is not a necessity.

For sheer visual impact, it would be hard to match the beach at Peñíscola, with Macho Castle commanding the view from the heights above the beach. The beach is wide and flat and the water shallow, clear, and calm for a hundred yards out. Sitting on the beach looking seaward, you always have the walls and ramparts of the castle in view. This is a scene not available just anywhere.

Built in 1966, Hostería del Mar, a four-star sixty-room hotel, is the largest in the area and offers the widest range of services. The Playa, a two-star affair and half the size, is only two years old. But your choice is not limited to these two; at least two dozen inexpensive hotel residences and pensions are available. And for those who want to stay only a night in the area, a four-star accommodation is the Albergue Nacional de Carretera about three miles north in Benicarló, a well-known beach resort.

The many beaches of the Costa del Azahar are to be found in small towns and villages—quiet, relaxing places. In some, such as Oropesa del Mar in Castellón, the beach is close to the town. And to accommodate the increasing numbers of vacationers who want the quiet of a small village, a high-rise apartment stands like a lonely beacon amid the vast surrounding plains. And in Gandía at the southern edge of Valencia province, the half mile of marble-tiled promenade along the beach passes a clutch of new high-rise apartments.

Still, this "fragrant coast" has many years before it becomes overcrowded.

Costa Dorada. The coastline of the provinces of Barcelona and Tarragona is known as the Golden Coast, Costa Dorada. Dana maintains that Sitges, twenty-two miles south of Barcelona, is the best teen-age (meaning thirteen to twenty-five) beach town in the Mediterranean. Lots of young people are there, along with other members of their families. Sitges is also a great place for older singles to meet, so the meaning is clear: Sitges can deal adequately with all ages.

Strangely enough, very little new building is going on in Sitges. It is a quiet residential area that becomes packed during the summer, yet the packing is not all-inclusive. For the most part it centers around Calle Bonaire and Hotel Calipolis, just about in the center of town.

Calle Bonaire is a side street near the four-star, 160-room Calipolis. But what a side street. While making our way through the throng, I commented to Anita that it reminded me of Chinatown. "That's it," she responded. "It's a Spanish Hong Kong." In fact, many of the leather shops will fit, cut, and put together most anything in twenty-four hours—à la Hong Kong.

Between the Calipolis and Hotel Terramar at the opposite end of town is the three quarter-mile beach—Playa de Oro. A little jitney bus, all seats, no sides, plies the Paseo Maritimo up and back all day and most of the night, for about a dime a ride. This makes getting around easy and suggests why parents don't mind the younger teenagers being out alone. Because Sitges is relatively close to Barcelona, you can expect the beach to be crowded on weekends. But again, if you wander in the direction of the Terramar, you do get away from the packed center.

The small side streets around Calle Bonaire—Calvo Sotelo, San Bartolomé, San Pedro, and Paseo Ribera, to note only a sampling—are crammed with small hotels, pensions, hostels, and residencias. None is more than a ten-minute walk from the beach, so it all depends on your preference and pocketbook. Both the Terramar and Calipolis are family-type hotels. Unfortunately, the Terramar is highly overrated. It's far too expensive for all its pretentiousness; the laundry prices, for example, are outrageous. And for a four-star hotel to supply thin slices of wood as toilet tissue is more than we can bear. After staying at the Terramar, the paradores are an incomparable joy. The Calipolis is much more friendly, less haughty, and more helpful.

Sitges is loaded with places to eat, and the food is good, even in the smallest most tucked-away places. If you're interested in something other than a typical restaurant, Go-Go's at Calle Parelladas, 35—just down from Hotel Bahía, is outstanding. Go-Go's is good food, good company, and it's right in the heart of "Hong Kong." Grilled barbecued chicken, salad, fried potatoes, and a glass of champagne for 75 pesetas—a little over a dollar, depending on the prevailing rates. Go-Go's has no doors, and the chickens are turning on spits right in front of you as you walk off the street. Go-Go's is a bar with stools. For our group, it was a nightly treat (Dana still hasn't decided if it was the chicken or the champagne). Johnnie, the hard-working, smiling manager, speaks English.

Sitges has another compelling feature: it's just a half hour by train from Barcelona. There's really no need to drive; the round trip costs 32 pesetas, or less than 50 cents. If you have nothing special in mind, get off at the new station, Paseo de Grazia. This puts you in the center of uptown Barcelona, in the vicinity of the better shops: Buntis, Pepe Martínez, Regents, Barcelona's "Fifth Avenue."

El Maresme is a fertile region between Badalona and Malgrat de Mar, named for the fact that its lowlands are easily inundated by torrential rains and crashing waves. Between the beaches and the highway are fig trees, palms, cactus, blackberries, and wild banana trees. In fact, this area is rightly called the "garden and market" of Barcelona. Its beautifully colored carnations are exported to Europe and South America by the thousands.

There are twelve picturesque towns within El Maresme, one following directly on the other. All appear to have been found by European vacationers seeking intimate touches of Spain. The beach at Masnóu, set against the smoothly sloping hills, has distinctly mustard-colored sand. At sunset the entire area takes on a deep red hue.

At Calella de la Costa the famous Roca Grossa forms several small beaches, separating them from the long stretch of beach in the main part of town. Each of the seaside towns—San Pol de Mar, Pineda, Malgrat, Canet de Mar, and the others—offers the American visitor a fresh vacation experience.

Costa Brava. The Costa Brava appears to have been chewed by a sea monster with bad teeth. In primordial terms, the tortuous crags rising from the water bespeak an incomplete creation. The wild cliffs shelter a multitude of tiny coves with crystal-clear water; on one side may be a sandy mini beach, on the other, rocky prominences or a beach squeezed between sculptured granite cliffs.

The Costa Brava is a contradiction. This seemingly inhospitable land is rich in old-world villages tucked in and around each bitten-out place, and along its shore are more hotels and guest houses than in any other area of Spain. In fact, primordial nature has lured the vacationer.

Lloret de Mar, for example, just becoming known to Americans, but famous as a beach resort for a century, at last count had 212 guest accommodations, from four-star hotels to one-star hostels. This beautiful little town swells from 4900 in winter to over 25,000 in summer. The attractions are many. More than a half mile of wide beach; calm, irridescent, crystal blue water; smaller beaches around any number of indentations along the coast; and the fine sea-front promenade, Paseo de Mosén Jacinto Verdaguer. "Cinto" Verdaguer to the Lloretans, is simple but lush. The gracefully lounging palms that line "Cinto" cast gentle shadows on the people eating and drinking at the outdoor cafés along its length. As if that were not enough, the altogether moderate prices of this resort add the final touch. But, as out-of-the-way and attractive as Lloret is, you've got to adore crowds.

On the other hand, about two miles south is the incomparable beach and bay of Santa Cristina, off the Blanes-Lloret road. It would be hard to find a more peaceful spot. Here is a golden sandy beach amid lush greenery and volcanic outcroppings. In the opposite direction, about two miles north of Lloret, is another delight of nature, Playa de Canyellas. Untamed Canyellas is along one of the most beautiful stretches of the Catalan coast, as the Costa Brava is called by Catalan-speaking Spaniards. The beach, shaded by oaks and pines, is divided in half by El Corquinyoli, a massive rocky ridge. Nature ran riot here. Around Lloret de Mar, you can almost have your cake and eat it, too. Crowds or isolation, the choice is yours.

The road from Lloret to Tossa de Mar, was obviously laid out by a confirmed drunk; there's not a single straight section in the eight scrambled miles. Of pre-Roman origin, Tossa has only 2500 inhabitants. But it has Vila Vella, a twelfth century Moorish Alcazaba—or fortress, containing the "old city," and protecting the sweeping horseshoe-shaped cove. What a sight! In back of Vila Vella is tiny Es Codolar beach, where the fishermen keep their small boats and where the rocky shoreline makes for secluded swimming. There are a number of small cove beaches around the walled fortress, as well as beyond the main beach.

Although not lacking for accommodations at any level, none terribly high in price, Tossa doesn't get the waves of people that pack into Lloret in July and August, when the French, English, and German invasion occurs. This is savagely beautiful country, and Americans ought to get to know it—while it's still this way.

San Felíu de Guixols and S'Agaró, at the tip of Playa de San Pol, are about fifteen miles farther north along this crazy no-name road. Just a little more heaving of the sea bed eons ago, and San Felíu would have been on a lagoon rather than the Mediterranean. The finger of land that almost closes it off to open water makes for a dandy sheltered beach, part sand and part rock. At the very edge of a glorious bay, San Felíu developed from an eleventh-century Benedictine monastery; today, it is the largest town on the Costa Brava. Considering that most towns here have 2500 peo-

A twelfth-century Moorish fortress on a rocky knoll at Tossa de Mar.

ple or less, San Felíu's 12,000 seems relatively large.

A mile beyond this big beach in the town is Playa de San Pol, open to the full force of the sea and simply great for swimming. It is a favorite of the Guixolis. The Gulf of San Felíu, which is dotted with small but impressive bays, ends at Cabo de Levante. The granite mound of the cape forms the southern boundary of San Pol, and the sands at the northern end blend into the gentle hillock of S'Agaró.

S'Agaró is unusual, as its teeming population of 160 will bear witness. This village is the summer residence of many Spanish and foreign luminaries, who have given the village an international reputation. It is a model of meticulous, strictly enforced city planning; a walk along the Paseo de Ronda will give you an appreciation of the planning involved—the well-tended gardens with fountains and statuary, the stately chalets, and enchanting intersections everywhere. And pine-bordered Conca Beach is one of the most attractive. As a luxury-class community, S'Agaró is a major center for both sporting and social events.

As if all this weren't enough for a village no bigger than a postage stamp, S'Agaró has a Hotel Gran Lujo, Hotel de la Gavina with seventy-three rooms, one of the six best hotels in all of Spain. Ask to be pointed in the direction of Plaza de la Rosleda, and you'll drive right up to the front door, just a whistle from the beach and the crystal aqua sea. Along the Costa Brava, the towns and villages are literally on the sea. You have to work at it, to get far from a good beach. For the most part the sandy beaches are small; it's the rocky beaches that are the larger, more inviting ones.

Consider Aiguablava. To do so, one must include Punta d'es Mut, a granite escarpment on which is perched the magnificent Parador Nacional Aiguablava. I suspect the Ministry of Tourism employs site locaters with goatlike climbing abilities. The site is sublime, but construction must have been an act of sheer courage. Today, the lucky ones, those able to wangle reservations—having written for them early enough—have both the sheltered sandy, mini beach 150 feet below and the weatherbeaten granite slopes slipping directly down to open water. For incomparable memories, don't forget your snorkeling or scuba diving equipment.

High on the granite cliffs, the parador at Aiguablava has an incomparable location.

The underwater world is lavish with colorful plants and small fish.

Across the cove from the parador are Los Olivos apartments. These should not be overlooked, nor should the guest houses scattered among the trees. Until you are close to them, the parador appears to be the only building in the area. Arrangements for the apartments and the guest houses should be made with the assistance of the Ministry of Tourism.

Bagur, with its 1900 people, is the big town hereabout, about two miles north of Aiguablava, and set in the hills edging the sea. Just south of Bagur is Tamariu (Catalan for *tamarindo* or tamarind, the trees that flank its beach). Although this is one of the most secluded and unspoiled of Bagur's beaches, don't expect to be alone—especially on weekends. The stark contrast between the bikini-clad vacationers and the black-draped Spanish women suggests that even without exposure, the native inhabitants love their beach.

On the other side of Punta d'es Mut, Fornells is characterized by its bare, creviced granite crags. Houses, pensions, and hostels are clustered at the base of the bluffs; steps cut into the rock lead down to the water.

Playa de Fornells has the four-star Hotel Aiguablava—not to be confused with the parador. The hotel opens April 1 and remains open until the end of October. In Bagur itself, the 235-room Cap Sa Sol is another four-star accommodation. Its wide range of services makes it one of the very few hotels along the Costa Brava that could be considered expensive. It opens on the first of June and closes at the end of September. These and a few others allow a choice beyond the parador at Aiguablava.

Sa Riera is an unusual beach due north of Bagur on the open sea. Facing north, it catches strong breezes that can bring the sea boiling onto the rocks. When the wind is from the south, the water is calm, transparent, and clear. This beach can't be seen from the road—you must leave your car and walk down a series of steps through the trees to where a concrete balcony has been built on the granite shelf. From here, another series of steps leads down to the sand and rock outcroppings. For quiet seclusion, few places can compare with Sa Riera.

While ancient remains of Roman origin are almost commonplace in Spain, Greek antiquities are indeed a rarity. Ampurias, some eighteen miles north of Bagur, was in fact Emporium of old—as old as 600 B.C., and much of it is intact. In addition to the excavations that cover several acres, the Archeological Museum displays a wide variety of statuary, amphorae, mosaics, and vases that have been unearthed since 1908, when the "dig" began. A day here is worth every minute.

But you need not be without a beach. Ampurias has its very own half mile of fine, white sandy beach, directly on the Golfo de Rosas, with the important fishing center of La Escala at the southern end and Rosas on the northern curve. Standing on the high ground of Ampurias, you can clearly see La Escala and its sand and rocky beaches. Between April and October, the winds and sea have subsided after a punishing winter, and the Mediterranean becomes almost motionless, shining with the blues and greens of precious stones. This is an area of fantastic sunsets that we have yet to capture on film.

Only relatively recently has our inebriate friend the crazy

Nature run wild is the theme along the Costa Brava; the beach at Sa Riera portrays this dramatically.

road builder brought two of his typical roads to Cadaqués: one from Puerto de la Selva, the other from Rosas. With these roads, however, Cadaqués has become less isolated; before the roads, the town was approached only from the sea.

Cadaqués is a special corner of Spain. It is Catalan, and its people reflect the austere life of those who extract their portion from a relentless sea. Although only several hours' drive from Barcelona, it is worlds apart in time and tempo. This is harsh country, and the hostile environment has fashioned a persevering, hardy folk. Yet they appreciate the "outsiders" who come to enjoy their beaches in the warmth of summer.

One's first impressions of Cadaqués is the stark contrast of the white houses clustered at the waterfront with the darkly brooding mountains encircling it on three sides. Quite unlike the other colorful towns along the coast. Is this why Salvador Dali loves it so, and has a home overlooking the harbor at Port Lligot? Or is it the coarse sand beaches—Playa de las Oliveras, Playa Gran, Playa Guillola, Port Algué—each a delightful cove with clear, clean water?

You can be sure that on the beach in Cadaqués or in one of its twelve certified lodgings, you won't be seeing anyone from home. Few Americans come here. It is that far out of the way, which is one of its great attractions.

Another, in these inflationary times, is that Cadaqués is one of the least expensive places to vacation in.

You must visit the seventeenth-century parish church right in the center of town and stand in fascination before the incredible baroque altarpiece. This is an unexpected place for such a work of art.

Cadaqués has yet another side; believe it or not, it's a swinging night-life town, replete with a bevy of small, all-night bistros. This is a good place for young people—and those who feel young.

Great days could be spent exploring the dozens of coves, inlets, and grottos between Rosas and Port-Bou, at the French border. It could be a little tricky, since the roads aren't all that great. At a number of places between Cabo de Creus and Puerto de la Selva, our friend the roadmaker has not yet done his work. This area is truly the *brava* coast.

Shopping. Spain can be a vast shopping spree. It is rich in regional arts and crafts as well as haute couture, and it has not yet been stripped of its antiques. There is a broad spectrum from which to select, and the range of prices you can expect to pay is at least as wide. Furthermore, your selections may come from places as disparate as the high-fashion house and the flea market.

A flea market is a joy to behold. The number and great variety of goods laid out on the ground never ceases to astound. Most interesting is picking your way through the maze, being careful to avoid stepping on an old clock or watch, a not-so-old collection of "ancient" keys, a converted fireman's helmet being sold as a genuine nineteenth-century cavalry headpiece, a bevy of oil lamps, and a thousand other things, from coins, medals, picture frames, and Spanish combs to bedposts and religious objects.

Flea markets are usually held on weekends. Try to get to the area early and watch the vendors unload their motorbikes, scooters, wagons, and automobiles. That in itself is a sight worthy of a prize photograph or a hundred feet of film.

Some markets such as the Rastro in Madrid's Plaza del Cascorro are well-established Sunday morning affairs; others you either stumble on in a vacation resort, or you are lucky enough to be around when handbills are passed out. You may see a sign posted that a flea market will be held every Saturday morning during July and August. In a town such as Mojácar, the entire place has a flea-market atmosphere.

Two things are necessary: a keen eye to distinguish between authentic and counterfeit, and a hard nose for bargaining. But if you like a piece, don't let its authenticity or lack of it deter you if the price is right.

If you see something you like, don't zero in on it. Pick it up, put it down, look at other things, come back to it, ask the price, put it down, walk away, frown, scowl. Then you either quote a price or ask the vendor his. Begin low enough so you can work up to a mutually satisfactory price. If you really want something, don't give up too easily. Remember, he wants to sell. The less he has to cart back home for next week's performance, the better he likes it.

Jewelry, including gold and silver filigree, is centered in Madrid and in Valencia, which is convenient to the beaches of the Costa del Azahar. Spanish craftsmen have a thousand-year heritage and produce excellent work. If you look at store windows, you will find that many bear a certificate guaranteeing the quality of the stones and metal. As with most jewelry around the world, prices in stores are not completely rigid; a reasonable offer may be accepted.

The province of Murcia along the Costa Blanca is justly famous for the delicate work of its jewelers. Along with the jewelry shops, the craftsmen's workshops are open to you.

Seville, less than an hour's drive from the towns of the Costa de la Luz, is one of Spain's three great antique centers. In its "Thursday" Market, akin to the Rastro in Madrid, you can buy anything from a Gothic panel to a piece of period furniture. In addition, a number of regular shops are crammed with authentic old pieces.

For some reason, visitors walking or shopping in Barcelona are usually directed to, or end up on Las Ramblas with its bevy of cheaper shops. However, Barcelona has some lovely shopping areas, one of which is Avenida del Generalísimo Franco. Ask to be directed to it. If you're anywhere near Estación del Norte, walk over to Paseo de San Juan. From here you can walk into Parque de la Ciudadela or over to "Franco." It's the Fifth Avenue of Barcelona.

There are still many alleys in Barcelona, Valencia, Cádiz, and Seville where patient craftsmen in their tiny shops produce pottery, guitars, toys, and forged iron work—marvels of originality and good taste. Walk around, follow the twisting narrow streets; you won't get lost, most come back to where they started.

On the other hand you must be wary of the "steerer" who, seeing your foreign dress and manner, spots you immediately for an American. They spot and steer any tourists they can persuade to "their shop," where great bargains in leather coats, perfumes, or other wares are promised. Unfortunately, the coats are usually second- or third-rate hides improperly tanned or dyed. Dry clean them once and they're two sizes too small. There is no charge for looking, but don't get pushed into buying if you're not a good judge.

For a look at the Macy's of Spain, be sure to walk into one of the five stores of El Corte Inglés in Madrid, Valencia, Barcelona, Seville, or Bilbao. Not only are there hundreds of departments and moderate prices, but the service is excellent. In addition they usually have a good restaurant with typical Spanish food, a *cambio* (foreign exchange at prime rates), post office, and information service. Don't pass them up.

The dollar still goes a long way in Spain. It's a shopper's paradise with lots to choose from. But do remember that Spain is where the *siesta* appears to have originated. Depending on where you are, *siesta* means "closed" from one to three or four P.M. So plan your shopping schedules accordingly. Happy hunting.

Food and Drink. The grape and the olive. Spanish gastronomy is firmly based on these two fruits—grapes for wine, olives for oil and condiments. Ever since the Phoenicians played "Johnny Appleseed" with olives, Mediterranean cookery has risen to the heights on olive oil. And although credit for Spain's viticulture cannot be so easily pinpointed, it is nevertheless extensive, with a diversity of types and flavors.

For example, as to strength of wine, the choice ranges from a lean *"churrillo"* from Burgos with less than ten percent alcohol, to the heady heavyweights from Jumilla, Cariñena, and Yecla. Not to speak of the world-famous sherries from Jerez.

As noted earlier, Spain is a large country, with a great diversity of flora and fauna and no less diversity of people. As a result, Spanish food is extremely varied: there are fifty recognized ways of serving potatoes and more than thirty well-known recipes for *gazpacho*—a cold soup delicious in any form. We've delighted in at least five types of onion soup, differing in color, contents, and taste. Rather then be surprised, expect to find a dish ordered in one town different from one with the same name that you had in another town.

Gastronomically speaking, Spain can be divided into five general gastronomic zones: the north for sauces, the center for roasts, the south for fried dishes, the east for rice cookery, and the Ebro

Basin of Zaragoza and Pamplona for the incomparable *chilindrónes*. But don't fret, there are restaurants in the south, around Almería and Málaga, that serve *chilindrónes,* and restaurants along the Costa Brava where magnificent roasts can be had, along with fish and seafood.

Should your eye catch *chilindrón* while scanning a menu, order the dish. The basis, of course, is finely chopped tomato and onion sautéed in olive oil, in which chicken, lamb, or veal is pot roasted. To this are added peppers, garlic, parsley, toasted saffron, paprika, and chili peppers. Try to imagine the aroma.

Entremeses are not to be confused with hors d'oeuvres or appetizers. If a comparison is helpful, they resemble antipasto. Five-star restaurants and wayside inns alike feature some variety of this national dish. The "dish" in this instance is uniformly large and overflowing with shellfish, such as mussels (*mejillónes*), pickled vegetables, green and black olives, sardines, anchovies, tomatoes, sliced hard-boiled egg, cold meats, usually several types of ham. Recently, hot *entremeses* have been added to the cold, including *riñónes* (kidneys), sweetbreads (*cridillas*), and spiced sausage (*chorizo*).

Garlic soup is not commonly served in American restaurants. In fact, few of us think of garlic and soup in the same breath. In Spain garlic soup is well known in several variations, including garlic with eggs, tomato puree, clear, and with meat. Most often it's served in earthenware bowls and eaten with a wooden spoon. Very Spanish.

One can't speak of soup in Spain, especially on a warm night, without mentioning *gazpacho,* an Andalusian-Moorish contribution. In restaurants the *gazpacho* base is brought to the table first, followed by the accessories: diced tomatoes, green pepper, cucumber, toasted bread cubes, onion, and chopped egg.

One night in Seville, at the excellent, moderately priced Via Veneto (upstairs), I began eating the *gazpacho sans* accessories, thinking this was the local variety. As I took my second or third spoonful, one of the assistants came up with a trayful of goodies. He pointed to each in turn, and I nodded yes, yes. In this way, *gazpacho* can turn into a meal by itself.

Although most restaurants add a ten to fifteen percent service charge, a small tip to the waiter and maître d' goes a long way, especially if you plan on coming back. They have good memories.

Although we are no more than moderate fish eaters at home, in Spain we invariably go on a fish kick. It's not unusual for me to have *lenguado* (sole), four nights in a row. It's always a little different, and always delicious. On the fifth night I may switch to *merluza* (hake) with a green sauce, garnished with asparagus and parsley. The little roast potatoes that are often served with it are mouth watering. Then, there's grilled sea bream, *besugo asado,* and trout, *trucha.* In some more creative restaurants, slices of ham are tucked into the trout, making it even more savory.

If you're along the Costa del Sol, try the Bodegón de Sancho Panzo in the Hotel Andalucia Plaza, between Nueva Andalucia and San Pedro in the direction of Estepona. The Bodegón is an authentic Spanish specialty restaurant, featuring traditional dishes from each of the culinary regions. The decor is pure, old Spain.

In the same area, on the main coastal road (N340) toward Marbella on the right side, is the very jet-setty Marbella Club. Although the restaurant is noisy, the food is quite good. At both La Pergola, the open-air terrace restaurant at the Marbella Hilton, and at the more formal Los Naranjos, the menus offer large selections, and you can be sure both food and service will be tops.

Of all Spanish dishes, perhaps the best known to Americans is *paella.* Although a good *paella* can be had in many areas, even Madrid, the best are acknowledged to be found along the Costa del Azahar and Costa Blanca, from Alicante northward through Valencia. Remember, this is the *Zona de los Arroces,* the rice area, and that's the basic ingredient in all *paellas,* of which there are many variations. *Paella* must be made in an iron pan, the *paellera.* The ingredients added to the rice include olive oil, chicken, lean pork, ham, eels, peas, beans, crayfish, snails, artichokes, green peppers, garlic, onion, spices, saffron, and herbs.

One of Spain's most typical dishes, not found too often along the coastal areas is *cocido* (literally "boiled"), a stew whose history is traced back to the fifteenth-century Spanish Jews. Often called *puchera,* for the pot it's cooked in, the dish contains chick peas, potatoes, cabbage, meat, and spiced sausage. Chicken giblets are added in some areas.

A discussion of Spanish food would not be complete without a word about *bocadillos.* Before we took Scott and Craig along on our trips to Spain, *bocadillos* didn't seem to exist. Somehow, those two found them wherever they went; I suspect they raised *bocadillos* to a new status. The *bocadillo,* Spain's response to the American sandwich, is a roll usually filled with cheese and tomato, or sometimes sardines or a slice of meat. I do believe Craig ate *bocadillos* from one end of Spain to the other.

As you drive along the open roads—and often they are open as far as the eye can see, unobstructed except for a mountain in the distance—you will feel the need for food and drink. But it isn't necessary to carry a canteen and pack lunch, as there are a variety of roadside "watering" places. Almost all towns have a *pastelería* and *confitería,* which sell tea, coffee, soda, cake, and *bocadillos* galore. We enjoy these shops most of all, as they allow us to get a glimpse of small-town life.

If you're looking for a complete meal along a highway in Spain, remember to give the albergues more than a second glance. Or, if you're the adventuresome kind when it comes to eating, stop at a typically Spanish roadside restaurant (more like an English pub) frequented by the local townsmen. Here you can eat your way through *Tapas* (hors d'oeuvres), picking from some twenty or thirty dishes that line the bar. Just point to this, this, and this, and you can enjoy a variety unlike anything you've seen elsewhere. On one occasion, six of us ate our way through about twenty different dishes—including anchovies, clams, squid, tuna, sausage, hard-boiled egg slices, potato salad, tomatoes, melon, asparagus, potatoes and tomatoes, clams, olives, string beans and tomatoes, pickled cucumbers, sardines, and cheese. With coffee and ice cream, our bill was 217 pesates—just a few pennies over $2! We paid four times as much for a tank of gasoline.

Most assuredly, you can eat well in Spain. If I could make only one recommendation about food, it would be to dine at the Spanish paradores. The food is excellent, moderately priced, and typical of its region; the service is as good as the food, and the decor is Spanish and elegant.

THE NEW RIVIERA

The Languedoc-Roussillon coast curves like a half moon around the Gulf of Lion for some 110 miles between the Spanish border and the Camargue (the Rhône delta) at Arles. And although the red wines of this region have been favorably quaffed for several hundred years, this area was long known as the land France forgot. But that has now changed; France has rediscovered Languedoc-Roussillon. Not content with one Riviera, they are creating a second here—a man-made French Riviera!

During the late 1950s, it became increasingly evident to a group of alert Frenchmen that the Riviera—the Côte d'Azur, between St. Tropez and Menton—had become popular to the point of overpopulation. They made plans to develop new beaches to accommodate the increasing numbers of sun-and-surf worshipers. A second Riviera would arise, not from ashes like a phoenix, but from swamp and marsh, far more difficult to deal with. And not one, but six new beaches were planned within the arch that embraces Montpellier to the northeast and Perpignan to the southwest. Resorts were planned for Saint-Cyprien, Leucate-Barcarès, Gruissan, L'Embouchure de l'Aude, Cap d'Agde, and La Grande Motte.

The idea was preposterous. Perhaps it had to be, if it was to succeed. Consider that 110 miles of low-lying, mosquito-infested swamp had to be drained, filled, and layered with fine, white sand. Hotels and complete beach resorts had to be constructed. But the idea was only preposterous, not absolutely impossible, so plans were drawn up. By 1963, derricks, earth movers, barges, and men had begun one of Europe's most massive earth-moving projects, on a scale reminiscent of Holland's development of its polders, by reclaiming land from the sea—an environmental revolution if ever there was one, and a beneficial one at that. Eight laborious years later, in place of sea, sky, and marsh, there had arisen near Montpellier a multipyramidal skyline that would make Tutankhamen green with envy. La Grande Motte was the first of the six beaches to reach a state of readiness for vacationers.

Although the entire project is under the general supervision of a ministry in Paris, each of the six resorts is being planned and developed by a different group of architects, and each will be uniquely different from the others. For example, La Grande Motte has taken for its motif a pyramidal style, and each building, while resembling a pyramid, is different from every other. Few areas of the world have given architects so grand a challenge and such free reign, and few areas can boast such elegant creativity.

Other beaches will cater to vacationers with a preference for boating and sailing. Accordingly, some of these new resorts have a built-in network of canals, allowing mooring almost directly at your front or back door. All the beaches have been planned to give preference to people; automobiles are banned all along the shoreline. It isn't necessary to keep an eye out for cars or motorcycles, and the noise level is low, which in itself should recommend it. Here we see total planning in action.

All that existed was marshy, irregular, lagooned coast. Architects and engineers had to plan roads, bridges, homes, stores, hotels, campsites, harbors, playgrounds, utilities, marinas, and reforestation; they did it all. Not only that, but each beach resort was planned to accommodate a limited and fixed number of people; each resort has a specific number of beds available in a fixed area, around which the architects had to plan. None of these beaches should become overcrowded in the future.

In addition to the six new beaches, a number of established sand, gravel, and even rock beaches that have long been used by the French and northern Europeans will be refurbished, while others will remain intact. Languedoc-Roussillon is emerging as a 110-mile resort with beaches to suit just about all tastes and preferences.

La Grande Motte is scheduled for completion by 1974. The others, in various stages of implementation and development, although beginning to accommodate increasing numbers of vacationers, should be completed by 1975.

Climate. Along this arch of the Mediterranean you can depend on at least a third of the total hours in the year to be hours of sunshine. The rain pattern here is a little like that of Miami Beach; in the fall, September through November, and again in early spring, there are heavy but intermittent short showers. Because there is a constant offshore breeze, the heat of summer never becomes unbearable. And the water is cooler and less placid than in many areas in the Mediterranean basin. Here you can expect rollers and deeper water, which also cools things off.

Transportation. Because vacationers usually have a limited time schedule, the planners of these beaches believed that getting there should be quick and easy. It was not whimsy that located these beaches between major air and rail terminals and linked them with major highways. And harbors and marinas were deliberately built early to facilitate arrival by sea.

Daily jet flights to Montpellier and Perpignan from Paris via Air-Inter take less than two hours. Half a dozen major European lines fly into Montpellier, Nîmes, and Perpignan. From London, BEA (BA) connects in Paris with Air-Inter, and from the United States, a number of international carriers provide service to Paris and Marseille.

Daily direct express rail service from Spain via Madrid or Barcelona to Perpignan, Narbonne, Béziers, and Montpellier is readily available. Similar rail service is available from Paris and

FRANCE

SPAIN

LANGUEDOC-ROUSSILLON

Nimes

Montpellier

La Grande Motte

Sète

Carcassonne

Cap d'Agde

RIVIERA

Narbonne

Gruissan

Leucate-Barcarès

Perpignan

Saint-Cyprien

Collioure

Rome. The eleven-hour train ride from Paris passes through lovely countryside and a number of major cities. By taking the train in the afternoon, you arrive in Perpignan in the morning and save the price of a hotel.

Once inside the French borders, all roads lead to the Mediterranean. From Spain, the N9 becomes the N113, which links all the beaches of the new Riviera. From Paris, take the N20 directly into Toulouse and the N113 to Carcassonne and Narbonne. From Marseille, drive north to Arles, then take the N113 down. Many good roads connect with the N9 and N113, which serve the entire area.

BEACHES

Leucate-Barcarès. About halfway between Narbonne and Perpignan is the new beach of Leucate Barcarès. In geographical terms, Leucate-Barcarès is a spit, five miles of white, sandy beach separating the Mediterranean from the huge lagoon of Salses. With "water, water everywhere," the architects designed this resort for sailing, motorboating, and yachting enthusiasts. Water skiers and fishermen will find that ample provision has been made for them as well. Not only have ports been constructed at each end of the spit, but a network of canals threads its way through and around it in a most ingenious fashion. No matter where a vacationer may stay, he and his boat are hardly parted and have ready access to either lagoon or sea.

Between Leucate and Barcarès is a vast common recreational area; the long, sandy beach stretches from port to port and is completely open to the public. Swiss, German, Greek, and French sculptors have created prodigious, brilliantly colored pop-art and free-form designs. Spaced at intervals along the beach, these sculptures are becoming known as the Sand Museum. Some weigh as much as five tons and may be twenty feet high. It's quite remarkable to come upon Herculean yellow and red electric plugs rising from the sand, or a series of intricately carved totem poles.

But it is no less remarkable to drive along the main road and come upon a steamship grounded on the beach. The *Lydia,* a ves-

The intricately carved totem poles are gathering places on the beach at Barcarès.

sel as large as those currently plying the Mediterranean, sails no more, but rather serves as a first-class restaurant, with fresh-water pool, bar, and nightclub. The *Lydia* is a symbol of leisure and relaxation.

The Marina Club of Barcarès (MCB) is one of the first to employ Teleski Nautique, an automatic device that can pull six skiers through the water at once, at speeds up to thirty miles per hour. Craig gave this a whirl and put his stamp of approval on it.

Along the beach, French school teachers have rented areas for day camps and for instruction in a number of sports. Swimming, for example, is taught in rectangular three-by-twelve-foot plastic containers. It's a great idea and apparently quite effective.

Mind you, Leucate-Barcarès is not scheduled for completion until 1975 or 1976, but people don't necessarily wait for the opening gun to sound. Many have come to buy apartments and "flats" ranging in price from 30,000 to 120,000 new francs—about $7000 to $30,000. Motels and hotels, with and without marinas, are becoming available in increasing number. Campsites are open, and

Scott and Craig sampling the children's play area at La Grande Motte's holiday village.

holiday villages are nearing completion. In all cases, real estate and rental agents, a local tourist agency, or the French Government Tourist Office in New York can be of help in arranging accommodations.

I might add that France is not cheap. Not only is gasoline expensive, but food is, too. For example, a bowl of spaghetti *Bolognese* at most restaurants is about $2; with a *salade niçoise* and dessert, which is not a large meal, the bill begins to add up. On the other hand, free wine can be had all over the countryside. Just watch for signs advertising this or that winery and suggesting you stop and taste. This is a good way to become an expert wine sampler.

We all agreed that Leucate-Barcarès (and the other beaches in this area) is, and will be for some years, very French. So it helps greatly to speak the language or at least make the attempt. It is obvious here that French high-school students learn about as much English as ours learn French. Although Scott and Craig found many teenagers here, and getting acquainted posed few problems, they pointed out that being able to speak French does make a difference.

At this point in its development, Leucate-Barcarès is definitely a family affair. It will be a few years before singles find this beach as inviting as St. Tropez and the other villages along the bustling Côte d'Azur.

Cap d'Agde. Béziers, about midway between the Camargue and the Spanish border, is only eleven miles from the new resort at Cap d'Agde. The nearby town of Agde has long been known for its fortified medieval cathedral.

The plan for this new resort calls for eventually accommodating 58,000 visitors—6000 in hotels, 15,000 in holiday villages and camps, 16,000 in individual villas, and 21,000 in communal blocks.

But so far, little has been said about Naturalist Camps. The fact is, facilities are being developed for 8000 nudists; when completed, this should be the largest nudist settlement in the world. Projections for the future indicate that it will eventually accommodate 15,000. This development fits right in with the growing phenomenon of nudity, and the French government, responding to the fad (?), has added this to the total planning for the new beach at Cap d'Agde.

Already constructed at the camp is a semicircular stadiumlike building that doubles as an apartment house and shopping center, but with nary a clothing store. When you see the sign of the Mermaid, you know you've arrived in the vicinity of Port Ambonne. So be prepared to disrobe, and remember, eye-to-eye contact is the rule.

Saint-Cyprien Plage. The beaches of Saint-Cyprien, Collioure, Argelès, and Banyuls-sur-Mer, all located just north of Spain's Costa Brava, collectively constitute the Côte Vermeille, the vermillion or ruby coast. Some eight miles south of Perpignan is Saint-Cyprien-Plage, southernmost of the six new beach centers, moving toward completion. Unlike Leucate or La Grande Motte, St.-Cyprien has a background of snow-capped mountain peaks, notably Mont Canigou.

The ancient fishing village and the nearby vineyards that almost border the sea form the nucleus around which the two-mile-long sandy beach will be built. Plans call for accommodating 24,000 people in a variety of single and multiple dwellings.

Collioure. It is the determined tourist who has sought out and come to know the quiet beaches of some of France's oldest cities. The beaches of Argelès, Collioure, Banyuls-sur-Mer, and Port Vendres have been vacation and work areas for a number of famous painters: Picasso, Matisse, Derain, Dufy, Gris.

At Collioure, three small sand and stone beaches curve around the now restored fourteenth-century château of the Kings of Majorca. This is a vividly picturesque setting, but it is far from being a bustling playground. A short walk away is the hostelry of the Templars, a two-star, fifty-three-room hotel. Its restaurant is undeniably dramatic. Scott felt as if he were eating in a museum, which in a sense it is; the walls are covered with sketches and paintings in water color, oil, and other media. And all are for sale. Here's a place to increase your art collection without the benefit of a middleman.

At Argelès, pine woods ring the long, wide strip of fine, sandy beach. Although not one of the new beaches, it is included in the refurbishing process. Its harbor is being extended to accommodate hundreds of yachts and light craft.

One can only wonder if the crystal clear water, now so inviting, will become hopelessly polluted from the thousands of boats to be berthed in the new areas. One can only hope the planners have considered this unfortunate possibility. As full development of this coast is not anticipated until 1975 or '76, there is still time to get in a good swim.

La Grande Motte. Instantly recognizable from sea or land by the distinctive pyramidal design of its dominant buildings, La Grande Motte is the linchpin in the chain of beaches that are fast becoming France's new "Riviera."

Between Le Grau du Roi and Carnon Plage, twelve miles east of Montpellier, on the fringes of Provence's Camargue, La Grande

La Grande Motte stretches for almost three miles along the coast.

Motte fronts the sea along two and a half miles of gently sloping soft sandy beach. Behind it are two impressive man-made lagoon-lakes and a natural rampart of craggy hills. Unlike most beaches, the result of nature's efforts over countless eons, this one is brand new; even the deep sand had to be trucked in.

La Grande Motte's 2000 acres, now almost completed, include apartments, hotels, shops, villas, restaurants, nightclubs, campgrounds, sports areas, and a thousand-boat marina. Here, the pedestrian is king. Although the main buildings have been laid out along broad boulevards, none is more than a ten-minute walk from the sea, and automobiles are relegated to the parking lots; none is allowed along the seacoast.

This was not meant to be an intimate hideaway beach resort but rather an action spot for everyone—singles, young marrieds, and families. It is so big and so well planned that there is a place for everyone. But you've got to be prepared for the high-rise, city-like atmosphere, which attracts a high-style international yachting crowd. The boutiques boast Paris originals rather than local peasant handicrafts, and the restaurants are staffed with trained chefs who delight in displaying their talents, which means, of course, inspired food. Be prepared for a relatively expensive sojourn.

Two hundred yards from the beach is the just completed 135-room, four-star Hôtel Frantel. Curiously enough, although the design is most contemporary, it is the only major building that does not follow the pyramidal motif. How did it pass the Central Committee?

Although this New Town has city qualities, it's unlike any city you've ever seen. It's like looking at abstract art—the design of the buildings, the colors, and shapes all have an unreal quality. This is a "city" without industry, without pollution; the sky is clear and deep blue. Because it is still in the first phases of landscaping, the trees are still small. But their greenery is beginning to add a natural touch. The water is clean, clear, and refreshing, not nearly as warm as the more southerly areas of the Mediterranean. And the beach is long and wide and relatively empty, sloping gently to the water. Consequently there are no sudden dips or drops, no shelves to walk off into suddenly deep water. Not only is this great swimming water, but the favorable off-shore breezes make this a sailor's beach.

Even in Paris, there are few places where you can walk up to a corner stall and buy a crêpe or crêpes with a dozen different fillings. Here you can. But like Paris and other French cities, La Grande Motte also has charming sidewalk cafés.

The planners haven't forgotten the evening. Along with well-lit shop windows, they have placed street lights strategically to allow strolling along the wide walks. The lights from the apartments and hotels add a touch of drama.

Places of Interest. The intentional development of the Languedoc-Rousillon coast has brought an added benefit. The whole of southwestern France, virtually off the beaten tourist track because of its distance and "out-of-the-wayness" from Paris, is now easily accessible. The ancient cities of Arles, Avignon, Nîmes, Narbonne, and Carcassonne, the châteaux of Quercy and Rouergue, as well

The sand is white and clean on the man-made beach.

The facilities for boating at La Grande Motte are extensive.

as the many Roman and prehistoric remains of Provence, become no more than one- to three-day side trips from the beaches.

For example, thirty-three miles from Narbonne, itself only eight miles from Gruissan, is one of the wonders of France. The thirteenth-century fortified city of Carcassonne in the department of Aude is perhaps the only one in Europe so completely intact and still in use. Within its formidable double stone walls, with towers and ramparts right out of the *Song of Roland,* are the old church of St. Nazaire, still used for daily worship, and the château museum, with an unrivaled collection of armor and seige weapons. There are fascinating antique shops and incredible photographic panoramas. Carcassonne has to be seen to be believed. Should you be in the vicinity on Bastille Day, July 14, stay around for the display of fireworks; the park in front of the main entrance is a good place to watch. Bastille Day is a national holiday, so you will probably find all stores closed but the food shops.

A completely different kind of attraction is the Aix Music Festival, held annually in Aix en Provence. From July 10 to 31, this ancient university town becomes host to music lovers from around the world. Performances are held in theaters, cathedrals, churches, cloisters, and châteaux. Organ, piano, and violin recitals; operas, concerts, and chamber music are in progress part of each day, and you can attend as few or as many as you like—as many as you can purchase tickets for, usually in advance.

Besides the music, Aix is a delightful university town. Especially charming is its Cours Mirabeau, a stately tree-lined boulevard with fountains, shops, and sidewalk cafés. A good deal of the night life for the teen generation begins at the Place de la Libération, where there are a number of noisy restaurant-cafés. The Rotande caters to the under-thirty crowd, while the Vendôme caters to the older ones.

During the music festival, hotel reservations become scarce. Nevertheless, keep in mind the four-star Hôtel Riviera in a wooded glade on the outskirts of town and the Roy René in town, just a three-minute walk from the center of the Mirabeau. If you haven't sampled old-world charm and service, try the expensive Roy René; there aren't many of this breed left. But ask for a room facing the park, in the rear, or you'll not sleep a wink. Unfortunately, the rooms facing the street are subject to the maddening traffic noise of trucks, taxis, scooters, and racing cars, all using the main road to Nice and Toulon.

Nîmes, in the lovely department of Gard, at the apex of the triangle of Nîmes, Montpellier, and Arles, is an easy one-day excursion from La Grande Motte or Cap d'Agde. Nîmes was already old when the Romans came through. Its amphitheater, dating from about the first century, is one of the largest arenas in the world, on a par with the Coliseum in Rome.

The Jardin de la Fontaine, at the end of Boulevard Jean Jaurès near the Temple of Diana, is a splendid example of a classic eighteenth-century garden meant for strolling. And La Maison Carré, in the form of a Greek temple, at the corner where Boulevard Victor Hugo meets the Place de la Comedie, is considered one of the finest Roman buildings in France. Today, it is a most interesting museum of antiquities.

Between May and October there are special events every week, including music festivals, agricultural fairs, folklore and equitation exhibitions and contests. To find out what events are scheduled for the time you expect to be in the vicinity, contact the Syndicat d'Initiative, Office de Tourisme de Nîmes, 6, Rue Auguste.

In addition, the French Government Tourist Office in New York City can provide information on the historic and religious sites and shrines in the entire region, as well as a list of the châteaux that are open to the public.

SARDINIA AND ELBA

SARDINIA

They say that Queen Eleanora d'Arborea, sailing to Corsica to marry Prince Brancaleone Doria, stopped briefly at the Bay of Capriccioli on the island of Sardinia. After taking a swim, she was combing her hair in the sun when her emerald bracelet came loose and fell into the sea. She began to cry because the bracelet was a present from the prince. Hearing her sobs, the sea told her, "Sweet queen, do not cry. The emeralds you have lost will stay forever in the color of my water."

People say this is the reason for the spectacular color of the sea along what is today called the Costa Smeralda, the Emerald Coast. Called Gallura by the Sards, this sea- and wind-carved coast in the northeast corner of the island has a profusion of grottoes, caves, coves, and bays. The many handsome beaches range from completely sheltered to totally exposed.

But the color of the water and the warmth of the beaches remained largely unknown until recently. Through the centuries of Sardinia's frequently turbulent past, Libyan, Punic, Phoenician,

Saracen, Roman, and Spanish invaders and pirates stormed across its beaches to pillage and plunder the towns. Small wonder then that the Sards took refuge inland, especially in the mountains. Unlike the people of other islands, they were not a seafaring race. The regular invasions from the sea pushed them steadily back to the midlands. They became farmers and herdsmen rather than fisherfolk, leaving the beaches to the sea. The result is that even now the Sardinian coast is largely uninhabited.

When Britain's Lord Nelson, ever with a keen eye for islands, chanced upon Sardinia, he wrote: "God knows, if we could possess one island, Sardinia, we should want neither Malta nor any other; this which is the first island in the Mediterranean . . . is fruitful beyond idea. . . ." Doubtless Nelson's interest lay beyond basking in the sun and swimming in crystal-clear, emerald-colored waters; but he did know a good island when he saw one. But even after Garibaldi, in 1861, helped bring Sardinia into the Kingdom of Italy, the island remained isolated. In 1948, under the new constitution, Sardinia became a self-governing region, but otherwise the

The emerald-colored sea gave Costa Smeralda its name.

island's status did not change.

In the early 1960s, however, a new invasion began, this time a beneficial one. When the Aga Khan dropped anchor in Cala di Volpe (Bay of Foxes) in 1961, he set off the most recent and welcome invasion of Sardinia. Prior to the arrival of Karim, son of Ali Khan, the area of the Costa Smeralda was inhabited only by a few herdsmen. There was no coastal industry, no communications, no public services, and no tourism. Impressed with the peace and quiet of the area, the beauty and unspoiled nature of the coast, the Aga Khan purchased land for a home of his own. So did several of his friends, and thus began the development of tourism in the northern part of the island.

Actually, Sardinia was ripe for "invasion," and a foreign presence was making itself felt on the opposite end of the island, as well. Some 160 miles southwest of the Costa Smeralda is Cagliari, the capital and largest city on Sardinia, founded by the Phoenicians more than three thousand years ago. Traces of this ancient heritage are still evident.

The quiet, unpeopled white beaches along the Gulf of Cagliari, between Villasimius to the east and Teulada to the west, have attracted Italians from the mainland for some twenty years. But now that the foreign invaders have brought admirable changes to the coastal areas, built attractive accommodations, combed and curried the beaches, and upgraded transportation, this part of Sardinia is becoming a splendid attraction to the vacationer who wants to get away from the continent. Sardinia is uncrowded, natural, and primitive, and it has some of the finest beaches in the Mediterranean.

Climate. The southern part of Sardinia has long stretches of sand beach, a less jagged coastline, and is more open to the sea than the north. But in both the north and the south, sea temperatures average 68° F. (20° C.) from May through October. Air temperatures do differ slightly between the two parts of the island. Along Cagliari's coast, June to September temperatures range from 78–82° F. (26–28° C.), falling to 62–64° F. in October and November. In the northern part of the island, the average seasonal tempera-

ture between May and October is approximately 73° F. Many people, including the Sards, say that May and October are the best months, because then the island is ablaze with the colors of luxurious growths of wildflowers.

Transportation. Sardinia is the second largest island in the Mediterranean. But where is it? Three points should help place it. The Strait of Bonifacio, seven miles of open, often choppy water, separate Sardinia from Corsica, its French neighbor to the north. The Italian mainland is approximately 115 miles northwest, and the north African coast is about 120 miles due south. This favorable position in the Mediterranean, coupled with its substantial size, 9200 square miles, makes it easily accessible.

By air, Cagliari is fifty-five minutes from Rome's Leonardo da Vinci airport, while Olbia, the main city serving the Costa Smeralda, is forty-five minutes away from Rome. BA (BEA) flies into Alghero, on the northeastern side of the island, in two hours and fifteen minutes from either London or Malta.

The Tyrrehenian Line provides daily (nightly) boat service to both Cagliari and Olbia from Civitavecchia. These car ferries provide four classes of accommodations, but as the fares are modest, we recommend a first-class cabin with private bathroom, at least on the twelve-hour Cagliari run. This allows a chance to get a good night's rest, have a *cappuccino* or *caffè latte* in the morning, and drive off refreshed. The Civitavecchia-Olbia run is six hours—just enough time to catch thirty winks in a reclining chair or cabin, depending on the state of your spine.

Although it isn't a requirement, it is a good idea to make reservations in advance and have your ticket with you when you get to the port. It saves a good deal of trouble at that end. In the States, the Italian Line can do this for you. Be sure to ask them to double-check the sailing times. In Italy, your hotel concierge is the best one to get tickets and reservations in short order, and properly.

Because we are so partial to boat trips, as a way of getting somewhere—especially if you can bask in the sun and swim in the Mediterranean at the same time—here's a highly recommended suggestion.

SARDINIA AND ELBA

Should you be in either Tangiers, Morocco, or Málaga, Spain, take the DFDS Seaways to Genoa. DFDS, a Danish company, runs two splendid sister ships, the M/V *Dana Corona* and *Dana Sirena*, 7600-ton vessels built in 1969. They are among the most modern, cleanest ships afloat. We discovered them accidentally, and what a happy accident they proved to be. Not only are the staterooms excellent, but they offer both restaurant and cafeteria-style dining. Imagine a car ferry with nightclub, children's playroom, duty-free shops, pool, and elegant service. It's a two-day run from Málaga or Tangier to Genoa and worth every minute and lire, which is the only currency used on board.

From Genoa you have two choices, a fast train (second-class is fine) to Civitavecchia and the ferry from there to Olbia or Cagliari, or another ship (Tyrrhenian Line) from Genoa to Porto Torres, Sardinia, a short ride from the Costa Smeralda.

Of course, all this is written for those who do not own yachts. Judging by the number of yachts berthed at marinas around the Mediterranean and anchored off the beaches, one can only wonder, doesn't everyone own one! The trick is that many, if not most, are rented. So—if you've always harbored a secret desire to drop anchor among a dozen other yachts, hire one, captain, crew, and all.

Civitavecchia, just far enough from Rome to be "countrified," offers a vivid and colorful picture of everyday Italian life and is worth the trip for that alone. Since you will be ready to eat well before you board, try Trattoria da Mentana, just to the left of the port building. Its open-air terrace affords a good view while you eat *spaghetti pescatore, fritto misto di pesce* (mixed fried fish), or *stracciatella alla Romana* (a delicious light soup). Remember, this is a fishing port, so the fish are really fresh.

After presenting your tickets for verification at one of the windows, you may check your bags or put them directly into the hands of one of the blue-frocked men, generally gathered at the entrance, who will have the bags placed on board. Do this early enough, and you'll have plenty of time to walk around the town.

If you arrive by train, you can drag your bags the several hundred yards to the Maritime Building, engage one of the blue-frocked men to pushcart them down and around, or take a taxi.

Since you shouldn't be in that much of a hurry, take the pushcart. But let him go off on his own; you horse-and-buggy your way around and arrive in style. Don't fret over your bags, they're safe.

BEACHES

Costa Smeralda. Sardinia's convoluted shore offers a variety of beaches. In the north along the thirty-five-mile Emerald Coast, fine, white sand gently shelving into the sea, is interspersed with ancient, weathered rocky areas. No matter what the shore is like, the water is an incredible iridescent shade. One afternoon, while snorkeling in the Bay of Foxes, I was struck with the depth of the water's clarity. I removed my snorkel tube and dove down; it was between fifteen and twenty feet deep, and clear all the way. The sea bed is smooth and firm with only a few plants and small fish. To see larger fish and a number of types of shellfish, you'll need to go scuba diving at least a half mile off the beaches.

Along the Costa Smeralda, most of the hotels have united in trying an interesting experiment; the hotel beach is entirely separate from the hotel grounds, so those who want to be on the beach are not bothered by other distractions. You have a feeling of being far away from everything, almost like being alone on a desert island. These hotels have motor launches that take ten to twenty people at a time to their beach, which may be around a cove or several hundred yards across the other side of a bay. In any case, the trip usually takes no more than five or ten minutes, and the boats go back and forth every half hour. The beaches are never crowded, but if you prefer to be completely alone, that's easy; take a short walk around a bend or over some rocks and you're invariably on a small, secluded beach—alone.

Some lover of statistics hiked (or swam) around the thirty-five miles of coast that make up the Costa Smeralda and found eighty-three beaches. Although we made no attempt to verify this, our sampling suggests there are many. Some are so tucked away that exact directions are required to find them. For example, a five-minute drive or a short walk from Cala di Volpe is the restaurant Il Pirata. Around a bend about fifty feet from the restaurant's en-

Free from all polluting influences, the water is crystal clear.

trance is a narrow dirt road. You'd surely pass it by, if you didn't know that it leads to three small but lovely beaches, separated by paleozoic rock outcroppings.

Around the shore, which is dotted with flowers, shrubs, cactus, olive trees, or cork oaks, are elegant villas built to blend in with the landscape. In fact, the rules are so particular about the type and placement of homes that you will notice now and then trussed poles, covering a plot or planned homesite. These indicate that a home or other building of the size and height indicated by the poles is intended for the site. They must remain in place for ninety days to give ample opportunity for someone to complain if the proposed building will be an eyesore or ruin the view. While we were there, one all-but-completed villa had to remove a wall that extended beyond its originally specified boundary. The residents intend for this area to maintain its natural beauty and also not exceed a rigid standard of population density. This is one coast that does not appear to be on its way to ruin as a consequence of the developers' "touch."

Cala di Volpe, Porto Cervo, Porto Rotondo, Porto di Pitrizza, Liscia di Vacca, and Romazzino. These are the new villages along the Costa Smeralda. Here is luxury in the true sense of the word, but not exclusively a rich man's paradise. Each of these villages is in fact a cove with fine, white sandy beaches and excellent accommodations.

For example, the layout of Hotel Pitirizza is unusual and charming: six flower-clad stone and wood villas grouped around a central building that seems to emerge from the surrounding cliffs. Each of the villas has a common sitting room, a patio, and from four to eight bedrooms, each of which opens onto a private terrace.

A swimming pool has been ingeniously carved out of the natural rock some hundred feet above the beach. The overflow from the pool cascades down a natural spillway to the beach below, where craggy rocks partition the beach into a rocky and a sandy area. Both areas are almost exclusively yours.

From the Pitrizza's terraced restaurant and pool you have a good view of the nearby islands of Caprera and Maddalena. As you might suspect from the separate villa design, Hotel Pitrizza is for

Hotel Cala di Volpe sits astride the bay, surrounded on the sea side by white, sandy beaches.

those fifty-two people who crave deluxe privacy.

On the other hand, hotel Luci di la Montagna, in the heart of Porto Cervo, is a small family-type hotel. Its eighty rooms perched high above the sea offer glorious views of the beach and sea.

At the head of Cala di Volpe is Hotel Cala di Volpe, surrounded on the sea side by a profusion of white sandy beaches. This is a bathers' and swimmers' paradise. And the accommodations are made to match. A shuttle-boat service whisks you to its main cloistered beach, a ten-minute ride away, or you can walk over the rocks to many smaller rock and sand beaches. The bay's calm water invites water skiing, sailing, and motor boating. For those who prefer fully provisioned cabin cruisers and yachts, both can be rented for one or several days.

In recent years French architects have added new dimensions to vacation resorts; the Costa Smeralda is an elegant example. And if it were necessary to choose the outstanding architectural design from the hotels, villas, and apartments these young wizards have produced, Hotel Cala di Volpe would be our choice.

In the early 1960s, Jacques Couelle was commissioned to design a villa for Karim, the Aga Khan. For this extraordinary mountainous landscape with the sea views and fiery sun, he blended stone, cement, wood, and glass to capture the flavor and style of a centuries-old Italo-Sardinian villa. Faded pinks, oranges, blues, and purples were blended into the white walls to give an aged look. At sunset this "coat of many colors" comes alive in a panoply of pastels that adds greatly to the pleasures of balcony sitting.

In 1963, the Khan's villa opened as a charming forty-room hotel. Room one twenty-one, was Karim's own bedroom. Couelle had done his job well. Full-length picture windows set in foot-thick cement walls provide views everywhere. No two rooms are on the same level, and each has its own staircase. Old rounded timber beams with carvings by some ancient woodsman were set in the ceilings.

Couelle's artistry was not finished. An additional hundred rooms were added, and in July, 1971, the new section opened. Cala di Volpe is the deluxe hotel of the Costa Smeralda. Its huge well-appointed lobby with bar and pleasant conversation corners makes this luxury highly informal. Add a number of outdoor and outdoor-indoor terraces set up for dozing, reading, talking, drinking, or just looking at the superb scenery. And topping it all is the dining room, where service and food are brought to new heights. Service is with a smile, cheerful and friendly, a cordial invitation to eating and drinking. It's so rare, but it's true.

Although Hotel Cala di Volpe is an expensive resort, others on the bay are not. For example, the Luciano Manchinis, Mr. and Mrs., opened the thirty-one-room Hotel Nibaru in July, 1972. It is just across the bay and about a third the price of the Cala di Volpe. There's nothing to prevent your living at the Nibaru, for example, and dining at Cala di Volpe or any other place in the area. This is a good place to stay while searching out the many coves and beaches nearby.

A short distance away at Romazzino is another great beach and hotel. Hotel Romazzino is in the contemporary style: the stark white concrete walls with pale pink-orange tile roof are in sharp

One of the many small beaches along the Costa Smeralda.

contrast to the green cliffs. It is built into the rolling hills, and the spacious green lawns slope down to the long, white sandy beach. Every one of its hundred rooms has a balcony overlooking the transparent beryl-colored sea. I suspect you could easily sit on your balcony and do nothing but look—and be satisfied.

    Both Hotel Cala di Volpe and Hotel Romazzino are quite self-sufficient, with bars, television, films, boutiques, hairdressers, and bookstores. But nearby is the newly created town of Porto Cervo. Here again, the architects have displayed their talents. Fronting on the bustling piazza of the town is the terrace of the Hotel Cervo, the Emerald Coast's center of activity. Although all age groups come together here, the teenagers are the most noticeable, with their casual but vividly imaginative clothes.

    The first-class, eighty-room Hotel Cervo is the popular, swinging hotel of the Costa Smeralda; it lays no claim to the romance of the Pitrizza or the dramatic quality of the Volpe. But sooner or later the guests at all the hotels as well as villa owners show up here to browse in the square's shops, try one of the restaurants or pubs, or chat over a cooling drink. It's all quite informal and friendly.

Two hundred yards and around a hill from Hotel Cervo is the Cervo Tennis and Yacht Club. In July of 1972, the Tennis Club opened its doors to yachtsmen, and now Cervo's marina is one of the finest in the Mediterranean. Although the club's facilities are private, daily membership allows use of its tennis courts, bars, restaurant, and indoor-outdoor pool. Across the road from the Tennis and Yacht Club is Club Ippico—a stable for equestrians who enjoy riding along the sea or up mountain trails.

An added attraction for beach people who enjoy an afternoon of golf is Pevero Golf Course, lying in a valley between the bays of Pevero and Cala di Volpe. This course has Robert Trent Jones's personal stamp; rather than blast away the boulders, he took advantage of the craggy landscape. Here is an eighteen-hole par-72 championship course measuring some 6600 yards. The sea views from a number of greens may make you want to exchange your golf clubs for a bathing suit.

Of more than passing interest to a number of people who vacation here are the islands of Maddalena and Caprera, which can be seen across the water to the north from Hotel Pitrizza. Both can be reached by small boat from the mainland, or by car ferry from the town of Palau to La Maddalena, which is linked to Caprera by road. To the thousands of Italians who make a pilgrimage here each year, Caprera means Garibaldi, and Garibaldi means Italy. Caprera has Garibaldi's home, tomb, and many relics of his exploits. It's well worth a morning out.

The Southern Coast. A number of modern hotels have sprung up along Sardinia's southern coast, but one of the most exciting concepts in beach vacations is the new fifty-five-acre Forte Village complex at Santa Margherita di Pula, sixteen miles from Cagliari. Even though the Village accommodates some 1500 guests, an incredible number at first glance, its half-mile-long, white sandy beach and its forty acres of pine woods, eucalyptus trees, and extensive flower gardens create a great feeling of space.

For the most part, the Village accommodations consist of some

Forte Village is tucked away between mountains and sea.

six hundred well-furnished bungalows, with either two or four beds, set in wooded glades. Along with the central restaurant, there are a number of pools and the Piazza Maria Luigia, with shops, boutiques, pub, pizzeria, dance floor under the stars, and nightclub. A half dozen all-weather tennis courts (with lighting) are also part of the grand design.

Overlooking the beach and the turquoise Mediterranean is the elegant, 118-room Hotel Castello, offering first-class service, food, and accommodations for those who want it. Thus Forte Village caters to those preferring a hotel vacation as well as those who prefer a private cottage in a rustic setting.

In the Castello's excellent Cavalieri Restaurant, Luciano Ramacci, the maître d'hôtel, dispatches his troops with flair, and his lieutenants can bone a sole, mullet, or any local fish with the skill and ease that makes dining a treat. As most of the people at this hotel speak English, there is no language problem here. Any Village guest can arrange to eat in any of the three Village restaurants, including the Beachcomber, which is run as a separate concession.

The view from the top of Hotel Castello.

Beyond the cottages and Castello, the many facilities are available to all—open-air cinema, discotheques, bars, beach and boating equipment, tennis courts, miniature golf, library, baby-sitting services, excursions—you name it. While not all services are free of additional charge, many are, including tennis and miniature golf. And it isn't necessary to walk, walk, walk, around the Village. If you're at the tennis courts and want to get over to the beach, just hop on one of the electric go-carts, and with a *"Prego,"* you're off. Unfortunately, this doesn't extend to the supermarket, which is a short walk down the road.

Activities at Forte Village center around its marvelous fully equipped beach. Particularly attractive is a well-managed scuba diving school under the direction of Keith Nicolson, former diving coach of the British Sub-Aqua Club. Experienced teachers take you by steady progression from snorkel tube to aqualung to sea diving. If you've thought of what it might be like to stare down a grouper or explore the wreck of a Greek or Roman wine ship, this could be your big chance. Should you prefer surface sports, pedal, sail, and motor boats, as well as water skiing, are available any time of day, as is a fast game of volleyball. For the less active, thatched umbrellas and beach chairs are yours at no charge. The sun shines on the beach for almost ten hours a day, so take advantage of it. Also, the children have a fully equipped playground in the woods, away from adults who may want to relax by themselves. This is a paradise for parents who have youngsters but don't want to shepherd them all day.

Ruling over this empire, is Comandante Leonetto Filippi, Direttore Generale of Forte Village, who was formerly manager of Venice's famed Gritti Palace. Assisting Signore Filippi is Signorina Caîra, Director of Hospitality, whose see-through office is just behind the grillwork in the reception building. She will greet you as you arrive, and will help solve problems that may arise; and she can do it in half a dozen languages. Even though Forte Village is a British enterprise and a fair number of Britons come here, you'll hear French, German, Italian, and other languages spoken. Most of the vacationers are anxious to make friends, so don't be deterred

The beach at Forte Village is made for fun and games.

by language.

Forte Village is open from March 23 to October 31, but their high season doesn't begin until July 15. During this period children aged two to nine get a 15 percent reduction, and pets come free. In mid and low seasons, reductions for children are up to twice as much. Rates in the Castello are substantially higher than in the cottages.

Currently, most guests are from Europe and come for two weeks or more. However, realizing the American desire to move around, the village will accept reservations for a week or less; one-night stands may not be accommodated. Nevertheless, you'll need to reserve at least three months in advance for the high season and two months for midseason, June 1 to July 14. Service charges and taxes are included in the per-person price, as are meals.

Tipping is not required at any time. However, if you want to reward particularly good service, a tip might be in order. Otherwise, no one expects to have their palm crossed. Hopefully this idea will spread.

Forte Village means dancing to an assortment of rock bands way into the dawning. It is for those who want to see and be with other people. Not so with Is Morus, also in Santa Margherita di Pula.

Is Morus (The Moors) is fifty-odd rooms of first-class sophisticated elegance, which could be described in one word as restrained. Is Morus is a rather expensive way of being alone. Although families do come to use its few bungalows, most guests are couples: young marrieds, newly-weds, and old-timers who want to be alone in quiet, unobtrusive luxury, who want every whim catered to. Even the grass is special here—it was imported from Kenya to withstand the long dry season. The splendid flower gardens, pine woods, sloping rock beach, and enviable sea view make this a splendid setting.

Is Morus has an arrangement with Forte Village, which is only a short distance away. If the guests tire of being alone, they can join the fun at the Village at no extra charge.

Because it's small and its devotees return year after year, reservations are best made six to eight months in advance.

On the road from Cagliari to Teulada, about half a mile up the beach from Forte Village, rising almost out of the flat-topped trees, is the second-class Abamar Grand Hotel. The eighty-room Abamar is relatively new. Its wide sandy beach sweeps around the curve of a hillside, which provides a sheltered surf. Here too, the beach has lots of rooms.

A good distance off the main road, but closer to Cagliari, is Hotel Flamingo, almost directly on the beach. The Flamingo is yet to have its first American guests. It is a cool, brightly decorated place widely known for its night life. Together with the Abamar it caters both to families and to young couples, as well as those who prefer a conventional hotel-type accommodation.

At this point, a word about the meaning of first- and second-class may be in order. It is generally understood that service distinguishes between a first-class and a second-class hotel. Although a pool—of any size—can often make the difference, the proportion of staff to guests is usually the major criterion.

In Italy, however, taxes play a pivotal role. Many hotel owners prefer not to pay the much larger tax required to have their hotel listed as first rather than second class. Accordingly, the notation second-class does not tell the full story, nor is it sufficient reason to shy away. Although vacations are always shorter than we'd like and don't always allow experimentation, you can save a good deal of money and be pleasantly surprised by trying some second-class hotels.

Information and requests for reservations can be obtained by writing directly to the specific hotel, or to Trust Houses Forte Hotels, 1290 Avenue of the Americas, Suite 4136, New York 10019 for Forte Village; and to Robert F. Warner, Inc., 630 Fifth Ave., New York for Hotels Cala di Volpe, Pitrizza, and Cervo.

It's easy to recommend Sardinia for a new experience in vacationing. And Americans are no longer as scarce as hens' teeth. We heard English, American style, at least once a day.

A final word about the character of Sardinian beaches. For those preferring to "take it all off," Sardinia is not yet ready for you. This does not mean that the scalloped coastline does not offer dozens of secluded places for skinny dipping; it most certainly does. What it does mean is that there are no villages, ranches, inns or hotels or other accommodations for the all-out nudist.

Places of Interest. Sardinia is famous for its characteristic prehistoric stone forts, the truncated conelike *nuraghi*, which are found throughout the island. Four hundred Nuraghic bronzes have also been found, produced by a civilization that apparently flourished for thirteen centuries from 1500 B.C. to 200 B.C. Most of these bronzes are images of men, animals, deities and boats; they show a startling likeness to modern art. Copies of the bronzes, made by a particularly capable and sensitive Sard artist, are available for sale in the major cities.

The Nuraghic period, about which little is known, is completely unique to Sardinia; nowhere else in the Mediterranean have such forts or bronzes been uncovered. At Barumini, thirty miles north of Cagliari, excavations have brought to light an entire prehistoric Nuraghic village. From Cagliari, take highway 131 to its junction at Bivio Villasanta; there you turn right on 293, which passes through Villamar and Las Plassas, just this side of Barumini. Take at least half a day for this interesting excursion.

An ancient site from a later period, which has been skillfully excavated, is Nora. This carefully preserved coastal city, which was old when the Romans began building, is just a few kilometers from Sta. Margherita di Pula. Of interest are the Roman streets converging toward the forum, the Theater, temples, and the remarkably intact mosaic-tile floors.

The National Museum in Cagliari is primarily of archeological interest, containing Sardinian artifacts that illustrate the history of the island and its various civilizations. This can easily be combined with a walking or shopping visit in the city.

While you are in Cagliari, walk up the Largo Carlo Felice past La Riniascente, an excellent department store, to the marketplace at the top. Look around, then continue up the short flight of steps to the entrance of the central market. Bring a camera loaded with color film, because this bustling place has all kinds of fish, seafood, meat, fruit, and vegetables—and most interesting of all, people.

If you are on the Costa Smeralda, take the main highway,

N125, into Olbia, a twenty-minute drive from Arzachena. Olbia is a good place to shop for Sardinian handicrafts, and it offers vivid glimpses into the lifestyle of the people.

From Olbia you can continue along the coast road to Siniscola. There, take the 570 for Nuoro, where you are in the rugged heart of Sardinia. There are remains of the Nuraghic civilization here, and you can sample typical Sardinian food.

Alghero, on the west coast, with stairs cut into the sheer face of a rock cliff, leading down to the Grotto of Neptune, is as exciting an experience as you can have anywhere. From Arzachena, take Highway 127, with all its curves and wrinkles, into Sassari, the second largest city on the island. From Sassari it's just twenty minutes to the center of Alghero. This outing should be planned to take at least a half day.

For an evening of loud music, both American and European "rock," try Disco Ritual just beyond the Costa Smeralda at Baia Sardinia, on the Palau.

Since 1657, May 1 has been synonymous with Saint Efisio's Day. For more than three centuries the Sards have kept their ancient vow made to their patron saint.

Each May 1, the island people, wearing their native costumes, come together in Cagliari for a great festival. The many different costumes give a complete idea of Sardinian national dress through the ages.

The festival procession consists of thousands on horseback and on foot, representing all regions, the administrative hierarchy, the armed forces—then and now—the gentry and the people. Few parades in Europe can compare with it.

Shopping. At La Riniascente, Cagliari's department store, you can buy exquisite Sardinian ceramic figurines, some of which are accented with gold. These pieces depicting Sardinian peasants in their native costumes are by the very talented Stelio Mala. He also executes these pieces in copper, and to me these are even more interesting.

At Boutique 75, on the Via Roma in the arcade some two hundred yards from Riniascente, elegant Italian-styled women's fashions are available. And at Emila Bonetti's on the Via Sardegna, a back street, you can pick up bargains in *capodimonte*, if you like these titillating intricate porcelain figures.

Sardinia has an abundance of good-quality clays, so you will find a great variety of terra cotta pottery, statues, and beads of typically Sardinian shape and design. Other crafts include baskets woven from rushes and dwarf palms, carved chestnut-wood pieces, cork, and most dramatic of all, multicolored hand embroidery with the typical geometric floral and animal motifs. These are worked on wall tapestries, carpets, bedspreads, pillows, and throw rugs.

Food and Drink. Although Sardinia is Italian, the Sards are quick to add, "We are our own," meaning that they have developed their own style of things, including food and drink. The Sardinian liking for sweets, for example, has resulted in some unique desserts and pastries. They combine sugar, bitter honey, wine, almond paste, and fresh cheese into a variety of goodies. One of the most delicious is *sebada*, a specialty of the district of Nuoro. When it was served, our first reaction was "Oh, an omelette." Not at all. There are no eggs in *sebada*—it's a cheese pastry fried with sugar and bitter honey. Try it, it's delicious.

In a typically out-of-the-way Sardinian restaurant you must at least taste *papassinos* and *zippulas*. *Papassinos* is a pastry containing a mouth-watering concoction of wine, walnuts, almond paste, raisins, honey, sugar, cinnamon, and fruit preserves. *Zippulas* is a fried-egg dish, combined with milk, orange peel, and an anise liqueur—believe that for an omelette!

One of the most flavorful cheeses is *pecorino* (sheep-milk), which is used in *sebada*; but *pecorino* is also great just to nibble with fruit and wine and a piece of *carta da musica*—"music paper," that foot-in-diameter, thin, flat, uniquely Sardinian crisp bread. With these, a bottle of S'Eleme, a full-bodied white wine, is a delight.

For meat or fish, try Jerzu, a heavy red wine. If you don't want a full bottle, most kinds also come in half-bottles. A good practice to follow in any restaurant is to ask for the local wine; it's usually exceptionally good and inexpensive.

As a matter of routine, stay away from the "specialty of the house" unless you know the restaurant and the dish. Too often these are prepared long in advance, anticipating the demand. The best dishes are those that must be made when you order them. Remember you're on vacation, so take the time to relax and enjoy.

On the Costa Smeralda in Porto Cervo, St. Andrews is a restaurant-grill where service and good food have been restored to their former glory. The barmen, waiters, and maître d' seem truly pleased at your expressions of enjoyment. It's a land of mutual pleasure. A new attraction at St. Andrews is Riccardo Donelli, an acknowledged champion in the art of legerdemain as well as a master of classic guitar. And he sings in three languages. What a magnificent accompaniment to a meal. Somewhere between main courses, try their spaghetti with tomato sauce and garlic, a real taste sensation.

At Capriccioli, about five minutes by car from Cala di Volpe, is Il Pirata. Go there for lunch for the magnificent view from the terrace.

In the back of Porto Cervo's piazza and down a flight of steps is the Red Lion Pub, a typical English pub. Best way to find it the first time is to ask for the newspaper shop; find that, and you're standing close to the Red Lion.

ELBA

It was April in Paris and 1814 when Napoleon was exiled to the island of Elba, at that time a French possession. None of the chronicles of the period state that Napoleon's sojourn there was calculated to turn Elba into a tourist attraction. But even today the memory of Napoleon lingers on, which makes Elba probably the only place within the Italian republic to have escaped the Garibaldi influence.

But Elba, eighty-six square miles of lush volcanic island, is an attraction in itself. "The jewel of the Tuscan archipelago" lies off the Italian coast six miles southwest of the ancient and still sleepy Tuscan village of Piombino. For the most part Elba is accessible by sea, and the first glimpse of the island suggests its natural di-

ITALY

ELBA

Cavo
Portoferraio
Spartaia
Procchio
Ortano
Porto Azzurro
Marina di Campo
Cavoli
Capoliveri

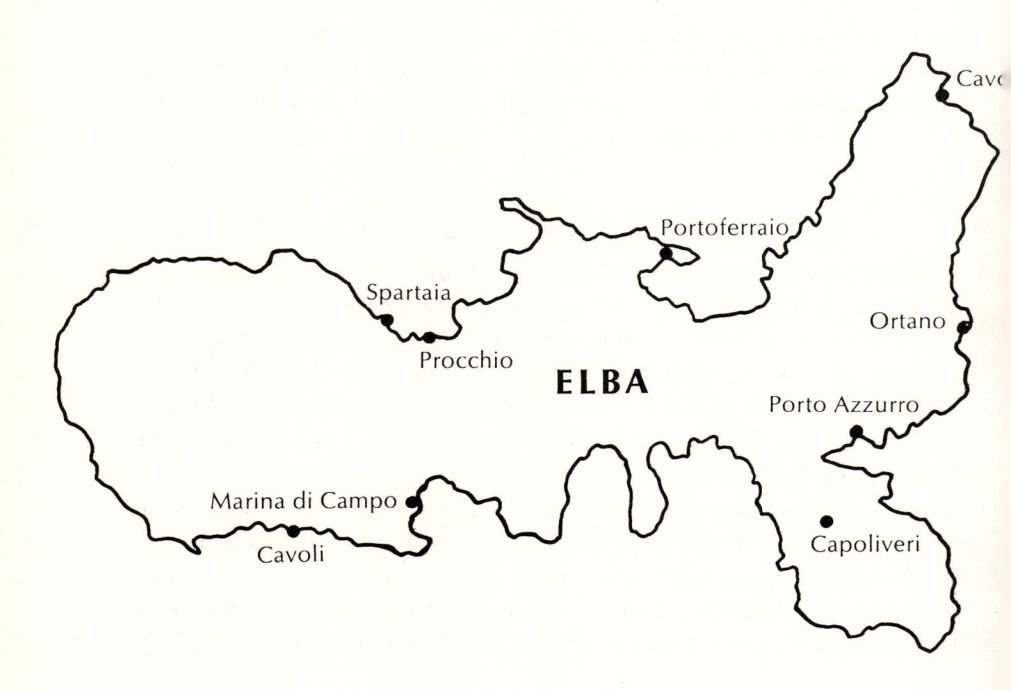

versity. Ravines, wooded valleys, reddish-blue cliffs, and in between, dazzling curved beaches where the water is so shallow as to be pale blue, almost white.

Elba's mineral resources, particularly its vast iron mines, were known and worked by the Ligurians, Greeks, Etruscans, and Romans, as well as by the French and Italians; smelting ovens dating to antiquity have been uncovered at several sites around the island. But otherwise the works of man are either invisible or have become an integral part of the landscape. Now, Elba has made the dramatic turn from mining to tourism as its primary industry, an excellent decision. On this tiny island one can find accommodations to suit all tastes: first-class hotels, small furnished villas for rent, rooms in pensions, or lodging in private homes. In 1952 there were seven hotels on the island, and by 1972 there were 162. But being so spread out on so many cliffs, beaches, and mountainsides, they are really far between and not easily seen.

Climate. Not far enough south to receive the most intense heat of the sun, yet not too far north, Elba compares most favorably with other resorts long celebrated for their balmy climate. Over the past ten years for example, Portoferraio averaged 167 clear, sunny days a year. For four of these ten years, 212 sunny days were recorded. Don't worry about rain, which is rare between May and September.

The island's average temperature is 60° F. In July, temperatures average 76; rare maximums of 88 have been recorded. As on many Mediterranean islands, spring, with an average of 60° F., and autumn with 63° are considered by Elbans to be the most pleasant and colorful times, as the hills, valleys, and roadsides are bursting with flowers.

Transportation. Elba is easy to get to from the mainland by car ferry or hydrofoil. Because of its small size, jets cannot land there; light planes carrying up to six passengers from Pisa, Rome, or other nearby airports can fly in, but this is expensive.

If you're driving (it's a good idea to have a car on the island, and you can rent one there), head for Piombino on the Via Aurelia, the main coastal road linking Rome with Genoa. You may take a car ferry from either Livorno or Piombino. But the Piombino ferry leaves every hour, every day, as compared to Leghorn's Monday-only sailing, so it's best to go from Piombino. The ferries carry a surprisingly large number of cars, and they cross so frequently that reservations aren't necessary.

By train, the mainliners from Rome and Genoa stop at Campiglia Marittima. Here, the local shuttles back and forth to Piombino Marittima, a fifteen-minute run. Be sure not to get off at Piombino; one short station beyond is Piombino Marittima. Remember this when purchasing your ticket. At the port, you have a choice of hydrofoil which crosses swiftly in thirty minutes, or the car ferry, which takes an hour. The car ferry costs $1.25, the hydrofoil $2.50. Crossings are made to Portoferraio, Elba's main city, where taxis, buses, or rental cars are available to whisk you off to your destination.

In addition to these frequent crossings, several daily crossings are made to Cavo on the northern tip of the island, and one crossing per day is made to Porto Azzurro, on the southerly fin of this fish-shaped island.

BEACHES

Portoferraio-Biodola. The backdrop for Elba's beaches are densely wooded coves, pine forests and boulder-strewn grassy hillsides. Few of the beaches are visible from the thin ribbon of road circling the island. A number are hidden between sloping hills that reach out into the sea to form sheltered bays. Some beaches can be reached only by roads that wind down 500 or 1000 feet of mountainside below the main highway. As you descend, the sudden spectacle of green cliffs and transparent blue water breaking on soft beige-colored sand is breathtaking.

The Hermitage (give it a French pronunciation) at Portoferraio-Biodola, with its ninety first-class rooms primarily in twelve large, well-appointed bungalows, is quite invisible. Even from offshore, only bits and snatches peep forth from the green camouflage. Should you be in Room 63, you'd be on the fourth tier along

The Hermitage at Portoferraio-Biodola blends into the landscape.

the cliff. From your private patio the sea is some 200 feet below, almost straight down. To bring you down gently and comfortably, terracelike walkways lace the cliff side. It's a uniquely clever woodsy setting. Even a portion of the dining room is entangled in semitropical trees and vines.

But this jungle atmosphere changes abruptly at the beach. For several hundred yards, the beach is clean, beige sand, flat and gently sloping into the Mediterranean. No steep drop here. The water is transparent and very clean, regularly sampled by the government for sanitary quality.

The Hermitage provides a beach umbrella and lounge chair with your room number prominently displayed, which means you'll have a place in the sun whenever you want it. No early-morning race for chairs here. Several hundred yards of this long curving beach are reserved for the hotel, but the entire beach is open to you, to swim or walk where you please.

The Hermitage is a haven for families and unusually good even for toddlers. It has been catering to a mixed continental clientele, especially Swedes, Dutch, English, Germans, and Italians from the mainland. That only an occasional American has set foot here is not for lack of welcome or because of language barriers—English is spoken here, and the welcome mat is out. However, it is off the beaten track, and a place for rest and quiet, with good service and food. For those who like to eat some of this, a little of that, and a good deal of those twenty-three other dishes, the Saturday evening buffet (with all the red or white wine you can manage) is hard to beat anywhere. Although many guests prefer to dress for dinner, that's strictly optional.

For music-lovers, Norman's Club is five minutes by car just off to the left as the Hermitage road meets the main highway. Norman, by the way, is Norman Lawrence, composer of "Jezebel." Many teenagers congregate at Club "64," about seven minutes away on the main highway.

The Hermitage is not cheap; it is expensive and not large. Add to this the fact that it has a devoted following, and you'll understand why reservations six months in advance are necessary for the high season—June 15 to September 20.

Should you want to beach it in this area, but are more interested in pension-style accommodations, Casa Rosa is within walking distance of the Hermitage. And, since Italian beaches are open to the public, you have the use of the big beach, although not the facilities of the Hermitage.

Although it's convenient to have a car at your disposal, buses are plentiful and inexpensive. From the Portoferraio bus plaza, you can take buses to most points on the island. For example, the eight-mile trip from Portoferraio to Biodola costs thirty-five cents, takes ten to fifteen minutes, depending on who is in front, and the bus drops you several hundred yards from the Hermitage or Casa Rosa. On the other hand, this same trip by taxi would cost five dollars. Of course, one of the best ways is to raise a thumb and hitch a ride. When a car or truck stops, just say, "Prego, Portoferraio favore," and smile—you'll get there.

Along the coast from Portoferraio to Biodola in addition to the first-class Hermitage, there are three inns, eight second-class, six third-class, and one fourth-class hotel. Information on any of these can be obtained by writing to EVE, Ente Valorizzazione Elba, in Portoferraio; ENIT, the Italian Government Travel Office, with offices in New York, Chicago, and San Francisco; or travel agencies for information on the larger hotels.

Procchio. The Gulf of Procchio, approximately five winding miles beyond Biodola, curves between Bagno, to the east, and Guardiola's hooked beak of land, to the west. Its shoreline of fine sandy beach interspersed with rocks stretches for miles, probably the largest and most picturesque beach on the island. The hillsides are bedecked with Spanish blade, prickly pear cactus (Indian figs to the Elbans), wild fig and cork trees, and crimson and orange flowers, in sharp contrast to the rocky slopes that merge with the water. Although the beach shelves gently into the sea, those who prefer to dive and snorkel can do so from the rocky headland closing the gulf.

Except for the village of Procchio, this area is sparsely inhabited. But overlooking a choice segment of beach is the first-class, seventy-five-room Hotel Del Golfo. If it's service you crave, remember that the classification of first class is the Italian way of guaranteeing it.

In the hotel's glass-walled dining room, just about every table has a clear view of the beach, the blue sea, and green cliffs. This alone ought to do something positive for the digestion, as might having one waiter for each two guests, parts of the first-class service. Although the hotel has tennis courts and a bowling alley, golf is nowhere in sight. (Hotel Del Golfo means Hotel of the Gulf.)

Should you feel the need to "hit a few," the golf club at Acquabona is only a few miles away. Because of Elba's climate, this is an all-year-round club. Particularly inviting is the fact that Hotel Del Golfo is just a few hundred yards from the center of Procchio.

As you walk around this area you are sure to see small yellow birds flitting from tree to tree. If you're wondering whether they are canaries—yes, they are. "Where the canary flies free" is a favorite Elban expression, and Elba is the only place where canaries are "wild."

If you prefer apartment-hotel living and like the idea of doing your own cooking every so often, with the option of room service, Residence Napoleon may be just what you're looking for. Residence Napoleon, which is not a *residencia* in the Spanish sense, is a wholly new concept for Elba. It is a six-story, 160-flat luxury apartment complex, complete with sea-water pools, restaurants, shops, bars, supermarket, tennis courts, and private beach.

The air-conditioned flats with four to six beds are fully furnished and equipped and are available on either a rental or purchase basis. Built into the wooded hillside, with flowers on all sides, with nothing to obstruct views of the very blue sea, Residence Napoleon is on its way to becoming a plush beach retreat.

At Spartaia, a short distance out of Procchio at the edge of a fresh green valley, is a delightful white sandy beach and clear, cool, calm water. This beach is for all intents the private reserve of Hotel Désirée. Named for Napoleon's first mistress, this is a thoroughly family-type accommodation. Not only does it have a roomy beach, with long pier for those who prefer to dive or jump into deeper water, but its location is just made for water skiing as well as underwater fishing.

A game of tennis can easily be arranged with the tennis pro, who appears to be especially able and patient with youngsters. Best of all are the new all-weather plastic tile tennis courts, which resemble sod. Provision is also made for golfers, for the Désirée is one of the hotels that belong to Golf Club Acquabona, a twenty-minute drive away. So that you don't have to keep one eye on the young, young set, a children's playground at the hotel is maintained under competent care. Parents can spend a relaxing day confident that the children are not only in no danger, but enjoying themselves.

The Désirée prides itself on the caliber of its bar service, under the direction of Umberto Vasporri. Although a second-class hotel, the seventy-room Désirée has a luxury look about it. It's small, cozy, and informal, and the owner makes a point of balancing nationalities in order to maintain an interesting group. Unfortunately, Americans haven't as yet found the Désirée.

By the time you've seen Biodola, Spartaia, and other beach

areas around the island, you begin to realize that Elba is all scenery. It is not a place you'd come to visit museums, cathedrals, castles, or great houses. Elba has none of this. It offers instead natural beauty, rest, excellent beaches, friendly people, and good food.

Marina di Campo. Almost due south of Procchio, across what might be termed the neck of the island, is Marina di Campo, where food, friendliness, beaches, and views are hard to better. Because of Elba's ink-blot shape, it has more gulfs than most countries can muster. Marina di Campo is almost at the head of Golfo di Campo.

If you stand at the old fountain in the square near the large public beach and look directly seaward, you can see the island of Montecristo, just as Alexandre Dumas must have seen it while writing his immortal *Count of Monte Cristo*. Strangely enough, Dumas never went over to the island, but you can, and should.

It's easy to understand why Dumas chose Marina di Campo in which to live and write—it's so picturesque. Except for the few shops and outdoor cafés, it probably hasn't changed a great deal since Dumas' day. Not many vacation resorts can make that statement. While this is a great gathering spot for teenagers, the pizzerias, food stalls, and pastry shops have an appeal for all ages. Speaking of pizzerias, do try a cold pizza with anchovy, tomatoes, and herbs. Although it's difficult to think of cold pizza, these are good.

Marina di Campo's waterfront, several hundred yards long, is an off-white, fine, sandy beach. Park yourself anywhere on the beach; rent chairs and umbrellas from one of the concessionaires.

Around the town and dotted in the hills around the gulf are three inns, a half dozen second- and third-class pensions, four third-class hotels, and three second-class hotels. The only first-class hotel in the vicinity, the Iselba, is the most expensive on the entire island. But at the other end of the price spectrum are the inns, which charge $3 to $5 per person per night without meals. Most of these accommodations provide no beach of their own. But that's no problem, because the public beach at Marina di Campo is more than adequate for the area. Most of the accommodations are within walking or bicycling distance.

The beach at Marina di Campo is a ribbon around the bay.

From the public beach you can look across the gulf to the beach and pine woods beyond. Almost directly at the head of the gulf, tucked into the cool piney woods, is Hotel Iselba. The main building contains common rooms, an open-air dining room, and a bar; bungalows are scattered among the trees. Walk a short distance through the woods and you're in the grassy flats at the edge of the beach. It's quiet here, a good place to read, unwind, and relax. This is a first-class hotel, which means you'll be catered to. Two lovely women see to that: Signora Conti, the manager, and Signora Banchi, the receptionist. Both speak English, but have few Americans on which to try it.

This rustic but elegant setting can only accommodate ninety-five people in its fifty rooms. Signora Banchi noted that for reservations in August it is necessary to write in January or February. But if you prefer to come in May, June, late September, or October, two to three weeks' advance notice would be sufficient.

If, while sitting on the beach or swimming in the cool water, you get an urge for town life, Marina di Campo is only a short distance away, either walking or by bicycle, motorboat, or car.

For us, Marina di Campo is Elba. It is pretty as a picture, with its tiny streets, colorful shops, and bright, sun-swept beach. There's music and excitement, and the atmosphere is informal, so come as you are.

Cavoli. Cavoli, approximately five miles west of Marina di Campo and diagonally across the island from Portoferraio, fronts directly on the open sea. As one travels westward across the island, the population (some 30,000) thins out remarkably. Cavoli is small, but its setting is breathtaking. The wide sandy beach appears to be set in a bowl below the surrounding mountain, and the water is incredibly clear and blue.

To make this beach more than a place to jump out of your car and into the water, Hotel Bahia was built. The Bahia is enveloped by mountains, boulders, and flowers both wild and cultivated. If you've never seen a pomegranate tree in full fruit, you can see it here. Bougainvillea, olive, prickly pear, Spanish blade, and bril-

The beach at Cavoli on a crowded afternoon.

liant scarlet fuchsia brighten an already colorful setting. The white buildings with orange roofs are grouped on several levels going down, down, down to the beach. On this beach, huge naturally smoothed boulders can be your basking chaise. What a scene in which to have yourself photographed water skiing, motor boating, or just draped on a rock. If you've ever wanted to learn sailing, this could be the place. They have a creditable school, and the location is made for it.

Hotel Bahia's all-night discotheque attracts "rockers" from around the island, so young couples should not feel isolated or out of it here.

As the Bahia is small, only forty rooms, and is rated second-class, which substantially lowers room rates, reservations for July and August must be made well in advance. But again, May and October are excellent months, and prices are literally half that of the high season.

Capoliveri and Porto Azzurro. Capoliveri and Porto Azzurro face each other across a blue bay on the lower portion of Elba's fishtail. In fact, it's not too strenuous a swim from one shore to the other. Usually the traffic is in the direction of Porto Azzurro, as Capoliveri is little more than a spot on the map; Porto Azzurro is a village at the base of a hill with a piazza where all ages congregate.

Someone thought the area attractive enough to put up the largest hotel on the island, Hotel Elba International. This is a 242-room American-style hotel with all manner of amenities, yet it is rated second-class. It has something few other hotels have: a funicular to take you down the mountain to a private beach. This is one of the few rock beaches on Elba, and from the concrete and rock ledges you go right into the water. The backdrop here is sheer cliff face. But this area is no place for toddlers and youngsters. For them it will have to be the hotel's large elliptical pool. Actually, the International is more for young marrieds and those who are vacationing without the children. It is only a short drive from Acquabona, so golfers can be on the greens in short order.

At Ortano, north of Porto Azzurro, in an area the Greeks and Romans knew well for its iron mines, plans for a beach resort are taking shape. Ortano Mare is to have private homes and rentables on its sheltered bay in a setting of fields, woods, and a wide sandy beach. Ortano Mare should be completed by 1974. If you go to Elba, be sure to look in.

Not unlike its sister island Sardinia, Elba has no accommodations for nudists. Here too, it's a problem that must be solved individually. And you're most welcome to try.

Places of Interest. Elba is even smaller than Malta, so all points around the island are within easy reach. Unless a flock of sheep block the road, it's no more than a thirty-minute drive to the farthest point on the island.

For gemmologists or anyone interested in literally picking up a bag of mineral ores, Elba is unsurpassed. For example, on the east side of the island at the abandoned Rio Marina mine in the Ortano district, limonite, pyrites, magnetite, and ocher can be found. In the western portion, serpentine, malachite, garnet, zircon, and clear, black, and yellow opals can be picked up with a little judicious prowling.

Art enthusiasts should find the Art Institute on the Portoferraio-Biodola road of more than passing interest. You can watch serious students at work, and you can enroll for as much or as little instruction as you wish.

The road to Ortano leads through some of Elba's highest mountains, an excellent way to get the full scenic impact. Shortly before the turn-off to Ortano, the road to the left takes you to the oldest village on the island, in fact an ancient Etruscan settlement.

Can a trip to Elba be complete without a visit to Palazzina dei Mulini, Napoleon's residence in Portoferraio? Hardly. But a word of caution about things Napoleonic: he didn't eat in every restaurant nor sleep in every wayside inn. But it does sound good, no matter how serious the guide may look as he says it.

Food and Drink. Elba is considered part of Tuscany, and its style of food preparation is primarily Tuscan, with a touch of Elban originality here and there. This originality can be seen in *agnellotti,* a chicken-and-veal-filled pasta that must be homemade. When it is, it is a pure delight.

Another Elban specialty is *cacciucco*, a particularly piquant variety of *bouillabaisse*. Just bear in mind that the waters around this island abound in fin and shellfish. With this, try a piece of *coaccota*, a cow and sheep's milk cheese, originally a Tuscan delicacy. And if you're a soup lover, *crema lamballe* is a cream of pea soup unlike any you've had at home. Bianco Secco is a local dry white wine with good color and bouquet to match.

For dessert, *tartufo* is the ultimate form of chocolate ice cream. Named for the truffle, it is deep, deep chocolate over a rich cream, with a grape and a dollop of liqueur on top. Failure to try this is worth three demerits.

The place to try some of these delights is the Acquabona Golf Club, on the main highway between Portoferraio and Porto Azzurro. This is a "must" for at least lunch or dinner.

MALTA

DEAD SMACK IN THE MIDDLE of the Mediterranean is the island of Malta. Its strategic location in the heart of the Mediterranean gave it command of the east-west trade routes. Every ship passing through the channel between Sicily and North Africa was at the mercy of Maltese galleys. Because of this fact, Malta is automatically associated with siege, warfare, garrison, and naval base. It is hardly ever thought of as a vacation resort, at least by Americans. However, Britons, Swedes, French, and Germans have been sampling Malta's beaches and outstanding attractions for years. Because of its distance from the industrialized cities of Europe and North Africa, its air and water are gloriously free of pollution.

Located sixty miles south of Sicily and two hundred miles north of the African coast, Malta is actually an archipelago, consisting of five islands: Malta, Gozo, and Comino, and the two tiny, uninhabited islands of Cominotto and Filfla. Altogether, they add up to a grand total of 120 square miles and 320,000 people. Malta, the largest island, covers less than ninety-five square miles. Its longest distance from northwest to southeast is about seventeen miles, and it is about nine miles across at the widest point. Gozo is less than twenty-six square miles (eight by four at its longest and widest dimensions), and Comino covers about one square mile. So all of Malta is within easy reach, and all the many things there are to see and do can easily be done.

Language should pose no problem in Malta, because English is one of the official languages, along with Maltese. It is rare to find someone who cannot at least give directions or aid in English. All hotels employ English-speaking staff. And because of 160 years of British rule, commercial and industrial dealings are conducted primarily in English.

The successive waves of conquering races have left indelible imprints of their cultures, imprints already old in 60 A.D., when St. Paul was shipwrecked here on his way to stand trial in Rome. The native language, Maltese, reflects these cultures. It derives from a Punic-Phoenician dialect onto which Arabic has been grafted. To this base have been fused liberal doses of Norman French, Italian, English, and Spanish. The result is absolutely impenetrable. However, the Maltese mercifully reserve it for their family and friends. Except for place names, you won't have to worry about the language; stick to English.

Climate. Malta's islands enjoy moist, mild winters and dry, hot summers. June and July are the driest months. Summer skies are almost cloudless, and even in winter, cloud cover is not a regular feature. The large amount of sunshine (ten hours a day), even in winter, mitigates the influence of the chilly northwest to northeast winter winds, and the cool sea breezes have a moderating influence on the heat of summer. From May through October, the daily temperature averages 72° F. This just about matches the average water temperature, providing a lengthy swimming season. And you can soak up as much sun as you care to.

Transportation. Malta is easy to reach. There are no direct flights from the States, but nonstop flights from London and Rome are readily available. BEA (BA) flies daily from London into Malta's Luqua Airport. The two-hour flight is accompanied by excellent food and service, with lots of leg room.

Malta Airways Limited, a subsidiary of BEA operates twice

The harbor and modern walled city of Valletta.

daily flights from Rome. In less than sixty minutes you're over Malta getting an all-over view of Malta, Gozo, and Comino. Should you require a slightly different schedule, two additional daily flights are available from Alitalia.

If you prefer the water route, car ferries operate daily between Syracuse (Sicily) and Valletta, Malta's capital city. Having made the trip both by sea and by air, we can attest to the relaxation offered by the eight-hour boat trip and agree that it passes all too quickly. For relaxation, little can compare to a sea voyage. Both first and second class are quite suitable, and the food, particularly soup and spaghetti, is mouth-watering. The ships are large enough to permit a stroll if you don't care to spend all your time basking in the sun.

If you plan to bring a car from Italy, it isn't necessary to book weeks ahead; several days advance reservation is all that's required as the ships not only are large enough to carry 300 passengers quite comfortably, but there is ample room for 40 cars. Without a car, advance reservations need be made no more than twenty-four hours in advance. Consider the evening crossing—there's something very romantic about a moonlit sea voyage.

For the past several years, the adult fare for a one-way, first-class accommodation has been less than fifteen dollars. Children up to twelve obtain a 50 percent reduction, and special reductions are offered to families and groups. Information on these sailings can be obtained from the Italian Line, which operates them through a subsidiary.

BEACHES

Malta is unusual in having two distinct types of beaches: sand and limestone rock. Each has much to recommend it; you should sample both.

Limestone is an extremely porous rock and not very hard. Over thousands of years of exposure to wind and rain, it has become smoothed and softly rounded. Interestingly, it doesn't absorb heat the way other types of rock do. Limestone is easy to walk on barefoot, and many find it comfortable to lie on even without a towel or mat. These are rocks, not stones or pebbles, and the sunbathers appear unperturbed by its hardness.

Rock beaches usually do not slope gently to the water; most often you will jump into water that is three to ten feet deep, depending on the area. Some hotels fasten ladders to the rock for ease in getting in and out of the water. The deeper water off the rocks is cooler and more refreshing after hours in the sun. In addition, there is no sand to blow or cling to wet skin and suit, and none to bring back to your room.

Rock beaches usually mean nearby coral, sea plants, and a variety of marine flora. A face mask and snorkel tube are all you need to watch the colorful underwater pageant hour after hour. The water is always clear, since there is no sand to be churned by water and bathers.

Many rock beaches have been "improved" by the hotels, with wood and cement decks for easier walking and setting of umbrellas, lounges, and chairs.

Sand beaches, on the other hand, allow you to walk into the

ITALY

CORSICA
SARDINIA

SICILY

GOZO

Mgarr

COMINO

Mellieha Bay
St. Paul's Bay

Golden Bay

Sliema
Valletta

Mdini

MALTA

water at your own pace, and for the less than great swimmers, it is reassuring to be able to stand on a smooth, sandy bottom. Sandy beaches are soft and easy to lie on and allow you to mold yourself right into the sand. Both types of beach appear to have their devotees. We came as sand-beach lovers and left with doubts, having sampled and appreciated Malta's rock beaches, too.

Malta. All in all, there are 110 hotels on Malta's three islands, ranging in price from $3 to $24 per person per day. With a little bit of asking and looking, you should be able to find what you are looking for.

Malta's newest hotel (opened October, 1972), which offers new standards of luxury, service, and comfort by any standard, is the Grand Hotel Verdala in Rabat, just outside Mdina. Its terrace restaurants and balconied rooms permit magnificent unobstructed views of the island as far as the eye can see. The Grand Verdala has two large swimming pools, one heated for swimming during the winter season, but the beach is fifteen minutes away by hotel bus. The management has arranged to use the beach at the Ramla Bay Hotel in Ramla Tal-Bir Bay at the northern tip of the island.

The Grand Verdala's high season extends from April 1 to October 31. During this period its best rooms, with balcony and panoramic view, including full board for two, are available for $40 per day, definitely a luxury classification.

Ramla Bay Hotel, owned and managed by the Holland family, takes its name from Ir-Ramla Tal-Bir, Maltese for Sandy Bay of the Wells. The characteristic lintel shape of old-style Maltese wells was used as the architectural motif for the hotel, which is set on a hill overlooking a small, secluded bay, with a fine view of Gozo and Comino. Bays and coves are around almost every bend in Malta, and each of them has a sandy beach. Few of the rock beaches are found in secluded coves. Consequently, the sandy beaches are matched with quiet water.

The Ramla Bay is small as hotels go, only fifty rooms, but well appointed and designed for coolness, with marble floors and stone walls. It caters primarily to families and those who want total rest and relaxation. But it does provide for all water sports, including

Mellieha Bay: flowers, golden sand, and an unspoiled landscape.

water skiing and sailing. By our classification, the Ramla Bay is a moderate-priced hotel.

Probably the largest of Malta's bays with sandy beach is Mellieha Bay. The English built a good-sized hotel here; in fact, Hotel Mellieha Bay has ten more rooms than the Hilton. Although this hotel caters almost exclusively to English vacationers, with package deals including air fare, Americans are entirely welcome. By our classification, this hotel dominating the bay is moderately priced.

The sandy beach is just a short stroll away, but it also has a rocky beach with steps leading directly to the bluest water. Or you have the choice of a pool. Here too, families and children are well provided for, and teenagers will find many others to socialize with, as will singles and young marrieds.

With the coming of sundown, the hotel becomes a swinging place. But the designers of the hotel took the noise factor into consideration, placing the disco and nightclub in the middle of the building, with the rooms stretching away to the left and right.

By the way, every room has its own balcony and a sea view.

Just outside of Mellieha Bay is the town of Mellieha, which according to historical accounts, was a flourishing town and harbor in Roman times. Legend has it that Saints Peter and Luke came here to preach.

From a belvedere above the town, both Comino and Gozo can be clearly seen. And from this vantage point, Mellieha Bay and the hotel make excellent studies for camera bugs.

Directly across the island to the west are the beaches with golden sands. In the immediate vicinity of Ghajn Tuffieha (the Spring from which the Apple came) are Golden Bay and Ghajn Tuffieha Bay; each is a sheltered cove with coarse cliffs for a backdrop. Here, the sands are actually golden—not tan or brown or yellow, but with a deep, golden hue.

Believing quite correctly that tourists would be attracted to these sands and their secluded coves, enterprising English hostelers built the first of Malta's resort hotels at Golden Bay. It was soon evident that the 22-room Côte d'Or was inadequate to the demand, so a second hotel, the 114-room Golden Sands, was built on a promontory overlooking the sea and the Côte d'Or.

From the Golden Sands high above the beach, you have two choices for getting down to the beach and the surf: an elevator on the side of the cliff or a long flight of steps. If neither appeals to you, an Olympic-size pool at the hotel may. Together, the two hotels offer a full range of aquatic activities, including speed boats, sailing, and deep-sea diving. Both hotels have a family atmosphere and offer English, continental, and Maltese cuisine. They are both in our medium-to-low-price category.

A cove and bay away is Ghajn Tuffieha Bay; and perched high on a cliff is Mr. Martin's Riviera Martineque Hotel. Unfortunately, Mr. Martin provided no elevator for the trip down to the beach—and we do mean down. We counted 280 steps, running all the way; going up was not quite on the run. However, it isn't necessary to go up and down often, with a snack bar, showers, and change rooms on the beach.

Among the things we liked so much here were the intimacy of the place (sixteen rooms) and the excellent buffets. Since the

The ruggedness of the countryside at Ghajn Tuffieha doesn't prevent it from being a favorite swimming spot.

hotel is only twelve miles from Valletta, getting into town is no more than a twenty-minute ride. On the other hand, the location is quite isolated for those who want that. A terraced double room with private bath and full board is delightfully inexpensive; it's in our low-price bracket.

On the northwestern tip of the island, just a short walk from the ferry to Gozo, is Paradise Bay, with a hotel whose prices go right along with the song, "Heaven can wait, this is paradise." Paradise Bay Hotel has only thirty-three rooms, but if reservations are made early enough, you should be able to get a room. In the high season, a twin or double room with full board—lunch, dinner, and English breakfast—is in our low category toward the budget end.

The hotel has a most unusual location on the very edge of a small, natural bay. Step outside the lobby, walk a few feet and down six steps, and you're in the water. Across the bay is a sandy beach, so here again, you have a choice of both rocky and sandy beaches.

Paradise Bay is directly on the bus run from Valletta, sixteen miles away. Even though this is the farthest point on the island, the bus ride into Valletta takes no more than thirty minutes—they do move along, and it's scenery all the way.

Amid rugged surroundings on high ground above St. Pauls Bay, between Qawra and Bugibba, is the gleaming, white Hotel Hyperion. The owners, the Murros and the Phillipses, have done a good job of creating a friendly atmosphere. The staff speaks not only English but also French, Spanish, Italian, and German.

For those who prefer a rocky beach, they've leveled off an area of the huge limestone rocks and have put in metal steps right into the sea. This bathing-basking area is no more than 200 yards from the edge of the garden.

In addition to a good-sized filtered pool, a children's pool, and a bar with poolside service is the Stable, a swinging discotheque. The Hyperion's per-day costs, including full board, place it in our low category. It is necessary to add, however, that its fifty-eight rooms are well known in Europe, which should indicate the need for reservations well in advance.

St. Pauls Bay has much to recommend it; it is one of the largest bays on the island, with sailing and speed boating, yachts available for charter, and the largest sandy beach on the island. It is also a historic and storied area. Salina Bay is just around the bend at Oawra; there, salt fans lie drying in the sun on the salt flats (*salina*). The Kennedy Memorial Park is located here, and the Salina Bay Hotel, looking down from its promontory like a large, brooding bird. This is the foremost summer vacation spot for the Maltese; the normal year-round population of 3000 swells to 30,000 in June, July, and August.

Perhaps some of Salina Bay's popularity rests on the Gillieru restaurant. With both a grand view of the sea and superb seafood lunches and dinners, this restaurant with its circular terrace hugging the rocky cliffs is a must for any visitor.

The 204-room Malta Hilton in St. Julian, directly on the Mediterranean, has a rock beach that offers a fantastic view of the entire waterfront. (Without the aid of binoculars you can follow the Spinola bus almost into Sliema.) From the beach you pop into

St. Paul's Bay has the largest sandy beach on Malta.

the bluest water imaginable. The Hilton has a large pool, tennis courts, gardens, and indoor and outdoor dining. Undoubtedly, its "8" Auberges Restaurant is the most elegant on the island.

However, it must be said that the Hilton, Malta's second largest hotel and one of its newest, simply doesn't have the disarming urbanity of some of the older Hiltons. It has a long way to go to approach the graciousness and fine service of the Hilton in Marbella, Spain, for example. It is large enough, however, to accommodate a variety of vacationers—families, young marrieds, and singles. Teenagers may find it a bit boring and a little too sophisticated. In our cost classification, the Hilton ranks as it should—in the luxury class.

The Hilton has the advantage of being within walking distance of St. Julian's shops and restaurants and the bus stop for Sliema and Valletta. Down a short road to the right of the Hilton, is the Dragonara Palace Casino, a magnificent birthday-cake creation set on a finger of land that juts into the sea. The casino offers a full range of gambling tables using standard European rules.

Along St. Julian's waterfront just about all the hotels have rocky beaches. These include the Sheraton (medium-priced), the Cavalieri (low), the Palms (medium), and St. Julian (medium). In this area, sand beaches are a rarity. All the hotels are within walking distance of the Dragonara Palace. Teenagers and singles from the hotels in the area congregate at the free disco on the Dragonara's rocky grounds. It's difficult to know where Dragonara ends and the Sheraton begins, but it really makes no difference. Everything is open to everyone; however, proper dress is required in the casino.

Gozo. Gozo is only twenty minutes and twenty-five cents by car ferry (the M/V *Jylland*) from Malta. Or you can make the trip even more quickly on a hydrofoil, clipping along at forty knots. Both leave from Marfa, at the northern tip of Malta, and put in at Mġarr. Buses, taxis, and rental cars are available in Mġarr (not to be confused with Mġarr on Malta, just a stone's throw from Ghajn Tuffieha). Victoria, only four miles away, is actually within walking distance. For real hikers, the most northerly point on the island is less than nine miles from Mġarr, and a walking tour is an excellent way to see many sights.

Surprisingly, most visitors to Malta do not think of the island of Gozo as a place to stay, which we feel is unfortunate. Those who have discovered it may want it to remain unknown, however. But we're agreed that that would be heartless.

Ta'Cenc is a most remarkable and unusual development. Using native limestone blocks in a most creative way, the architect-designers have produced a self-sufficient village or, as they say here, an isle within an isle that is truly idyllic. Ta'Cenc, less than a mile southwest of Mġarr, is considered a first-class "A" hotel. But it isn't a hotel in the usual sense. Set among fig, carob, and prickly pear trees, on the edge of the Mediterranean, it is a collection of splendid cottages, each with its own unique design and private garden. In addition to the individual cottages, there is a series of connected single and double rooms, which create a charming courtyard effect. The shopping center, tennis courts, pool, and restaurant make Ta'Cenc a world in itself.

Ta'Cenc on Gozo has a private beach as well as a pool.

The sandy beach and transparent sea are completely isolated—in fact, off-limits to all but its guests. If you want a combination of charm, luxury, and isolation, consider Ta'Cenc. A *camera singola* (single room) with full board in high season is midway in the luxury price range, while a *camera doppia* (double) is just about at the top of the class. A cottage suite is higher than anything else on the island, $60 to $70 per day.

Places of Interest. The islands of Malta offer the vacationer a wide diversity of interesting attractions—religious, historic, and archeological—as well as the indigenous handicrafts. Even dedicated beach people will want to see the sights, and because Malta is so compact, points of interest are easily accessible from most beaches.

For example, in 1883 in the Basilica Ta'Pinu on Gozo, a peasant woman named Carmela Grima reported that the Virgin Mary had appeared to her. Ta'Pinu, in open country a short walk from the village of Gharb near the northern tip of the island, became a religious attraction when reports of miraculous cures reached the continent. Since then, what was once a tiny chapel has grown into a cathedral-sized stone church and an attraction for tourists from all over the world.

The capital of Gozo, Victoria, also called Rabat (not to be confused with Rabat near Mdina on Malta), is the site of the Gran Castello—the Citadel. Within its ramparts are a museum, ancient cathedral, and remains of old buildings.

To get to the Citadel, turn right at It-Tokk, Victoria's main square, and walk or ride up the asphalt road. You'll know you're at It-Tokk when you see the bronze statue of Christ, a memorial to those who died in World War II.

A walk around the ramparts of the Citadel provides a panoramic view of the entire island. It's perfect for camera buffs.

The Citadel's museum houses a fine collection of Roman antiquities unearthed in this area. Those Romans must have been as enchanted with Mediterranean beaches as we are.

Gozo has much more to offer: prehistoric temples dating to 3000 B.C., alabaster caves, and some unbelievable views from cliffs above the sea. Malta is widely known for its handmade lace, which is made primarily on Gozo. Don't fail to watch the lace workers. As they work, the dozen or so bobbins fly with incredible speed. Nevertheless, the patterns they weave are so intricate that the edge of a handkerchief may take a full day to complete.

A word about Malta's buses. Because the country is small, buses have evolved as the primary means of mass transportation. They are in good supply, fast, and the fares are low. And they are unique in being color-coded. It is only in relatively recent times that literacy has become widespread. To help those who could not read, the destination signs on buses were color-coded, and the custom remains today.

In the bevy of buses lined up at Kingsgate Terminus, just outside Valletta's walls, anyone can tell at a glance which bus to take if you know the color. If, say, you've just come from St. Julian, you were on the Spinola bus—green with a light green stripe. Dark blue buses ply the road to Rabat. Red buses with blue stripe go to Żabbar; orange, to and from Żurrieq. White buses with pale blue stripe will take you to Marfa, and on the way, to Mellieha Bay and Gahjn Tuffieha.

In Gozo, light gray buses with red stripe run from Mġarr to the bus terminal on Victoria's Main Gate Street and from there to Gharb and the beach at Marsalforn. In addition to this sampling, there are a dozen more bus routes. A note of caution. When paying your fare, which depends on the destination, you'll be given an almost tissue-paper-thin receipt; don't throw it away until it is torn down the middle by one of the two conductors. To help keep employment up, both a "tearer" conductor and a driver usually work each bus.

In Valletta you will avoid undue confusion by using either the Kingsgate or Castile Terminus, which is inside Kingsgate to the right of Queensway, in front of the Auberge de Castile, as your base for any trip, rather than switching buses on unfamiliar streets. If you plan to drive yourself, you'll need an International Driver's License and a Maltese police permit (free). Remember, drive on the left, English-style, and always expect the unexpected. Why not take a bus and leave the driving to them? All those religious symbols and holy medallions in the buses may not be for effect alone.

Let's consider the attractions on the island of Malta. Although not listed among the Seven Wonders of the ancient world, the Hypogeum in Paola is surely a wonder. Discovered in 1902 by a builder digging a foundation for a house, the Hypogeum (literally, "beneath the earth") is the only known subterranean neolithic (2400 B.C.) temple in the world. It was actually hollowed out of solid rock, an incredible feat that must have taken ages to accomplish. The ancient workmen were not content with hollowing out a single room; in fact, the Hypogeum consists of three levels, with the lower level forty feet below ground. In the Oracle chamber, when a man whispers into a cutout opening in the wall, his voice becomes fantastically magnified and booms throughout the structure. For some unexplained reason, a woman's voice does not produce this effect. This sexual difference has defied explanation. Perhaps the ancients were trying to tell us something.

Paola is easily reached from the Kingsgate Terminus; take the pea-green Cospicua bus right to Paola's main square. If you prefer to go with someone who can explain the historic sites, certified guides are available. Just phone the government tourist board or drop in at 9 Merchants Street in Valletta. Guides and cars, or chauffeur-driven cars will be provided for a set fee, according to the size of the group and the length of the tour.

At Tarxien, just south of Paola, a group of four Stone-Age temples, discovered by accident in 1913, stand intact today. This cluster of four interconnected buildings is formed of enormous, evenly cut stone blocks. Some are ornately decorated, the work of highly creative mason-artists. Considering that these date back to 2400 B.C., the civilization that produced them must have been quite advanced. The fact that no one knows how the blocks were lifted into place makes Tarxien all the more marvelous.

Tarxien is reached by bus from the Castile Terminus. Take the red bus with green stripe going to Żejtun, and ask the ticket tearer or conductor to let you off at Tarxien's police station.

Additional examples of prehistoric monumental structures are at Ħaġar Qim and Mnjadra on Malta and at Ġgantija on Gozo.

For the less archeologically inclined, a number of attractions can vie for your beach time. One of these, older than all the megaliths, was carved not by man, but by the forces of nature. On the southwest coast, a short way from the picturesque fishing village of Wied-iż-Żurrieq, is the Blue Grotto. Similar to its namesake on the Isle of Capri, this grotto is even more spectacular, as artificial light is not needed to set off the brilliant colors of the marine environment.

The grotto can be entered only by boat—nothing fancy, just a rowboat. You can arrange to hire one in Wied-iż-Żurrieq. One person may go alone, but the rate drops considerably for a group. One person will pay close to $1.40, half a pound; four people can hire the boat for about $2.80, or a pound at current rates of exchange.

Here again, to get to the grotto, take a bus from Kingsgate Terminus, the orange one to Wied-iż-Żurrieq. The best time for a visit is early in the morning when the sunlight best sets off the colors of the grotto. Plan to leave some time for poking about the village and taking pictures.

Should you prefer, a phone call to the Tourist Board will produce a chauffeured car and arrangements for a boat. A number of the hotels will also make these arrangements for you. If you're staying at one of the larger hotels, just let the concierge know time and place—he'll do the rest. (The knowledgeable concierge is an indispensable institution and often makes the difference between a so-so vacation and a great one.)

For garden *aficionados,* Buskett Gardens of Verdala Palace in Rabat is a beauty spot on the island. This "Little Wood," although no Versailles, is a lovely public garden containing groves of orange and lemon trees, gigantic ash trees, Aleppo pines, cypress, olive trees, and grapevines. Here one can walk, sit, or sketch in quiet relaxation.

Verdala Palace, built by Grand Master Hugues De Loubenx-Verdalle in 1588 as a summer residence, overlooks the garden and is open to the public. On an island with no mountains or rivers and few trees, Buskett Gardens is indeed, a sanctuary, a unique patch of green. The Grand Master obviously thought ahead when he had this garden planted. A touch added long after Verdalle had gone to his reward, is the terrace restaurant and snack bar, serving visitors on their way up or down from the palace.

If you're staying at the new Grand Verdala Hotel, you're within easy walking distance of the palace and gardens; if, however, you're booked at one of the beach areas, take the dark blue bus from Kingsgate or drive, a short trip from most anywhere on the island A visit to Mdina is a must, so plan to do both on the same day. It's really worth while.

Called the Silent City, Mdina, the old capital of Malta, speaks quietly for itself. When the Romans referred to Malta, they called it Melita (their word for honey), and they were referring to Mdina. It's easy to understand why. As you walk through its quiet streets, which are empty even though the city is fully inhabited, you are struck by the golden hue of the place. Honey-colored is about right.

Being only seven miles from Valletta, Mdina offers those who can afford it a quiet retreat. Many high-level government officials, members of Maltese nobility, and other influential families live

Mdina, Malta's capital until 1570, dominates the coastal plain.

here. But the exteriors of the fortresslike houses give no indication of their splendid interiors. This is one place you'd want to go with a competent guide, as explanations are needed.

A word of caution. Both Andrea and I were wearing shorts when we visited Mdina and consequently, we were barred from the Cathedral. As Anita was wearing something that could pass for a skirt, she was allowed to go in. So it's long trousers for men and skirts or a reasonable facsimile for women, if you want to see the Cathedral. Dominating St. Paul's Square and being on high ground in open country, Metropolitan Cathedral offers an unobstructed view for miles in all directions, so bring lots of film.

After the earthquake of 1693 the Cathedral was restored in the Renaissance style it now bears—for the most part. Its ceiling is superbly painted and Petronilla, as the huge bell is affectionately called, cast in Venice in 1370, is one of the oldest in Europe.

Despite looting by the French during their short occupation (less than two years) there are many beautiful treasures still to be seen both in the Cathedral and in the nearby museum.

At Ta'Qali, on the road between Mdina and Rabat, is the Mdina glass factory on the site of an abandoned RAF Base. Here, you can watch glass being made by hand, and you can buy some of the loveliest glass objects you've ever seen. Mdina glass is famous for its splendid mixture of colors, representing the blues and greens of its waters and the tans and gold of its rock. Don't pass up this opportunity to buy some Mdina glass. We did not buy any, and we're sorry; we haven't been able to find this glass anywhere in the States. (According to the Malta mission, however, Mdina glass should soon be on sale at the United Nations.)

In Valletta, St. John's Co-Cathedral, built between 1573 and 1577, offers a completely different type of attraction. Unlike traditional sixteenth-century European cathedrals, this one's magnificent interior belies its rather drab, fortresslike exterior. Tucked away on St. John's Square amid Valletta's cramped streets, it is not visible from a distance. However you will recognize it by the eight-pointed cross of the Order of Knights of St. John atop the building.

This unusual cross, seen often in Malta, is packed with meaning. The eight points are reminders of the eight beatitudes, and the four arms speak of the four virtues: prudence, temperance, fortitude, and justice.

The cathedral's interior walls and ceilings are richly decorated with paintings, tapestries, and carvings, giving much of the colorful history of the knights. Here, too, proper dress for both men and women is called for. Shorts and bare feet are definitely out.

A word about the Auberges of Valletta. During the 218-year presence on the island of the Knights of St. John, eight different Auberges, or inns, were established as residences for the knights of different nationalities. The knights of each Auberge were responsible for the defense of a certain section of Valletta and Grand Harbour. Today, five of the eight original Auberges remain and all are open to visitors.

For a good close-up view of Grand Harbour, Fort St. Angelo, and the three cities of Vittoriosa, Senglea, and Cospicua, take a water taxi—a *dghajsa*. The rower pushes rather than pulls on the oars, enabling you to get a good look at the harbor defenses. Again, don't forget your camera.

Food and Drink. There are a number of good restaurants in Malta that serve home-grown versions of English and Italian cookery, but there are also some typically Maltese dishes. Each successive wave of foreign domination appears to have dropped something into the kettle.

Torta tal lampuki is a particularly delicious concoction, consisting of slices of fried fish, *(lampuki* is a local species) covered with a pastry crust, then baked with tomatoes, onions, parsley, and cauliflower. Wild strawberries in cream are often served with it as dessert.

Maltese bread is good, but only when fresh. Try it with sheep's milk cheese—*gbejna*—that has been ripened with or without black pepper and vinegar.

Bebbux, snails in a peppery sauce, should appeal to most seafood enthusiasts. Other Maltese specialties include fried or stewed rabbit, *stuffat tal-fenek,* and widow's soup, *Soppa tal-armla,* made with eggs (often poached), vegetables, cheese, and spaghetti. *Timpana,* a kind of meat and vegetable pie, contains macaroni, liver, eggs, onions, and eggplant. Some menus note *aubergine.* This should not deter you. It is only a Catalan-Arabic version of Alberginia, eggplant, which the island grows lots of.

Artichokes stuffed with chopped olives, bread crumbs and parsley are called *Qaqoec Mimli.* Even if you're not normally an artichoke devotee, give this pleasant minglement a try.

YUGOSLAVIA

The Socialist Federal Republic of Yugoslavia may not be the most exciting name, but this mountainous country, with its secluded, sun-warmed, tree-lined beaches, certainly is compelling. Yugoslavs are big people, and Yugoslavia is a big, sprawling country made up of six seemingly disparate republics that often find living together difficult. Yet the country has the spirit and humor of big people, the ability to laugh hard, work hard, and drink hard. The national drink, slivovitz, a fiery plum brandy, is a measure of this hardiness. And Yugoslavs are friendly and open, in the style of Americans.

The republic of Montenegro, a bit of Bosnia and Hercegovina, and the province of Dalmatia (part of the republic of Croatia) extend along Yugoslavia's Adriatic coast, that calm, sun-drenched extension of the Mediterranean. Although this coastline meanders some 600 miles, from Rijeka and Trieste in the north, to Ulcinj, on Albania's forbidden border, it is the area between Dubrovnik and Ulcinj, some 135 easily covered miles, that we are concerned with. Hidden away in sheltered coves and bays along this prismatic shore are a number of spectacular beaches.

This is ruggedly beautiful country, with craggy, scabrous

mountains sloping to the sea; with trees and shrubs growing almost to the edge of its primitive beaches; with pines, tall firs, and olive groves; fragrant orange and lemon trees, and the minty scent of rosemary mixed with lavender and oleander. This vivid sea and landscape, far from the industrial cities of Belgrade and Zagreb, invites the vacationer to its pollution-free air, to swim in its crystal-clear water.

The argosies (galleons) of Ragusa, now Dubrovnik, no longer enter that city's medieval walled harbor. But thousands of vacationers headed for Dalmatia's beaches do. Until now, few have been Americans. But if you're looking for a new experience, don't hold back because of the language barrier. English is spoken in all hotels, most restaurants and shops, and by many of the young people generally. John Wayne is a household word; western movies are favorites in Yugoslavia.

Serbo-Croatian is the chief language of Yugoslavia, but because four of its republics belonged to the Austro-Hungarian monarchy, it has remained a German-language area. As a result, many German tourists flock here to take advantage of the warming sun, as well as to make their marks go a long way. The dollar goes far, too; you'll get good mileage for your money in Yugoslavia. And even with all the tourists from West Germany, Belgium, Austria, and Italy, there is more than enough beach to go around.

Climate. Because Yugoslavia is only beginning to emerge as a vacation land for Americans, few realize that in terms of weather, it compares favorably with both the French and the Italian Riviera. Somehow, these places have come to be the standard by which all else is judged.

During June, July, and August, the sun shines an average of eleven to twelve hours daily along the Dalmatian and Montenegrin coasts. In fact, that is substantially more than either the two French Rivieras or the Greek islands.

During the same period, the air temperature may vary between 66° and 85° F. (19° and 29° C.), but the mean daily temperature is approximately 77° F. (25° C.). The temperature of the sea water remains between 72° and 76° F. (22° and 24° C.), which permits

AUSTRIA HUNGARY
RUMANIA
ADRIATIC SEA
BULGARIA
ITALY
ALBANIA
GREECE

Zagreb

Belgrade

YUGOSLAVIA

Dubrovnik
Budva
Ulcinj

swimming until October.

Although it can get hot, hot, hot in July and August, this is a dry corner of the world, so the heat never becomes oppressive. There is so little rain during this period, it isn't necessary to drag along umbrellas, raincoats, or other foul-weather gear.

Transportation. Lack of familiarity with Yugoslavia may make you think it is difficult to get to. No trouble at all; you may travel there by land, sea, or air; by train, plane, car, or boat. There are excellent direct-access roads and trains from Italy, Austria, Hungary, Rumania, and Greece—all the countries that have a common border with Yugoslavia. Flights from each of these countries aboard their national carriers arrive daily in Dubrovnik. From the United States, all carriers flying to Rome include Dubrovnik in the price of the Rome fare. From England, BA has five weekly flights to Zagreb, Yugoslavia, and from there to Dubrovnik. Altogether, and counting the one-hour time-zone difference, the elapsed time from London to Dubrovnik is approximately three and a half hours. In addition, BA flies to Dubrovnik directly every Saturday.

Should you be in Italy, the most relaxing, although time-consuming, route to Yugoslavia is by car ferry across the Adriatic. The crossing takes eight or fourteen hours, depending upon point of embarkation; this gives you an opportunity, if you sail on a Yugoslavian ship, to sample Yugoslavian food and to talk with Yugoslavs and get your ear accustomed to the language. Of course, our prejudice toward ship travel is clear by now.

The *Sveti Stefan,* a Yugoslavian car ferry, makes the crossing from Bari, Italy, to Bar, near the southern tip of Yugoslavia, in eight relaxing hours. From June 1 to July 14, it leaves at 10 P.M. each Monday, Wednesday, and Friday evening. From July 15 to August 31, you have the choice of Monday and Tuesday mornings at 10 A.M. or Wednesday, Thursday, and Friday evenings at 10 P.M.

Accommodations on the deck, including use of all common rooms, are all you really need for either the day or evening crossing. For $6.50 this has to be a bargain. You may have a stateroom and bed for approximately $9 to $15, depending on class (first or second) and the number of people in the room. Small cars (up to

2100 pounds) cost another $14 to $15. Passage can be booked in Bari through Morfimare at 18 Via Melo, directly across from the pier. The scene becomes rather hectic as sailing time approaches, so it pays to be early. And don't worry; even though the wait appears interminable, your passport will be returned on time.

If you're farther north on the Italian boot, or on your way south from Venice, you can cross the Adriatic from Ancona on either of the seven-hundred-passenger car ferries M/S *Liburnija* or *Ilirija*. These put in at Zadar, from where you can drive south along the Dalmatian coast. Or you may remain on board, as the ship calls at Split, Hvar, and Korčula before arriving at Dubrovnik. Of course, this trip is longer, but these ships have outdoor pools, so it's worth considering. Port agents for the shipping line, Jadrolinija, are G. Radonicich and Company in Venice, Agenzia Marittima in Ancona, and P. Lorusso and Company at 18 Corso Cavour, Bari.

Additional sailing schedules and ports are available through Linee Marittime Dell' Adriatico, an Italian company that operates M/S *Tintoretto* and *Tiziano* from Ancona, Pescara, and Bari. In the United States, information can be obtained from their representative, Atlantic Holidays, Inc., P.O. Box 2525, Grand Central Station, New York, N. Y. 10017. Port agents are easily located in the Italian cities noted.

Camping. In Yugoslavia, camping is not allowed outside of properly designated camp grounds. Between Dubrovnik and Ulcinj, eight campsites have been established, all close to the sea. They are located in Kupari, Cavtat, between Sutomore and Petrovac, Budva, Sveti Stefan, Bar, and Ulcinj. All charge about the same fee: 4 dinars per person per night (approximately 25 cents) and about 37 dinars ($2.50) per car. However, they do not all have equally good facilities. The Automobile Association of Yugoslavia publishes a guidebook listing all the camps and their facilities.

Camping equipment may be brought into the country duty-free, provided you take it with you when you leave. The authorities don't take kindly to the idea of selling your equipment after it has been allowed into the country. A number of camps grant discounts to holders of International Camping Carnets. Before you leave the States, it's a good idea to get one from our State Department or the American Automobile Association.

BEACHES

Dubrovnik. We were about to leave Dubrovnik, secure in the knowledge that sandy beaches were not part of the landscape, when a shopkeeper told us about Kupalište Sumratin. Because of the geological nature of Dubrovnik, this sand beach is indeed a rarity.

As the Dubrovchani much prefer rock beaches, Sumratin, which is both long and wide, is never crowded. Because of the thick stand of trees that grows right to the edge of the sand, we're tempted to call it Green Beach. The pines and firs all but conceal the hotel, villas, and a few guest houses at the base of the mountain.

Tucked away among the greenery to the left of the beach is the seventy-room, class-B Hotel Sumratin. If you want a sandy beach and yet still be almost in the heart of Dubrovnik, this may be the place for you. This beach has a good, firm, smooth sand bottom and clear, clean water. Beach umbrellas are provided by the hotel, and wood platforms allow you to sleep or sunbathe off the sand, if you prefer.

Dubrovnik itself is small, having a population of about 25,000. From the Rector's Palace at one end to the fountain at the opposite end, the main street is perhaps a few hundred yards long. But it conjures visions of knights on horseback clattering along cobblestones. From the roads above the town, one sees the massive ramparts, bastions, and towers of this beautifully preserved walled town and the cramped houses with their red-tiled roofs.

Where are the beaches in relation to the heart of town? Actually, they are outside the walls, which means outside of Dubrovnik, but remember, this is not a large city. For example, Hotel Excelsior, one of Dubrovnik's half dozen class-A hotels, is firmly planted in the face of the cliff right on the coast, less than a quar-

The Hotel Argentina is built on shelflike rocks.

ter mile from the city's walls.

The Excelsior, the Argentina, Hotel Villa Dubrovnik, the Neptun, and the Novi Belvedere are built on rock beaches; not pebbles, not stones, but big, naked, shelflike rocks. Many hotels have paved a portion of the rocks with cement to provide places for beach chairs, umbrellas, and steps to the sea. Villa Dubrovnik, with a walled esplanade above its sea wall, has steps leading down to a tunnel that opens to the rocky beach.

The recently completed Hotel Dubrovnik Palace, on the Lapad Peninsula just north of the city, was built into a scooped-out portion of the cliff face. Even though its 325 sea-view rooms with balconies make it a sizable affair, it seems quite unassuming, set into the mountain. Its beach is directly below the face of the cliff. Also on this peninsula, but sufficiently removed from the Dubrovnik Palace by thick, unbroken pine forests, is Hotel Neptun. Most of its 220 rooms are in a central, multistoried tower. And although it has a commodious pool, guests usually prefer to jump into the sea from its cement-paved rocks or step down the ladders provided. The Neptun is a good example of a modern class-B hotel fitted out with discotheque, café, and restaurant.

The water around the rock beaches is first-rate for snorkeling and scuba diving. Marine life is abundant, colorful, and harmless. Bring along at least a pair of goggles and a breathing tube. The underwater parade can be watched for hours on end.

Speaking of marine life, for those professionally or otherwise inclined, a superb public aquarium as well as the world renowned Biological Institute are housed in the fortress of St. Ivan, within the walls of the city. Additional institute facilities are maintained on the island of Lokrum. An impressive collection of mounted fishes and birds is on display in the island's Benedictine monastery. If you need an excuse, try the picturesque and romantic restaurant on the island. From the restaurant there is a sweeping view of the old section of the walled city.

A poll of our intrepid little band elicited the belief that most beach areas were quite suitable for teenagers, singles, and families. According to Dana and Andi, if a hotel didn't have a disco, there was sure to be one nearby. Teenagers, they felt, would have no language problems. They also noted that boys were everywhere and were friendly, good-mannered (a characteristic they miss at home), and good dancers; best of all, they are anxious to meet Americans. A number of hotel resorts have pools and bathing areas for youngsters, so parents should have no worries on that score.

Few coasts anywhere in the world have such a chain of islands as does the Dalmatian coast. Some can even be reached by car, but most require a short ride by ferry or motor launch. It is on these islands that sandy, hideaway beaches can be found. The islands of Lopud and Koločep, seven and four sea miles, respectively, out of Dubrovnik, have incredibly clear, calm water gently lapping at sandy beaches.

On these islands, hotel prices are far lower then on the mainland. For example, Hotel Koločep on Koločep and Hotel Lafodia, Hotel Dubrova-Pracat, and the Grand Hotel on Lopud are in our low category. If you don't require a private bath, the room charge can be 30 to 50 percent less.

At Kupari, four miles south of Dubrovnik, a hotel and tourist combine (a Yugoslavian form of capitalism) has developed an imposing resort complex. However, the dimensions of the Pelegrin development don't become apparent until you drive into the compound and find yourself in the middle of the Kupari campsite, one of the eight between Dubrovnik and Ulcinj. Beyond the campsite is Hotel Pelegrin, a concrete and glass, tiered trapezoid tapered so that it's narrower at the base. Built on the slope of the Pelegrin Hills, which form the cove of Kupari Bay, three of the hotel's four sides have an unrestricted view of the bay.

A few hundred yards away is the smaller, quieter Hotel Goričina, where the elegantly polished wood interiors contrast sharply with the lush surrounding vegetation—cactus, Spanish blade, and pines.

The clear water of Kupari Bay is darker blue than the water in Dubrovnik, and there are two beaches to choose from: one pebbly, the other a long concrete ledge curving with the shoreline.

Leading from the Pelegrin are two paths, one for cars, the other a foot path. General public use is restricted. The foot path leads to New Beach, while the automobile path brings you to the parking lot on a level with the top of the twenty-two-room Hotel Galeb in an extraordinary, sequestered woodland setting. The hotel is well appointed, with service and food to match. Outside its front entrance is the cement walk to New Beach, and just off the walk are a series of nicely planned wide marble steps built among the boulders leading down to the concrete platforms that make up New Beach. Here, you can skinny dip, bask in the sun, or just be alone. The setting, except for the ladders into the water, is authentically primeval: bare rock surrounded by lush undergrowth and evergreen woods.

As if all this weren't enough, beyond the Galeb, cloistered among the fir and pines are two wholly unexpected contemporary villas, Jadranka and Boruvka, which are Yugoslavia's last word in luxury. Jadranka is usually kept in readiness for use by Marshall Tito, should he feel the need to get away from Belgrade. But both can be available for tourists. Though only two in number (more are in the planning stage), they are not on every tourist agency's list. It appears that their availability is kept "close to the vest." When we were there, Elizabeth Taylor and Richard Burton, on location for a film, were occupying one apartment. Nevertheless, if this kind of accommodation in the setting described appeals to you, it could be worth an inquiry at the Yugoslav Tourist Information Office. This applies to Hotel Galeb as well. I'd be surprised if the Galeb is known to the general run of tourist agencies.

This suggests a cautionary note. For reasons we've not discovered, the Yugoslavs who name hotels have a predilection for repetition. We've come across at least seven Bellvues, three Galebs, a number of Adriatics, several Albatrosses, and so on. Accordingly, we suggest you be sure to specify the city as well as the hotel you're interested in. Don't say Hotel Galeb and leave it at that. Given the ubiquity of Murphy's Law, "If a thing (reservation) can go wrong, it will," be sure you indicate which Galeb or Bellvue.

The Yugoslavs also have a penchant for big hotels. Perhaps because of the huge mountains all around them (80 percent of the country is mountainous), the Yugoslavs don't realize how large some of their hotels really are.

Around a few bends off the road leading south from Kupari, about ten miles from Dubrovnik, is the 650-room Hotel Plat—a "mother house" with nine satellites. But as big as it is, it doesn't look it. You wouldn't guess that it could accommodate 1200 people, if you strolled its half dozen beaches: they are not crowded. These rock and pebble beaches snaking along the waterfront must be over a mile long, broken by outcroppings of rock and trees. But if you prefer to bask around a pool, then jump in—they've got that, too, and one for toddlers.

Mlini, at the head of Zupa Bay, about a mile up the road from the Plat, is the site of the new class-A Hotel Astarea, which has a stony beach with some of the clearest water we've found anywhere. Stony in this instance means fist-size stones, smooth and not so smooth. This is splendid snorkeling ground, so bring your gear along. One afternoon I trailed several multicolored fish for half an hour. Although Anita and I disagree on the need for bathing slippers for walking in and out of the water, many of the Eu-

Although the Hotel Plat at Mlini is big enough to accomodate 1200 people, it is dwarfed by the mountains.

ropean men and women wear them; not all the stones are perfectly smooth. These slippers are readily available in Dubrovnik, and most of the larger hotels stock them, so it isn't necessary to bring them from home. Besides, they're cheaper here.

The Astarea is set into the hillside in such a way that from the beach below, a number of floors appear to be unsupported, shooting off into space. A third the size of the Plat, the Astarea is much cozier—even though a 220-room hotel is not exactly a monastic retreat.

It was at the Astarea that I met a *Feldsher* for the first time. In eastern European countries, a *Feldsher* (from the German for field barber or surgeon) is a kind of physician assistant.

Various kinds of assistants have the title of *Feldsher*. At the Astarea, the young woman *Feldsher* was the first-aid nurse in charge of the infirmary as well as the masseuse, which was how I met her. Her massage technique, which I wholeheartedly endorse, consisted of applying various oils to your body all over and giving a vigorous massage. A wide variety of massages are listed, but I suggest the full treatment; it's well worth the few dinars. Our *Feldsher* friend is also in charge of the sauna, so you make appointments through her for these salubrious sessions. Her office is just before the indoor pool and showers.

As you walk down the path to the village of Mlini, you'll pass an open-air beer garden restaurant that doubles as a discotheque. Lots of young people here and lots of fun. The village draws a number of British tourists who like music, beer, and people. You'll get on famously together.

Cavtat, on the point of land that completes the semi circle of Zupa Bay, is approximately twelve miles from Dubrovnik and six from Čilipi Airport, a good location. It is far enough from Dubrovnik to be away from the crowds, but it's only a brief, twenty-minute drive into town. As most hotels provide a shuttle service at regular intervals, a car is not a necessity. And because Cavtat (Epidaurus during the Roman occupation) is off the Adriatic Highway, fewer people make their way here.

To get to Cavtat from Čilipi, turn left as you approach Zvekovica. You may think you've come to Cavtat several times as you drive the narrow road along the bay. Around a bend here and there, you will pass a villa or hotel, but not until you see the two very modern five-story A-shaped buildings, are you in Cavtat. This is the class-A Grand Hotel Albatross. From the sea you get an exceptionally good view of this Arcadian sand and pebble beach resort. And the sea is another way of getting here from Dubrovnik. I must interject at this point a strong recommendation to take a boat ride along the coast, to see the beaches and the nature of the coast and obtain the pleasure of an offshore view.

One of the most striking features of Yugoslavian resorts is the size of the grounds around hotels. To their everlasting credit, they haven't skimped on either grounds or common rooms. The Albatross offers a good example; in addition to its 250 rooms and apartments (with refrigerator and TV), it has a large but elegant dining room, a huge, glass-enclosed indoor pool, and a tremendous, well-appointed lobby. The outdoor pool (with heated sea water in winter) is surrounded by spacious promenades and sunning areas.

In the past, Cavtat's villas and pensions were for those seeking

A cement beach; this one at Cavtat means no sand between your toes.

sylvan solitude. But with the coming of the Albatross and, most recently, its gambling casino and all-night eatery, the Chuckwagon (a revolutionary idea in Yugoslavia), Cavtat may emerge as the most swinging beach resort on the Dalmatian coast.

In the summer of 1971, at the invitation of the Yugoslavia Ministry of Tourism, American entrepreneurs (promoters?) set up a Las Vegas-type casino in the Albatross and began training "table" and "dice" men. By the summer of 1972, the young, eager Yugoslavian boys had learned English as well as "21," chemin de fer, roulette, poker, and all the other games. Admission of course, is free.

The Croatia, an American-style hotel with twenty-four-hour service (another revolutionary import) and a casino, opened in July of 1973. It is one of the most modern and luxurious hotels in the Mediterranean basin. Time and tide have carved the Cavtat area into a horseshoe-shaped piece of land that just misses being an island, so the Croatia's beach on the Sustjepan peninsula is extensive, private, wooded, and on the open sea.

Cavtat offers scuba divers and snorkelers an exceptional opportunity to swim among the underwater ruins of the Roman city of Epidaurus; it offers all swimmers calm, crystal waters. It also has the impressive Račic family mausoleum at the point of the peninsula. A creation of Ivan Meštrović, an acclaimed master in Yugoslavia, the mausoleum, although not big, is impressive. Its bronze doors, between two caryatids, portray Cyril, Methodius, Gregory, and Sava, the four Slavonic apostles. The ceiling is highly decorated with figures representing members of the Račic family, along with the apostles and their animals.

Montenegro and South. "What country, friends, is this?"
"Why this is Illyria, lady."
"And what should I do in Illyria?" The response should have been, "Relax on the beaches at Sveti Stefan or Budva and be sure to view the Boka Kotorska from on high."

It never occurred to me that Shakespeare was referring to the Dalmatian coast when he wrote those lines in *Twelfth Night*. It was not until we visited the admirable but miniature Maritime

Museum in Kotor that I learned that here, in fact, was Illyria.

Traveling the Adriatic Highway (*Autoput*) south to the beaches of Budva and Sveti Stefan, you must pass through Kotor, a most pleasant "must." The road girdles the entire margin of the Gulf of Kotor, which is in no sense an ordinary gulf. It is the enchantingly lovely Boka Kotorska and the gateway to Black Mountain, the republic of Montenegro. If you cannot take the time to drive around the four bays of the Boka, there is a small, six-car ferry at Kamenari which crosses to Lepetane. From there it's just a short drive into the heart of Kotor.

If you're not in a rush, drive the full way around. Along the bays of the Boka you'll pass through several villages, each with its own beach and small hotel or guest house, which are not on any travel agent's list. If you're inclined to get away from cities, people, and things, try your German, French, or even Croatian, with your *Say It* book in hand, to negotiate for room and board. Not to be ruled out is "Molin vas, govorite li Engeleski"—Pardon me, do you speak English?

Historically, Perast is the most widely known town of the Boka. The fame of its sailors and sea captains is legendary. It's worth stopping here just to walk around and see its old palaces and the aristocratic homes of a bygone age. Risan, just north of Perast, is magnificent for boating and swimming and is agreeably secluded. Farther along are Morinj and Strp, both with lovely, small, clean, quiet beaches—a little sand, a bit of stone interspersed with rock ledges and hemmed in by mountains and greenery—a real postcard setting come to life.

Had you driven into Kotor from Cetinje over the snaky, S-curved road across Mount Lovćen, you would not as yet have seen the Boka. Instead, coming around the first of the S's at the highest point on the road, you'd suddenly see, a thousand feet below, one of the world's great natural panoramas, a stage setting only Hollywood could dream up—except it's real. The setting is Kotor on its flat blue, mirrorlike bay, held fast by the surrounding mountains.

If a coastal passenger ship is in the harbor, you'll wonder how it got in and how it expects to get out; it seems an impossible fit.

Kotor Bay is like a movie set, too perfect to be real . . . but it is.

Between wondering and attempting to keep the car from going off the cliff, don't forget to photograph this incredible sight. Better yet, someone other than the driver had better take over the photographic assignment!

Kotor itself is not for beaching. It is a lively and colorful walled market town with cobblestone streets dating to the Middle Ages. If you don't mind a few flies and hornets hovering over the succulent watermelon, peaches, and grapes, here's the place to fill up. The streets outside the wall are lined with all manner of vegetables, fruits, peasant art, clothing, and knickknacks for the tourist. As in most markets you'll deal with the women. Remember, haggling is an age-old, honorable practice. So practice.

The Cathedral of St. Tripon is an outstanding example of twelfth-century Romanesque ecclesiology and quite different from the cathedrals in western Europe. It houses a substantial collection of religious art and relics.

From the cathedral square you can easily get to the plaza of the Maritime Museum. Its collection filled in gaps in our scant knowledge about Yugoslavian and southern European history; it's well worth an hour's visit.

From Kotor it's twelve miles, about a twenty-minute drive, to Budva. Because of its sheltered position on the Montenegrin littoral, its pleasant climate, and windless, almost two-mile-long sandy beach, Budva has become a haven for Europeans. It should now be sought out by Americans. The mountains descending to the water have divided the sandy shoreline into several beaches. Two of these, Slovenska and Bečići, offer remarkable examples of big Slavonic beaches.

Sharing Bečići beach are hotels Bellvue (Bellvee, according to local pronunciation) and Montenegro. Together, they have about a dozen low-profile buildings that can accommodate some 1700 people. The Montenegro's dining room can seat a thousand. This complex is so new that its gardens are not yet fully grown.

Although the coarse, multicolored sand can get hot, the water is invigoratingly cold; not bone-achingly so, but colder than the Mediterranean around Spain and Portugal. Recall, this area is a few degrees of latitude farther north.

Don't wait to rent a sun chair or beach umbrella *after* you get down to the beach. The beach boys require a ticket before they hand out equipment, and unfortunately, tickets can be purchased only at the main reception desks. To avoid walking back, purchase tickets at mealtime—preferably breakfast and no later than lunch. For some unfathomable reason, the reception desks are closed between two and six in the afternoon. Bring beach towels, as these are neither supplied nor rentable at the beach.

A mile around the mountain in the direction of Budva is Slovenska Beach with its complex of three hotels: the International, the Adriatic, and the Slavija. Of these, the International is the most outstanding, and the clientele is more English and American than anywhere else except Dubrovnik. The International has a large outdoor dance floor and discotheque. And if our teenagers are any judges, they have a reasonably good rock group that favors American music. All these hotels cater to all types of guests: families, singles, and couples.

In addition to daily boat trips to Dubrovnik, there are excur-

Sveti Stefan, a fourteenth-century fishing village, is now a modern resort.

sion buses, which leave regularly for day and half-day trips up and down the coast. Motor boats are constantly skimming across the water to Sveti Stefan, and the walled medieval town of Budva itself is within walking distance. There is only one entrance in the wall, and cars and buses are barred. The narrow, winding streets are crammed with people, snack bars, restaurants, and inviting specialty shops. On display in the town are archeological finds from the Illyrian, Greek, and Roman periods.

Five hundred years ago, as a defense against buccaneers and plunderers, the fishermen of Sveti Stefan built a fortified village on a coastal reef connected to the mainland by a narrow causeway. Today, this whole village is an elegant hotel. Few other hotels can boast solid rock walls up to eight feet thick! Not only does it make for quiet rooms, but for coolness on the hottest days—without the need for air conditioning.

The individual houses have been transformed into 116 well-appointed rooms—23 singles, 70 doubles, and 23 suites. Anita and I both marveled at the size and splendid decor of the bathrooms.

We've come to believe that bathrooms are a good indicator of a hotel's character; Sveti Stefan gets high marks for character.

Having been a village, the hotel continues to provide just about everything guests may want and need—gardens, open-air restaurants, café, bar, nightclub, hairdresser, and a variety of small shops.

Sveti Stefan's twin beaches, mirror images of each other, are private, pebbly, and unpopulated. The turquoise sea is made for water skiing, sailing, and snorkeling. The whole place is beautifully quiet, "English is spoken here," and it is one of the few hotels in the entire country given a deluxe rating.

Of late, a new attraction has come to Sveti Stefan. Harold's Club of Las Vegas, at the invitation of the government, has opened a gambling casino. It is anticipated that this will attract tourists from a wide area, including many from Dubrovnik who will be able to yacht on down and tie up at its pier facilities. Apparently, the government is seeking to attract a more jetty set. The evenings should prove to be livelier than ever before.

In case you didn't notice, the water begins at the dark edge; it's that clear!

On the mainland, a short walk from Sveti Stefan's beaches, is an even more exclusive beach, part of a lovely park with flowers and shrubs. The park and beach are part of the extraordinary "courtyard" and playgrounds of Hotel Miločer, formerly the summer palace of the Queen Mother during the 1940's. Fortunately, Tito's government has seen fit to maintain a number of palatial estates, even though they are reminders of the monarchy; they make excellent accommodations. In the case of the Miločer, six stone buildings have been converted to villas—luxury apartments with a total of seventy-seven rooms (fifty-three doubles, six suites, and eighteen singles).

From our point of view, the splendid grounds and beach are the drawing card. The gently sloping, pebbly beach is just made for youngsters, and the water here is unusually still, because of the deep cove created by rock outcroppings on each side of the beach. For tennis players who like to bat it around in the hot sun, the cool water is a great refresher. And there are no crowds here. There is a second beach, larger, not as private nor as quiet, but better for speed boating and water skiing. This one is at the edge of the park.

The park consists of fifteen acres of private walks in, around, and through the woods and alongside the sea, a number of buildings, and a charming, arbor-trellised, restaurant by the beach. You can't get lost here, but you can surely find a place to be alone. And you can always walk over to Sveti Stefan and use its facilities.

Close to the Miločer, enveloped by olive groves on three sides and bordered by a very private beach, is Hotel Maestral, named after the cold, dry wind of the Mediterranean basin. Although Louis XVI's influence can be seen in the hotel's design, I'm sure he would applaud the fact that each of its 154 rooms has a private bath, balcony, and sea view.

These three hotels share a most exceptional area of the Yugoslavian coast, just between the rocky beaches of populous Dubrovnik and the low-lying, sandy beaches of southern Montenegro. They are secluded, private, and fairly expensive.

Ulcinj. The southern Montenegrin countryside is dotted with mosques and minerets, reminders of Yugoslavia's Turkish and Ottoman heritage, an entirely different landscape than we have seen thus far. It is quite common to see Montenegrin peasant women in their colorful and billowy costumes, different in each area, prodding a flock of brown or black goats, working in the fields, or just walking what seems to be interminable distances.

The south is unique because of its fine, sandy beaches, a rarity for Yugoslavia. The south also appears to be the favorite area for nudist beaches, which are not unusual in central and southern Europe. Considering the variety of interests in the south and the apparent fact that few Americans have taken a beach vacation within sight of the Albanian border, it may be that Ulcinj, the southernmost town on Yugoslavia's Adriatic coast, is a good place to jump in.

Ulcinj is a peasant world of sheep and goat herders, of mustachioed men in traditional costumes; Moslem šiptars with colorful turbans; and women with white, shawllike headdresses or pancake hats and colorful aprons selling fruit and vegetables in the marketplace. Little remains of Olcinium of Roman times. The present atmosphere of the town stems from three hundred years of Turkish rule, lasting into the latter part of the nineteenth century.

The most famous sandy beach in Yugoslovia, Štoj beach, is in Ulcinj. Its fine sand, all seven miles of it, is reputed to be therapeutic for rheumatic ailments. Having arrived with an aching back, I was told to cover myself with the warm sand, which contains salt and iodine. Unfortunately, I was unable to follow the advice for more than a few hours, so I can only suggest you try it and let me know the results.

Štoj Beach, also called Velika Plaža (the Long Beach), is not only long but several hundred feet wide. Here, where Montenegro meets Albania, the mountains are off at a distance. Closest to the water the sand is dark golden, while the hundred yards between the hotels and the sand has grass and trees. So when you wish to, you can get out of the hot sun and under more shade than is offered by a beach umbrella. The area in front of the hotels is, of course, the most crowded; but as you walk a few hundred yards toward Albania, you have miles of beach all to yourself as well as lots of lovely palm trees. Down here the sand can get very hot, so be sure to carry slippers or sandals.

The water is clear and calm the entire length of the beach, good for swimming, floating on a raft, water skiing, and speed boating. The beach slopes so gradually that the water isn't over your head until you've gone a hundred yards out.

As noted earlier, clustering of hotels seems to be a typically Yugoslavian pattern. Fortunately, with dominating mountains and trees surrounding them, the hotels do not overcome the landscape.

The complex on this beach consists of the new class-A Olympik and class-B Lido and Bellvue.

The Olympik represents the best in this part of the world; it boasts a year-round, glass-enclosed pool, not in the hotel itself but connected by a fully enclosed walkway. Obviously, this hotel will be of interest to people who can travel in the so-called off-season, when the rates are about 50 percent lower than during the June 16 to September 30 peak season.

In our opinion, the Bellvue and the Lido offer accommodations equally as elegant as the Olympik. The difference between class A and class B seems to be in the price of the single room and whether the rooms have bath or shower. Families and couples should be comfortable here. Teenagers will find their generation well represented, with little difficulty in meeting one another; their music transcends all barriers.

These hotels and Štoj Beach are a short ride (by bus, taxi, or car) from the center of Ulcinj, with its bustling marketplace, souvenir shops, municipal beach, and a number of good hotels.

As you enter Ulcinj by the main road, you pass through a jam-packed peasant-type marketplace which, according to Andi and Dana, is a dandy for browsing and buying locally handicrafted items—baskets, peasant hats, hand-carved musical instruments, four-foot-long cigarette holders, rugs, and more.

Keeping to the left and along the major left fork, you come directly into Hotel Mediteran's parking area. Seven years old, it has a large, immaculate dining room, an ample reception area, and suitable common rooms. We agreed we were not smitten by the

The public beach in the heart of Ulcinj. Hotel Jadran sits on the promontory at the curve of the beach. Hotel Galeb is tucked into the hillside.

room decor or plumbing, but the price is right.

Just a short walk from Ulcinj's market and shopping area are the class-B Galeb and the class-C Jadran, built during the reign of King Nikola of Montenegro, in the years before World War I.

The Jadran, on a promontory overlooking the sea and rock cliffs below, now also overlooks Municipal Beach. The hotel has actually created its own "beach" by hollowing out a section of cliff near the water and pouring a set of six steps, or tiers, each of which—I didn't measure them—must be twenty feet long and four feet wide. Leading from these large steps are several small steps that take you right into the sea. It's an interesting development and only for the Jadran's guests. If you prefer sand, the municipal beach, which can get quite crowded, is just a short walk away.

The Galeb (no relation to the hotel of the same name outside Dubrovnik) has also created its own beach. Although similar to the Jadran's—a half dozen, strategically placed, concrete tiers—it's more extensive and done with an eye to blending nature and contemporary design. Seen from off shore, it's a most impressive sight.

Hotel Albatross, a short walk from the center of Ulcinj, is probably one of the most modern and luxurious hotels. On top of the huge, craggy rocks that jut into the sea has been built a lounging and sunning area, a rock-walled, concrete affair with spiral rock stairs leading down a series of terraces to the water. Below the tree line, a most unusual and dramatic beach has been created by pouring an irregular series of concrete ledges between boulders.

Hard by the Albatross is Women's Beach; its water, with unusually high sulfur content, is said to be therapeutic for women unable to conceive. Also in this immediate vicinity is an active nudist beach. If you're so inclined, it is open to anyone who plays by the rules. This means you can only enter if you are prepared to "take it all off," leave your camera behind, and maintain the proper eye level and decorum. In this part of the world, nudist beaches are not group sex or group contact therapy sessions. That's strictly *verboten*.

Still in the planning stage is a nudist settlement for this area.

These women are on their way to the nudist beach. See the sign.

Apparently German sponsored, it will be a village composed of bungalows, stores, markets, and the like, similar to the one Scott and Craig visited in France. The Tourist Ministry expects it will accommodate up to 3000 nudists. If you want to know more about this, check with the Yugoslav State Tourist Office in New York.

If you had driven the *Autoput* south from Budva, you would have passed through Petrovak and Sutomore on the way to Ulcinj. Had you arrived in Bar via car ferry from Bari, Italy, these resorts would be a short drive north. Both towns are rather tiny and too crowded, but if you just want a dip to cool off, either place is suitable.

Should you need a pharmacy or a physician, Petrovak has both. Some three hundred yards up the dirt road from the town "super" market is a State Clinic. Being in need of aspirin, I stopped in; a box of twenty cost ten cents. A *Feldsher* is on duty most of the time, but a physician can be summoned if necessary. By the way, visit the supermarket, and try the quite good cold fruit drinks—they go a long way toward slaking a thirst. You can also pick up a variety of goodies for a roadside picnic. Don't even consider the language problem; just pick out whatever you want and bring it to the check-out counter. If you don't know the prices, put down a bill or hold out a handful of change, and they'll do the rest; you won't be overcharged.

The last word in nudity and nude beaches is to be found a few miles below Ulcinj, hard-by the Albanian frontier. Here, the river Bojana forms a tiny island as it flows into the Adriatic. Deran Sveti Nikola makes an excellent hideaway. It's a brand new settlement; so new in fact, it hasn't been named yet. It is a B category village with 30 single and 360 double rooms, accommodating about 750 people.

For information on this village write to the Montenegro Tourist Bureau, Budva, Yugoslavia.

Places of Interest. As the total driving distance between Dubrovnik and Ulcinj is only 135 miles, you will find many attractions within easy striking distance, no matter where you may be.

It is quite obvious that the walled city of Dubrovnik is itself a well-preserved museum, and the museum atmosphere is used to good advantage during Dubrovnik's yearly summer festival, held from July 10 through August 21.

The Divona Palace (also known as the Rector's Palace) is part of the summer festival; the atrium is used for musical and theatrical performances. Stadiumlike seats are erected on two sides of the arches, with orchestra and players between. By the way, if you look closely at the capitals of the arches, you will see that each one is different and that they are quite unlike the typical Greek and Roman designs. In the evening, with spotlights playing on the building, it's quite an impressive sight.

During the festival the Shakespeareans take over, with a number of outdoor productions both concurrently and in succession. Also during the festival you can see outstanding folklore ballet, with dancers from all of Yugoslavia's six republics. Performances take place at the Placa on Main Street of the Old City. Tickets for all festival activities are available at most hotels, and at the Tourist Office on Main Street.

Speaking of folklore, two artists must be mentioned, and their work should be seen: Jovan and Lazar Običan, father and son.

Jovan Običan, whose studio-home in Dubrovnik is at Supilova 69, opposite Hotel Argentina, is one of the country's acknowledged folk artists. Lazar Običan, following a proud Montenegrin tradition, translates his brightly colorful folk art into collages, textiles, and toys as well as canvases.

To bring Yugoslav folklore to life, plan a visit to Mostar, northwest of Dubrovnik on the road to Sarajevo. On the way there, you drive through the Neretva Gorge, as primitive and primordial as any place on earth. One wonders if this was what the earth looked like at the time of creation. Along the way you might stop and look at the Turkish and Yugoslav tombs, which are curious and unorthodox, as tombs go.

Mostar's claim to fame is its bridge. In Croatian, *most* means bridge, and the town takes its name from the sixteenth-century Turkish bridge that spans the emerald Neretva River. Linger awhile in this quaint and lovely little town; the Turkish influence is everywhere, especially in its marketplace. From the handicraft shops you should be able to find gifts to bring home to friends and relatives, as well as a few for yourself.

A trip to Mostar can be a half-day affair, or combine it with an overnight trip to Sarajevo, the city that lives in history as the place where World War I was sparked by the killing of the Archduke Franz Ferdinand. Today, Sarajevo (in the republic of Bosnia-Hercegovina) is a blend of old and new. Here too, the strong Turkish influence is evident.

You may think you've seen and explored underground caves, but you haven't until you've seen Vjetrenica, which must be one of the world's largest caves. About one mile of the twelve that have been explored has been provided with lights and paths. Its galleries, waterfalls, lakes, stalactites, and stalagmites are a photographer's dream. The caves are in Zavala, in Bosnia-Hercegovina, so plan on a half day or more.

It goes without saying that a seafaring city will offer several cruises up and down its coastline. If there is time for only one, and you should try one, at least, may we suggest a cruise around the Boka Kotorska. Here again, information, reservations, and even tickets can be obtained at most hotels.

If you are jaded with history, and the cultural you needs refurbishing, stop in of an evening at Hotel Orlando and compare Yugoslavian strip artistry with that of nonsocialist countries. Somehow, political theory doesn't seem to interfere with or dull the performance.

You can cruise along the coast to the beat of rock music every night except Monday or Tuesday on the S/S *Antika*, a cruising discotheque. Tickets are available on board ship. If you like your music loud, this is one place to get it.

Cetinje, pre-World War II capital of Crna-Gora (the Serbo-Croatian name for Montenegro), is some twenty scenic mountain miles from Budva by a road that is one breathtaking hairpin turn after another. Not as high as Denver, Cetinje is on a plateau about 2000 feet above sea level. In the town are the Palais Biljarda (Palace of Njegoš), the Vlaška church, and the monastery. These are really worth a morning's outing, not for their palatial qualities, but for what it must have taken these people to build them. This is harsh country and has developed a hardy folk.

The Biljarda was built in 1838 by Peter II to serve as his royal palace and the meeting place for the Montenegrin Senate. It is an austere palace, called Biljarda because of the billiard table that had to be brought up the mountain from Kotor. Imagine that, as you drive the twisting road! Today the palace houses a museum devoted to Montenegrin ethnography and exhibits of national costumes, agricultural tools, and musical instruments. In one section are displayed items pertaining to the War of Liberation and some gruesome reminders of man's inhumanity. The section that was Peter's quarters may be seen also. He is remembered today as one of Yugoslavia's great poets.

Behind the Biljarda is the monastery, built in 1484, and still in use; it can be toured most any time. It has an impressive collection of jewelry and icons and the *Oktoih*, one of the first books to be printed in the Slavic language. The oldest building in town, the Vlaška church, dates from 1450.

The drive back to Budva is even more dramatic; when you suddenly emerge from the rocks, the sea below is an inspiring sight.

From Ulcinj or Budva, Titograd and Lake Scutari are short drives, easily worth a half-day excursion. Titograd has replaced Cetinje as the capital of Montenegro. This has embittered a lot of good people in Cetinje and there remains a residue of ill-will between the towns. However, this in no way affects the tourist. A visit to Titograd and the shores of the huge lake, a third of which belongs to Albania, will give you additional insights into the culture of Yugoslavia. It isn't necessary to rent a car; regularly scheduled bus tours are available. The buses are large and comfortable, and the drivers are professionals. The natural beauty of Yugoslavia is so compelling that it is a pleasure to leave the driving to them and just sit back and relax, taking it all in.

Food and Drink. Food in Yugoslav hotels is for the most part fair to good. You may find by chance an exceptionally good hotel dining room, but if you have gourmet tastes, you won't find it in Ulcinj, hardly in Budva, and infrequently in Dubrovnik. The hotels seem to have adequate dining-room staff, but service generally is not yet Continental, although they are trying. Hopefully, these two observations won't deter you; they shouldn't.

On checking in to most hotels, you will receive a set of meal tickets, one for each meal for your stay. Don't lose or misplace them. Some hotels issue tissue-paper-type tickets, others are similar to theatre tickets. Your waiter, headwaiter, or the manager of the dining room will ask for one at each meal.

Then there are the games played at lunch and dinner called, "What will I feel like eating tomorrow, today?" and "What did we order yesterday?" At each lunch you'll be asked to choose a main course for the following day's lunch and dinner. The fun comes the following day when you sit down at the table, thinking what you'd like to have, and your waiter brings yesterday's choice. Invariably everyone says, "Did I order that?" I might add that there are quite a few choices, and they are all good. You might try a different one each day.

Not all hotels use meal tickets and require prior selection. The Excelsior, Argentina and Dubrovnik Palace have mercifully escaped this convention. Why, remains a mystery. It may just be that once beyond Dubrovnik the "game" goes into effect.

All hotels require that you dine at the same table for every meal. This can be difficult if the people who share your table are less than congenial. On this point, I'd suggest a firm but friendly approach to the hotel manager if the headwaiter proves intransigent.

You may be surprised to learn, and better now than later, that along with wine, beer, and mineral water, coffee and tea are not included in "full board." Another surprise could come when you are handed a slip at the end of each meal requesting that you pay for such extras. And they mean pay now. Thus far, they do not have meal checks to sign. In addition to Coke, Pepsi, and Schweppes, there is an indigenous drink called Upi that looks like 7-Up but is actually a quite respectable orange soda. Although these drinks are extras, dessert is not.

As is the case in many hotels in other countries, many items are not served automatically but are available. It is anticipated that guests will ask, so ask. For example, butter is often not placed on tables unless specifically requested, and the same is true for jam, jelly, mustard, and ketchup. And ask also for a number of dishes whose ingredients cross cultural lines. The Serbs, Montenegrins, Croats and Moslems have each added their own touches. For example, *Cevapcici* can be eaten at street corner stalls or in the best dining room. Somehow though, eating these spicy meatballs on a picturesque street in the middle of the day, is more appealing than in a restaurant.

Djuvec, a down country-type specialty, is a hearty mixture of rice, pork or veal, tomatoes, onions, peppers, eggplant, dill and squash baked together to make a stew Dinty Moore would be proud of.

For those who prefer home-type cooking away from home, *omlet sa sirom* found on most menus is usually a creditable cheese omelet. Of course *Tunina* is tuna fish, and for lovers of sole, *Morski List* is regularly available. It would surely be a gastronomic crime to be in Yugoslavia and not sample *Kackavalj*, the understandably renowned Serbian cheese. Again, if you don't see it, ask for it.

No meal in any of the six provinces can even be considered complete without coffee—*kava*. You might not believe it, but coffee is the national drink, and being patriotic, Yugoslavs drink it day and night. There are at least three varieties to choose from. The very black, strong enough to walk-on variety *Turska kava* is a constant reminder of Ottoman heritage. *Bela kava*, light, with cream, is more on the American style. It's a dead give-away when you order it. *Ekspresna kava* (espresso) is a reminder of the Italian contribution to Yugoslav cookery.

Claiming pure Yugoslavian lineage is that drink for brave men only. Sljivovica (slivovitz), a plum brandy, sounds harmless enough, but more than one at a sitting is, as Scott ventured after he recovered his breath and composure, "undiluted dynamite." And don't forget, Yugoslavia is the land that made fermented milk famous, claiming it responsible for long life. You can spoon or drink yogurt all along the Dalmatian coast.

TURKEY

Turkey's uncommonly wrinkled Aegean coast provides a great many naturally sheltered coves; its southern, Mediterranean coast offers long, long stretches of sandy beach. From ancient times this shoreline has been invaded by conquerers from East and West. Each established themselves and the heritage of Hittite, Mamaluke, Greek, Roman and Seljuk, remains in the heritage and culture of southern Turkey.

With its dissolution in the late 19th and early 20th century, the Ottoman Empire lost its vast political hegemony, and in spite of its splendid beaches, modern Turkey became better known for its shish kebab, belly dancers, and mustachioed men than as a choice vacationland.

With over ninety-five percent of its land mass now in Asia Minor, Turkey is considered a Middle Eastern country. However, it does have a toehold in Europe. Istanbul, its largest city and most bustling commercial and tourist center, is divided into European and Asian sections. Should you fly into Istanbul you'll land in Europe, as the airport is in the European section. But if you arrive by boat, you disembark in the Middle East. At first it seems complicated; it really isn't. The complications are left to the politicians and statesmen; for the visitor it's pleasantly romantic.

Climate. Turkey's climate is pleasant the year round. In the south, the Taurus Mountains form a natural wall against the harsh inland Anatolian winds.

Along both the long Mediterranean and corrugated Aegean coasts, summers (May through September) are hot and dry. Just right for swimming, sunning, shopping and scrutinizing some of the best preserved antiquities in Europe and the Middle East.

Although the climate calls for lightweight clothing, a jacket or sweater should be part of your wardrobe as hot days (75–80° F.) can give way without warning to cool evenings.

During the spring and autumn be prepared for rain. Although these are not the torrential or chilling variety, just intermittent showers, it does mean an umbrella and raincoat, in most areas.

Air and water temperatures for the Aegean and Mediterranean coasts, during the months of May through September, can be represented by those in Izmir and Bodrum.

In and around Izmir the air temperature ranges from 77–87° F. (25–33° C.). During the same period the sea hovers between 68–77° F. (20–25° C.). In Bodrum and east along the coast, both the air and sea are warmer, from 76–95° F. and 66–75° F., respectively.

Transportation. Pan American's direct flights from New York to Istanbul take about eleven hours. Another airline to consider is BA, British Airways. Its jet fleet of Tridents and Super 111's has flights from New York via London to major and minor cities of the Mediterranean, including several flights a week to Istanbul.

Arrangements and reservations on BA can be made through any of its offices or your travel agent. We've traveled BA a number of times and find them outstanding; the roominess, food, and in-flight service make them our choice. If you are already in Europe and want to go on to Turkey, any BA office can make all arrangements, including assistance with hotel reservations.

Trains from western Europe and the Balkans (except Albania) and ships from Italy, Greece, and North Africa put in at Izmir and Istanbul. Information about them can be obtained from

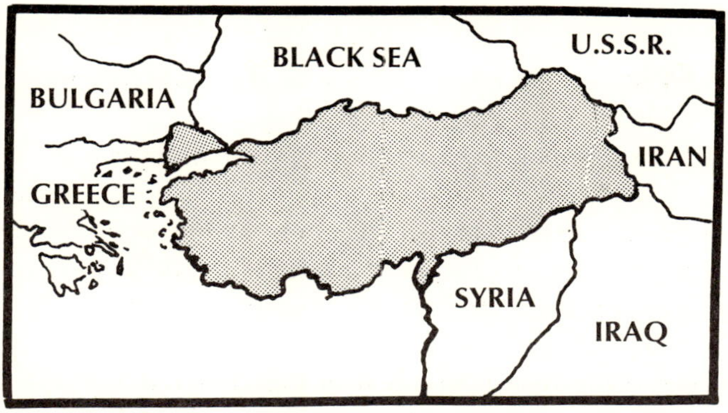
BLACK SEA
U.S.S.R.
BULGARIA
IRAN
GREECE
SYRIA
IRAQ

Istanbul
Ankara
TURKEY
Izmir
esme
Kusadasi
Bodrum
Antalya
Alanya
Marmaris
Mersin
Silifke

the Turkish Government Tourism and Information Office, 500 Fifth Avenue, New York, N. Y., 10036.

Although Ankara is the administrative capital of Turkey and Istanbul its most fascinating city, neither is convenient to the Aegean and Mediterranean beaches. The best jumping-off point is Izmir (Smyrna of old) an attractive city built on hills that surround a magnificent harbor and shimmering bay.

Camping. One aspect of vacationing that has been brought to a fine art in Turkey is camping, which is in style throughout the country. Especially along the as-yet-undeveloped southern coast, with its beautiful beaches, there are many areas where you may camp.

However, another dimension of camping has been developed by the British Petroleum Company (BP) through a subsidiary, the Kervansaray Company. Mocamps (the name is derived from motel-camping) combine the comforts of a motel with the outdoor pleasures of camping. Sites have been chosen for the dozen or so Mocamps near principal tourist areas, and all modern facilities have been provided. Each Mocamp has a permanent building containing a restaurant; facilities for (hot) showers, washing, and laundry; tiled bathrooms and kitchens; and, of course, a BP gas station. Other amenities include swimming pool, 220 electric current, ice machines, and plenty of space for parking and pitching tents.

In the beach areas, there are two Mocamps on the outskirts of Izmir, one in Kuşadasi, one thirteen miles from Alanya, and one at Silifke on the road to Mersin. The cost of a night at these camps is about $3 per person. For complete information and descriptive brochures, write to: Kervansaray A.S., P.K. 211 Sisli, Istanbul, Turkey.

Izmir. In spite of the number of smart hotels in Istanbul, we were not prepared for Izmir's elegant, 296-room Büyük Efes Oteli—the Grand Efes Hotel. Surrounded by lush gardens some 300 yards from the sea wall, the Efes, open year-round, is among the most modern hotels to be found anywhere.

When I peered over our balcony the first day we arrived and

caught a glimpse of the headwaiter inspecting his "troops" and issuing orders, I knew that dinner would be a memorable event. We had already seen the impeccable service in the lobby, at the pool, and throughout the hotel. By the time we left Turkey some weeks later, we had learned that good food and gracious service were standard.

The price of rooms at the Efes is equally memorable; during the high season, April 1 through October 31, a room for two with a view is less than $10. From November through March, the winter season, these same rooms are $2 to $3 less.

Although these prices do not include breakfast, a variety of breakfasts are available from 60 cents to $1.20, for which you can just about eat until noon. Don't pass up Turkish peach juice. Thick and delicious, it is quite unlike anything we have in the States. According to Dana and Andi, our hamburger experts, the Efes served the best hamburgers in the entire Mediterranean region. They ought to know, having sampled them from one end of the Mediterranean to the other. Wanting only a snack one afternoon, we tried a couple at the poolside snack bar and found them to be a meal in themselves. In addition, you may order cheeseburgers, iced tea, ice cream sodas, and just about anything else you might feel homesick for.

Across the street from the Efes, just beyond the Statue of Kemal Atatürk on Cumhuriyet Square, is the nine-story, 112-room Hotel Taner (Taner Oteli), the second largest hotel in Izmir. Here the best rooms are less than $10 per night for two in high season. Like the Efes, the Taner is a modern, fully air-conditioned structure only recently completed; it also offers splendid views overlooking the harbor.

In addition to the Efes and Taner, we suggest the following hotels in the moderate-to-low price range; the Kismet, Anba, Kilim, Billü, Kâhya, Badaban Palas, and Kabadayi offer rooms at $4, $5, and $6. Just write and request a rate card and brochure from the hotels or from the Turkish Government Tourism and Information Office in New York City. But do it early.

Lining the waterfront boulevard are a number of private apartments, hotels, restaurants, snack bars, and coffee houses. Each evening at six P.M., Atatürk Boulevard is closed to automobiles and carriages; people of all ages gather here for sociable strolling, meeting, and chatting till dawn.

Dinner in Turkey is a late event, with people dining in hotels and sidewalk cafés until eleven at night. As you walk you will be enticed by the desserts displayed in refrigerated cases in the restaurant windows. We all agreed that the cakes, pastries, and other desserts in Turkey tasted as good as they looked. That is more than can be said for the desserts in some other countries, where looks and taste do not always go together.

A carriage ride along the waterfront or through the streets to the bazaar at Konak is a great way to get to know Izmir. There are no meters or fixed fares for these carriages; all are negotiable. The idea is to keep the bargaining friendly and within reason, but the stress is on friendly. For example, from Cumhuriyet Square or the vicinity of the tourist office to Konak, a 15-20 minute ride, two people should be able to get a carriage for 7 to 10 TL (at current rates of exchange, 15 TL is approximately equivalent to $1). Keep the figure of 10 TL in mind as the highest, and base your negotiations on that.

It is an art that must be cultivated. Remember, don't get angry and don't walk away for good; keep the channels open for the next move.

So it's off to Konak to try your tactics in the bazaar. If you are looking for gold or any other jewelry, which is what to shop for in Turkey, don't panic when the item is put on a scale. All jewelry is priced according to weight. Since Americans are known to agree on the first price, let me caution you once again. The seller is testing you. A grimace or a hurt look will tell him that you are not one of those gullible types, but are ready to "play." This also holds true for leather coats, copperware, carpets, evil-eye bracelets and necklaces, sandals, old guns, coins—in short, just about everything. Speaking of coins, Turkey has had such a varied succession of rulers that it is a haven for collectors; Lydian, Greek, Roman, Byzantine, and Assyrian coins are available in many shops, but you must be careful, since counterfeit coins abound.

Other items to watch for are onyx and alabaster from the region of Cappadocia in east central Turkey. Items made from these materials can be found in shops and stalls throughout the country. Alabaster, a form of gypsum, is the less expensive.

After walking through the bazaar, you may very well be hungry. If so, it isn't necessary to leave the area; try the Sukran Lokantasi (restaurant). The Sukran offers salads, kebabs, desserts, and drinks in an open-air section on Anafartalar Street. A section reserved for more substantial meals is through a corridor to the rear. And here, too, meals can be eaten outside in a shady, secluded area.

Turkey's greatest hero of modern times and first president (1923–38) was Mustafa Kemal, called Atatürk—Father of the Turks. Kemal Atatürk freed the Turks from the shackles of the past by compelling adoption of western dress, the Latin alphabet, the Gregorian calendar, and most important of all, universal education.

In Izmir, is the Atatürk museum, formerly Kemal's summer home. A visit to the museum is a must.

Should you want to follow your visit with a cold drink or ice cream while you relax in cool comfort, take a carriage or walk over to Kültür Park. Retrace your steps to the intersection, then walk one block to Ziya Gokalp Street, which will take you directly to one of the park gates.

While you're at the park, look in on the Archeological Museum. It contains a substantial collection of Greek and Roman objects, including a bronze bust of Demeter and a statue of Aphrodite, all unearthed in and around Izmir.

To get a small taste of Turkish ruins, take a leisurely stroll or ride to the Agora, hard by the Konak district (by now, you should have established a working relationship with a carriage driver). The Agora is a second-century Roman building; the well preserved arches and columns that were part of the first floor and the statues of Demeter, Poseidon, and Neptune in the far left corner give hints of the past.

For those who enjoy views from on high, one viewpoint that captures almost the entire city and the surrounding bay is Kadifekale atop Mount Pagos. The fortress walls were built by Lysimachus, one of the generals of Alexander the Great. I'm told that by night this view from a parked car or carriage can quicken the blood.

Should you prefer to make this a daytime trip, you might try a more mundane form of transportation—the *dolmuş* taxis, which are quite similar to those in Mexico City. These taxis drive a set route, stopping to pick up and discharge passengers at designated points. This route simply brings you near your target. In Turkey, the *dolmuş* can be a minibus or a standard taxi with a yellow band around the body just below the base of the windows. Often the word *dolmuş* is written on the vehicle. Of course, these are much cheaper than regular taxis, which are not expensive to begin with.

We'd also like to recommend one of the ferry rides across the bay. On a warm day the breezes are particularly welcome! At dusk the setting sun is a photographer's dream. You may board the ferry at a pier near the Clock Tower or at a pier directly in front of the Atatürk Monument in Cumhuriyet Square.

BEACHES

Although we would like to explore Istanbul, we are in a hurry to get to the beaches. To avoid the thirteen-hour train or bus ride over the mountains from Istanbul to Izmir, we decided to sample one of THY's (Türk Hava Yollari—Turkish Airlines) domestic flights. It would be hard to improve on covering the 300 miles in thirty to forty minutes. The bright red and white jets are as modern as can be found anywhere. And the price is right: $10.25 for students carrying a bona fide student travel card, and $15 for adults.

Incidently, the Ministry of Tourism maintains an office at Istanbul Airport staffed by volunteer university students who speak English and are generally knowledgeable and helpful.

At the Izmir Airport, THY provides a bus for 5 Turkish lira (35 cents), for the twenty-minute ride to the center of town. Taxis are also available, for a bit more money. Often these are old Chevrolets and Plymouths, since Turkey has apparently bought up a huge number of our used cars. Either the Turks are the world's best repairmen or these cars have more left in them than we care to admit.

If you're not planning to stop over in Izmir, but are anxious to get to the beaches, pick up a car near THY's office-terminal, next door to Hotel Büyük Efes, or hire a taxi. On both sides of the street about a hundred taxis are waiting to whisk, (and I do mean fast, very fast) you to any beach—ten, fifty, or one hundred miles away.

Directly across from the main entrance to the Efes is the office of the Ministry of Tourism. Some of the people here are fluent in English and do very well in French or German.

Nebioglu. If you're driving from Izmir, follow Atatürk Caddesi in the direction of the Clock Tower until it becomes Mithatpasa Caddesi. This in turn becomes the major highway, stretching fifty miles to the tip of the peninsula at Çeşme. About ten miles (sixteen kilometers) from Izmir on the road to Urla, you'll pass the village of Inciralti.

Although you're heading toward Urla, you should turn off to the right at the sign for Çeşmealti village, which is just before the left turn to Urla.

Drive into the village slowly to avoid colliding with the goat flocks and to savor the atmosphere of a typical Turkish village.

As you come within sight of Nebioglu, your first remarks will almost certainly be some variation of "What are those!" No, they're not diving helmets worn by giants of another epoch; nor are they Brobdingnagian tea cups or soup bowls. They are Mr. Ziya Nebioglu's idea of what vacation cottages should be. And with credentials such as his, they have much to recommend them.

As if "Son of the Prophet" (translation of Nebioglu) were not enough, Mr. Nebioglu is an architect and engineer. In fact, it was during his tenure as assistant professor at the University of Florida that he met his "Georgia cracker" wife. Having spent a lifetime architecting and engineering for others, he did what many of us only dream of; he designed and built his own vacation hideaway. The architecture and the sign at the entrance, "Vacances 2000," go well together.

Mr. Nebioglu's vacation village is strikingly different.

Nebioglu's concrete and glass bungalows and common rooms—restaurant, disco, game room, and snack bar—are laid out in tiers along the hillside. As a result of nature's chewing away of the coast, the water at the beach is calm and nontidal. The "Son of the Prophet" has thought of everything. He has designed a smooth stone ledge for sunbathing that is a step up from the beach proper. The relatively narrow beach is a thin layer of sand over a rock crust. Here, when you lie down after swimming, you don't acquire a layer of sand.

Nebioglu is open from May through October, and high season extends from June 15 to September 15. During this period, a room with twin beds, far larger than might be suspected from the exterior design, is less than $8 per person per day with full board: three full meals! During May and October, you can expect a 30-percent reduction. If you're considering a "family affair," note that children up to six are given a 25-percent reduction. Mr. Nebioglu made a point of telling us that the high season notwithstanding, he believed that September and October were the best months in this area.

The village appears to be a harbor for singles and young marrieds. There is an atmosphere of friendliness and camaraderie, even though the guests are from such diverse countries as Switzerland, France, Holland, Belgium, and Germany. Americans will find the welcome mat out too.

While most guests come for one or two weeks, there is no minimum period. However, in order to ensure a reservation during high season, better request reservations two or three months in advance. Reservations and additional information can be obtained through your travel agent or by writing directly to: Nebioglu Village, Urla, Iskele, Izmir, Turkey.

By the way, Nebioglu Village is particularly well located to enable you to enjoy a number of national festivals. For example, Izmir is one of six cities throughout the country celebrating Navy and Merchant Marine Day on July 1. Boat races, aquatic sports (including water polo—a national pastime in Mediterranean countries) and parades provide a variety of colorful diversions. For three days, between July 18 and 20, the Festival of Aquatic Sports, with a great number of competitive events, takes place in both Izmir and Foça.

Foça. About thirty-five miles northwest of Izmir, tucked away in the foothills surrounding Foça, is one of Club Méditerranée's more romantic vacation villages.

Not only is it tucked away, but it's strictly "no admittance" without membership and reservation. And if you think you can slip in by spinning a yarn at the entrance about wanting to see your cousin or great-aunt, forget it; these people have heard them all. We do, however, understand completely why people try to get in for a day.

The success of the Clubs (at this writing there are fifty-nine in twenty-one countries) is directly related to their operating philosophy that people who work in cities want to vacation in a radically different environment. Although this doesn't seem to be a very radical concept, Club Méditerranée has developed it to the ultimate: no barriers, no rules, no restraints. A vacation here is an escape from the cares of everyday life. Accordingly, all of Club Méditerranée's villages have done away with the necessity for lavish wardrobes. Bikinis and pareos (colorful lengths of cloth worn sarong style) are the order of the day. Radios, TV, and newspapers have been banished, and only a single telephone is available in the director's office for emergencies and for arranging transportation.

The Club's formula includes accommodations, unlimited food at each of the three meals with all the wine you can drink, free sports and facilities (horseback riding is the exception in most clubs), and entertainment. Drinks at the bar are paid for from a string of plastic poppit beads, which everyone wears as necklaces or bracelets. There is no need to carry cash, or even to have it in your room.

Vacations at Club Méditerranée are open to members only; however, membership is open to anyone. The initial cost is $10 for singles and $14 for families. These fees become $6 and $10 thereafter, renewable yearly. Club vacations and memberships can be obtained through any American Express office or travel agent.

Staff at the Clubs are referred to as G.O.s (*gentils organisateurs*). They live and eat with the members, participate in all activities, and generally enjoy the privileges of the G.M.s (*gentils membres*). Their participation on an equal basis and as friends appears to be an important element in the unique character of the clubs. The G.O.s do not accept tips; in fact they are obliged to refuse them.

Club villages are of two styles. In the hotel-type villages, rooms with bath range from semiluxurious to good quality by hotel standards. In the traditional villages, the Polynesian-style thatched huts have minimal furnishings and community toilet and bath facilities. The idea here is one of total escape. But other than this, the programs are the same for both kinds of accommodations.

Foça is a hotel-type village. The existing buildings, erected in 1966 (new ones are planned for the next two years), can accommodate approximately 650 guests. Although this may seem like a lot, the spacious grounds and large common facilities handle everyone easily and comfortably.

The village is so well designed that it seems to blend into the hills and crags. White-washed stucco buildings give it a Foreign Legion appearance; and each one has either a French or a Moslem name. All the rooms are large and airy, designed for maximum coolness in the heat of summer.

Foça's Club Med is open from May 16 to October 15, and August through September is considered high season. Two types of accommodations are available; the "A" buildings of Olive Village and the somewhat smaller "B" buildings in Arab Village. Both have single and double rooms.

The Club accepts children from age five and gives a substantial price reduction to those from five to twelve. Beyond twelve, it's full price. However, there are no special facilities for children.

Each newly arriving group gathers in Foça's own Roman-type mini amphitheater to meet one another. At this time all the G.O.s, as well as the *chef de Village,* are introduced, so that everyone is quickly oriented.

Foça, in the style of all Club Méditerranées, has fantastic meals. The buffets seem endless—salads, vegetables, meats, fish, fruit, wine, cheese. But meals are not simply eating contests; there's much talk and entertainment. They are lively affairs to which everyone contributes. It would be unthinkable for anyone to go to a Club Méditerranée and remain out of it.

Social activities go on and on from noon to the early hours of the morning in the open-air nightclub. If you prefer, however, you can spend your time swimming, scuba diving, spear fishing, water skiing, or sailing in the bluest, clearest water with some of the most primitive country for landscape.

The two beaches at the base of the foothills are splendid. Although you can swim from both, one is primarily for sailing instruction (at no extra charge), a special attraction at Club Med. So if there is some water sport you're particularly eager to learn, this is a good place to do it.

In addition, tennis, archery, judo, yoga, chess, and just plain old-fashioned lounging are all part of the colorful scene. Each Saturday evening the guests put on a show, produced and directed

Sailing is another activity that makes for togetherness at Foça's Club Méditerranée. The resort is on a wide bay north of Izmir, facing the Greek island of Lesbos.

by themselves. And every two weeks there is a Turkish night with singers and dancers performing typically Turkish entertainment.

Although there are many guests over forty, Foça is primarily a holiday village for the eighteen-to-thirty-five group. There does not appear to be any division along age lines; everyone mingles freely and comfortably.

Unfortunately, a note of caution is called for. Foça is a French-speaking village, and all posted and verbal announcements are in French.

Scott and Craig spent a week at the Club Med in Kuşadasi, south of Izmir. According to Scott, who approaches fluency in French, and Craig, whose French is limited to *"Ou est la salle de bain?"* French was not absolutely necessary there. But the rest of us agreed that Foça required a right-smart conversational ability. Recall, Club Med is a French invention.

Should you decide to give Foça a try, bring towels and soap, as neither are supplied. If you bring an electric razor, do not forget an adapter for the 220 voltage. And remember, it's informal;

leave dressy clothing home. Just bring enough for excursions around the coast. For this, plan on easy walking shoes, sport shirt, and either long or short trousers, for men; women should wear either a casual summer dress or slacks, *not* shorts. Turkey is not yet ready for short shorts on women.

For full details on Club Méditerranée generally or Foça in particular, contact Club Méditerranée, 516 Fifth Avenue, New York, N. Y. 10036, or your nearest American Express office. You may also write directly to: Chef de Village, Club Méditerranée, Foça, Izmir, Turkey.

Çesme. About forty-eight miles (eighty-eight kilometers) west of Izmir, on a finger of land jutting out into the Aegean, is the beach resort of Çeşme. The water is lime colored where it meets the white sand, blending to shades of blue and aqua farther out.

The name Çeşme means "fountain," and the village received this name because of the many fountains that were built long years ago in and around the town. Although this is a quiet part of

An uncluttered landscape stretching away to the mountains serves as a backdrop for the elegant Hotel Çeşme.

the world, it does offer a variety of opportunities for exploratory sightseeing excursions.

Five miles beyond this picturesque village, with its intact fourteenth-century Crusaders' castle, is the luxurious Hotel Çeşme. Once again, we were agreeably surprised as our taxi drove through the colorful flower-lined drive leading to the entrance of this 124-room contemporary building, almost at the edge of the sea.

The hotel belongs to the Emek chain, which also includes the Efes in Izmir. It has its own white sand beach with cabanas, outdoor snack bar, and promenade. The rooms are well appointed, and the food and service are excellent.

Unfortunately, even though the weather is fine year-round, Hotel Çeşme is open only from May through September. When you consider that a room for two in this luxurious hotel is about $8 per day, and that a sumptuous meal for two in lovely surroundings costs less than $6, you'll have to agree that Turkey has to be one of the great bargains in the entire Mediterranean area. Considering the type of hotel, its impeccable but friendly service, and the kind of food served, one must ask, "How do they do it?" As yet, I don't have a satisfactory answer, but here the dollar goes a long way.

Although a first impression may suggest formality, at Hotel Çeşme you are free to choose your own style of dress. It is as informal or formal as you care to make it. Should you be staying elsewhere but want to spend a day at the beach here, you can rent a dressing room for about a dollar. And the dining room is open to all, so take advantage of it.

Don't be surprised by pockets of bubbling warm water as you swim along this beach; the entire area is studded with sulfurous hot springs. As a result, both Çeşme and Sifne have become well known for their "medicinal" springs. They advertise that these natural waters have proven healing powers to aid in the recovery from such ailments as rheumatism and kidney stones. There are also special mud baths in Sifne, beauty baths popular with visitors who wish to have their wrinkles disappear.

Opened in August, 1971, Hotel Sifne, nine kilometers up the road toward Ilica, caters to thermal-spring devotees. The hotel has only nineteen rooms, each with plumbing connections that bring the hot sulfurous water directly to individual bathtubs. The hotel has built rooms directly over the thermal springs, which in point of fact are small indoor pools. And a large outdoor pool a short walk from the beach is actually hot. Visitors of all ages were swimming, wading, and just lolling around, testifying to the popularity of the waters.

The hotel's prices are unbelievably low. A room for two with full board—three meals—is approximately $12. By the way, for about fifty cents, guests at Hotel Çeşme can use the hot-spring facilities at Hotel Sifne. As for reservations, bear in mind that with nineteen rooms, it doesn't take many guests to fill the hotel.

From the promenade at the rear of Hotel Çeşme, you can look along the shore line and see Hotel Balin. The Balin has fifty-two twin-bed rooms, each with its own entrance. All have balconies and bath facilities. It offers a playground for children, a private beach, and a spacious dining room. With full board, rooms for two are approximately $10 per day.

A ten-minute walk from Çeşme village is the modern Motes Motel, with fifty bungalows facing the sea and the quiet water of a natural cove. Extending from shore is a long dock from which you can jump, dive, or just step into the water. From the stone veranda-lounge, steps lead down to a flat stone sun-bathing deck, some six feet above the sand and rock beach. Steps lead down to the private beach, so you will share this beach with few others. If this is not private enough, simply walk around any of the hillocks that slope to the water's edge, and you are alone for skinny dipping or an undisturbed snooze in the sun.

Down the road from the Motes is Hotel Turtes, with a discotheque and American bar. This new group of buildings situated amid multicolored gardens offers a magnificent view of the sea, a private, uncrowded beach, and the usual bargain in well-appointed room and good food. These are not luxury establishments, but they are clean, simple, and well located for local exploration. At a motel of this type, reservations are usually unnecessary. Two people can expect to pay less than $15 per day with full board, and to make it even more inviting, there are usually no service charges tacked on.

The area around Çeşme offers quiet relaxation. Except for the discos that each hotel believes their guests want, little entertainment is available, aside from exploring nearby antiquities. These are not action places; from Izmir to Çeşme, the night life is pretty quiet. But if you want to get away from it all and swim in clear, clean water, these are places to consider.

From Çeşme, you can visit the nearby Greek islands or even take the two-day boat trip to Brindisi, Italy, by way of Piraeus and Patras. The Ertürk Lines operate a car ferry between Çeşme and the Greek island of Chios, and from Chios there are regular sailings to Piraeus. Ferries leave Çeşme every day except Monday at 4 P.M. A one-way adult passage costs $7. For children up to twelve it is approximately $3.50. Motorcycles and cars are charged from $10 to $30, depending upon their weight.

The trip is quite short, just an hour and a half. This gives you a chance to see a good bit of Chios before dark, which falls about eight in the evening. The boat returns the following morning.

Kuşadasi. To head south to the Mediterranean proper, it's necessary to start from Izmir. But just before we reach the Mediterranean area, there is an Aegean beach resort that must not be overlooked. Kuşadasi (Bird Island) is almost due south of Izmir, but the road does not follow the path of the crow or any other straight-flying bird. The sixty miles of road winds through olive groves and tobacco fields on its way to Selcuk, just bypassing Ephesus (Efes) the site of some of the greatest antiquities in the world.

Kuşadasi, with its long stretches of golden sandy beaches and crystal-clear water, offers more night life than is available in Çeşme and Izmir. Although it is a resort well known to northern Europeans, Kuşadasi has maintained the character of a sleepy fishing village, modern hotels notwithstanding, and has yet to receive many American tourists. Don't hesitate to try this corner of Turkey, so close to the magnificent antiquities of Ephesus, Didymi, and Priene; there are a number of excellent hotels in and around the town.

The seventy-two-room Kismet boasts a terrace restaurant with an unobstructed panorama from every table. In fact, matchless views of the water and landscape are seen from almost all its rooms.

An interesting feature of the Kismet, as in a number of coastal hotels, is its daring perch above the sea. Steps cut alongside the cliff lead down to a cement promenade, from which you can step right into the clearest, cleanest water imaginable. The sandless beach allows you to bathe and bask in the sun without sand clinging or blowing. This water is also great for scuba diving and snorkeling; the variety of colorful aquatic plants and fish can keep you submerged for hours.

On another promontory, this one overlooking Kardinlar Plaji, is the very contemporary Otel Imbat. A series of two-story dwellings flanks the geodesic-domed restaurant, lobby, and recreation area. It has steps built into the cliffs, leading down to the beach. But you have a choice: to the left, you have a sand beach, and to the right, a cement promenade.

At the Imbat you can choose either the half or the full pension

Hotel Imbat has a gleaming beach all to itself.

plan. The half pension offers breakfast and one meal, either lunch or dinner. With the full pension plan you get three excellent meals along with your double room. All for less than $20 per day for two people.

With eight hotels, the Tusan Hotel-Motels is the largest chain in Turkey. Its fifty-room Tusan Oteli in Kuşadasi is one of the most modern. In addition to private bath facilities, each room has its own balcony with sea view. At the beach, for those who prefer to come out of the water without getting sandy and for those swimmers who insist on the "toe in the water" before jumping or diving, a long cement walk with steps and handrail has been built out from the shore.

On this shore of the Aegean, which many refer to as the St. Tropez of Turkey, is Kuşadasi's Club Méditerranée, situated below the ramparts of an ancient Ottoman fortress that crowns the village. Its cluster of white-washed concrete building units can accommodate some 900 guests. But the vast grounds include a huge ampitheater, dining facilities, and a long, wide beach and lengthy shoreline, providing more than ample room.

Meals are an indelible and profound experience; all the wine you can drink (at no additional charge) and all the food you can possibly eat, laid out upon table after table. If you're the dieting type, think twice before signing on.

Each bungalow has accommodations for two and is equipped with shower, sink, and toilet. Bed linen and blankets are provided, but towels and soap are not.

In addition to sailing, high-caliber instruction is available in water skiing and swimming, with all equipment provided. Many guests prefer just plain exercise, otherwise known as *gymnastique,* but there are tennis courts and pingpong tables for those who want a little more exertion.

To round out the days and nights, the Club provides a library, a weekly newspaper, dancing nightly (and in the afternoon, or whenever you please), and social activities, including spectacles befitting the Roman-style amphitheater. Once you arrive here, no additional charges are made for anything except liquor and whatever you buy in the shops and boutiques. The only other costs would be for sightseeing excursions.

Club Méditerranée at Kuşadasi is also a French-speaking village. But after spending a week there, Scott said that fluency in French is not a prerequisite. Again, as with Club Méditerranée at Foça, the primary age group is twenty to forty. Children from age five are admitted, but no special facilities are provided. Here too, because of the demand, reservations must be made early. Write either to the Chef de Village at Kuşadasi to Club Méditerranée in New York.

If you're not in a great hurry, and you shouldn't be, take advantage of the splendid antiquities at Priene, Didymi, or Ephesus. The ancient Ionian city of Ephesus is the most outstanding, and it is close to Kuşadasi. On the road you'll spot ancient columns and buildings; stop and take a look. Many of these uncared-for ruins are extraordinarily well preserved. They make great photographs, with you in them, of course.

Bodrum and Marmaris. Bodrum, at the edge of the Mediterranean on the southwest corner of Turkey, is in fact Halicarnassus of the ancient Greco-Roman world and known as the birthplace of the Greek historian Herodotus. Its whitewashed, red-roofed houses encircle twin harbors dominated by St. Peter's Castle, a fortress of magnificent proportions built between 1402 and 1495 by the Knights of St. John as a backup to their fortress on Rhodes. When the castle was completed, the Knights dubbed the area Petronium in honor of St. Peter. In 1523, when Suleiman the Magnificent captured the city and once again dislodged the Knights, the name was changed to Bodrum.

Today, Bodrum, nestled in Kemre Bay, is still a long way from the mainstream of world tourism. As a consequence, it offers tremendous value and quiet vacations to those who find their way here. Northern Europeans discovered Bodrum years ago and until now have had it almost all to themselves.

As I noted, St. Peter's Castle dominates the two harbors. Cumhuriyet Caddesi rings the exterior harbor, and Neyzen Teufik Caddesi follows the interior harbor. Around Cumhuriyet are some half dozen hotels and pensions, including the Kumsal, Neveid,

The ancient city of Ephesus, just outside Kuşadasi, is an antiquarian's treasure trove.

Halikarnas, Artemis, Mercam, Balikei, and Dinc. Pension Herodot, one of the larger, is on the waterfront of Interior Harbor, just a stone's throw from lovely Tepeçik Mosque. And in the same general area are the Deniz, the Orfoz, and a dozen or so others.

A glimpse at prices of a random sample of these hotels may show you what you've been missing. The Halikarnas Pension, Bodrum's most posh public house, offers among its twenty rooms a single with bath and full board for about $4! Should you care to take all your meals out, deduct 50 percent.

A short walk down from the Halikarnas is the Artemis, where a triple room with bath costs $3 to $4. A single room without bath is $1, and a double is about $2. At the Herodot on Neyzen Teufik Street, doubles with bath are offered at $2 and $3. Many of the others are even less.

If you are not in need of luxury, you can live like the mayor himself on $100 a month (the mayor's salary is $100). If you don't mind accommodations with local color, you can rent a room in a private home for 40 cents a night, eat a shish kebab for 25 cents and purchase a bottle of local wine for the same price.

For $35, four people can enjoy a day's sailing and fishing (a full twenty-four hours), including breakfast and cold beverage. A year's rent for a good stone house, with kitchen, bathroom, and sleeping accommodations for four, can be as low as $50.

Bodrum's waterfront plaza, where many of the cabin cruisers are berthed, is a meeting place for vacationers and townspeople. Particularly popular is Dimitrakopulo's open-air bar adjoining the Smyrna Rug Shop. In the rear is Restaurant Korfez, where excellent salad, fish, shish kebab, and melon are available for less than a dollar.

The Ministry of Tourism maintains an office on the square. If you're looking for a place to stay, they can usually help. But it will be a very tight squeeze in July and August if you haven't made prior arrangements. As I mentioned, many Europeans descend on Bodrum to take advantage of its beaches, impossibly low prices, and quiet.

Bodrum has a fascinating (and free) museum within the walls of the castle. There is an outstanding collection of objects found underwater, including amphorae, statuary and other objects recovered from sunken vessels. Of special interest is a frieze from King Mausolus' mausoleum, erected in 352 B.C., which was one of the seven wonders of the ancient world.

Tepeçik Mosque, a favorite attraction at the water's edge on Neyzen Teufik Caddesi, was built in 1152 on the site of the ancient Doric Agora. Bombardments by the Allied fleet during World War I partially destroyed it, and the minaret was replaced in 1957.

The entire coast in and around Bodrum, with its many coves and bays, is one big beach area. All you need do is find a piece of shoreline that you like and make it your own. Camping is perfectly acceptable here.

Across Kemre Bay to the east is the small beach resort of Marmaris. Unfortunately, on maps it looks deceptively closer to Bodrum than it is. Whether you head there from Bodrum or points north or west, you must first go to Mugla and pick up state highway 23. The first section of this road is a series of hairpin curves, winding up and down mountains; that part of the trip slows you to a snail's pace. As there is no way to race over this road, just relax and enjoy the breathtaking views.

When Suleiman the Magnificent decided to expel the Knights of St. John from Rhodes (1522), he had a castle-fortress built in Marmaris as a base of operations. Today it still overlooks this sleepy village. Because of its closeness to the Greek island of Rhodes and its lovely bay area, Marmaris has become an attraction for vacationers on Rhodes who want to spend at least a few hours in Asia Minor.

Each morning except Wednesday the boat from Rhodes arrives at about ten-thirty. Those who make the two-hour trip have until three-thirty in the afternoon to sample coffee shops and Turkish food, or shop in the marketplace and bazaars. The other way around, vacationers in Marmaris can take the three-thirty boat to Rhodes, spend the night there, returning the following morning on the eight-thirty run to Marmaris. The round-trip fare is $4 for students and $5 for others.

Should you be interested in a cruise around the harbor or the coves near Marmaris, either ask one of the fishermen whose boats

The Marti Motel in Marmaris resembles an ancient Turkish inn.

are available for hire at about $2 to $3 per day, or have it arranged by the tourism office, just a short distance from the pier where the Rhodes boat docks.

The coastline around Marmaris is even more jagged than Bodrum's. Almost every bend hides a sheltered cove with a lovely expanse of beach. On one of these is the four-year-old Marti Motel Marmaris, a striking hotel designed to resemble an ancient Turkish caravansary, or inn. Green-blanketed mountains rise in the background, and the pine woods come down almost to the water's edge.

The motel-hotel offers rooms with modern shower and bath facilities, and each has a private sun deck. The Marti is another one of those surprising hotels with elegant dining and impeccable service, which one does not expect to find in a remote corner of Asia Minor. Their chefs have learned well the art of grilling as well as the preparation of delicious hors d'oeuvres, vegetables, and pastries. The dining rooms are open to the public.

In the high season, July 1 through August 31, a double room

with full board is approximately $17 per day for two. This is among Turkey's highest-priced accommodations. The Marti is a particularly desirable hotel and is booked well in advance, so you would do well to write for reservations at least three months prior to your planned trip.

According to its owner, Mr. Memduh Moran, the finest time of year in Marmaris is September and October. The sea is calm and warm, and the fishing is excellent. And in the off-season, prices drop 15 percent.

The wide private beach is sheltered by the islands in the bay. The sand is dark, almost red, probably containing substantial amounts of iron oxide. I suspect it is the iron that absorbs the sun's heat and makes the sand a "hot spot." But the water is cool and refreshing, a good place to spend your time in the heat of the day.

To augment its present facilities, the owners are building a small village, which will have sixty-seven bungalow accommodations for some 140 people. With narrow streets, minarets, coffee and tobacco shops, it will have the flavor of a typical old Turkish village.

In August, 1971, a spanking new resort, the Marmaris Tatil Köyü, opened its doors to visitors. Spread out amid the pine-covered hills on another cove of Marmaris Bay, the Holiday Inn is of a very different nature, more like a summer camp for adults. The concrete bungalows are designed for coolness under Turkey's hot August sun. Some are units of two, others of four, but with individual entrances and private shower and sanitary facilities.

For this type of accommodation you can expect to pay from $9 to $11 for two, with full board, in high season. The $2 spread represents differences in the size of the rooms. To make it even more enticing, there is no tax and no service charge.

The main building includes a dining room, disco, dance area, and bar and lounge, all overlooking the bay. For some strange reason, the reception building is shaped like a huge wigwam. In it are barbershops for men and women, gift shops, and offices.

Meals in the dining area are served cafeteria style. There is no menu and no choice, but the food is good and in good supply. Be prepared to eat Turkish cheese and olives for breakfast, along with strong coffee. Most of the young high-school and university boys working in these hotels speak some English, so you should have no difficulty getting along.

Directly in front of the dining room, at the water's edge, is a red-brown cement sun deck, somewhat cooler to lie on than the sand. A crib-type swimming area is provided for young children and nonswimmers. This is great snorkeling and scuba water, so bring your gear along. The crystal clarity of the water allows almost unlimited viewing of aquatic flora and fauna.

In addition to Holiday Inn's own disco, which operates full blast from nine to midnight, there is another at the Hotel Lidya, just a five-minute walk away. Admission is free, and soft drinks are inexpensive. Santana disco, also close by, is on a boardwalk in the bay. These places swing until six in the morning with taped music, usually American.

The well-established Hotel Lidya has its own beach and, like the Holiday and Marti, transports its guests to Marmaris in awninged launches. These boats pick up passengers several times a day, obviating the need to take taxis the eight or ten miles to the center of town. For 15 cents, the boats are quite a bargain.

In 1973, the Lidya opened its new multistoried annex, giving it a total of 85 rooms. In the high season double rooms without meals in the brand new wing range from $5.50 to $9.50 per day. Even if you demand more than three meals a day, this has to be one of the least expensive places to spend a great vacation.

Antalya, Alanya, and Mersin. Between Marmaris and Antalya, about one hundred fifty miles to the east, as the crow flies, is a great expanse of open country. Unfortunately, most of it can be crossed only by a jeep. Many Turks still travel by camel or on horseback. From Antalya to Alanya to Mersin, the long southern coast of Turkey is called the Turkish Riviera. Virtually the entire coastline of the province is a sandy beach. Only a few beaches have been developed; most are still pristine and primitive, for use mainly by the transient camper. It will be several years before adequate accommodations are available along much of this verdant, tranquil shore, which has known Persian, Roman, Greek, Seljuk, Byzantine, and Ottoman invaders.

There are three ways to get to this area. The most direct is by plane from Izmir to Antalya. The second, by car, say from Marmaris, is long and tiring but a great way to see the country. The third route, scenic, relaxing, and inexpensive, is via ship from Istanbul or Izmir.

If you are driving from Marmaris, you must first drive to the inland city of Denizli, since many parts of the coast are impassable or roadless. Before leaving this area, stop at Pamukkale, about fourteen miles north of Denizli. This area is often called the Cotton Castle because of the white limestone terraces formed by overflowing mineral waters. It is truly a remarkable sight. The White Cliffs Motel of the Tusan chain provides excellent food, a swimming pool, and mineral springs. Across the road at Hierapolis are interesting ruins left by the Romans.

From Pamukkale, return to Denizli, then drive toward Acipayam to pick up state highway 81. The last stretch of this highway, from Korkuteli to Antalya, is a tangle of single, double, and triple hairpin curves through the Taurus Mountains. This will soon tell you who the good drivers are. The road workers who are widening the highway must have little regard for their lives, since many stretches of the old highway are nothing more than goat trails clinging to the sides of mountains as high as 6500 feet, right in the clouds.

Consequently, one must not be deluded into thinking that what appears to be a short distance on the map can be covered rapidly. It can't; the word is "slowly!" And the drive is up and down mountains with breathtaking views and roads to match. It wasn't long before Craig exhorted us, "There's no giving way here." The car to the left has the mountain on his side, "He can give way." These roads are not to be traveled at night. We've seen the results of too many cars slamming into horse-drawn carts, trees, and boulders. Besides, Turkey is far too lovely to miss by traveling at night.

Should you decide to drive, get an early start, a full tank of gas, and pack a lunch. You'll be on the road at least eight hours—

possibly nine or ten. There are gas stations here and there, watering holes, and farmers selling melons and fruit; make use of them all.

For a more relaxed trip, the Turkish Maritime Lines operates eleven-day cruises from Istanbul to Iskenderun (just this side of the Syrian border) and back. Ports of call are Izmir, Kuşadasi, Bodrum, Marmaris, Antalya, Alanya, and Mersin. This is an unusually good combination of boat trip and beach hopping. Perhaps the fact that that it is poorly advertised in the United States may account for so few Americans taking this pleasant cruise around the Turkish Riviera.

Of the ships that make this run, the M/V *Marmara* (there are also M/V *Samson* and *Iskenderun*) is the deluxe ship of the line. This 125-foot, 6000-ton vessel is fully air-conditioned, has a pool, pleasant dining and common rooms, and a staff that keeps up a full program of fun and games for those who care to join in.

At each port, the ship stops for at least half a day, and at Izmir and Kuşadasi it stays a full day. At Kuşadasi, a tour of Ephesus is organized. Passengers disembark at Marmaris to shop at its bazaar and bathe at its beaches.

A round-trip fare with accommodations on "A" deck is about $56, not including food. The meal fare for the round trip is another $20 per person.

But less elegant accommodations can be obtained for as little as $33 (plus food) for the round trip. A one-way passage (on "A" deck) is about $40, and passage between ports Izmir and Kuşadasi or between Marmaris and Antalya, for example, can be arranged for a proportionate amount.

In Antalya, a visit to the old quarter is well worth the time, as is a meal at the Derya Hotel. Their *lagos* (a type of fish), chicken kebab, and pastry are yet another sample of the excellent food available just about anywhere in Turkey.

While in Antalya, walk to Belediye Park at the end of Atatürk Caddesi. The view of the mountains and the Gulf of Antalya is a picture you'll want to bring home.

Ten miles east of Antalya and off to the left of main highway E24, is the ancient city of Perge. This walled city, complete with baths, stadium, and theater, was a cultural center in Hellenic times, and it was from here that Paul and Barnabas began their pilgrimage through Asia Minor.

However, if you have to make a choice, continue east another twenty miles and stop at Aspendos (Belkis) three miles to the left off the main road and just six miles this side of Side. The Roman theater at Aspendos, over 1800 years old, is just about intact. Few antiquities anywhere are this well preserved. And it is free standing, not built into a hillside as many Roman theaters were. The stage and entrance ways for both major and minor actors remain as they were originally. If you're a camera bug, be sure to have a wide-angle lens. And should you be one of the lucky tourists who can vacation in May, keep in mind that every year at that time, classical plays are presented in the theater as part of the Antalya-Aspendos Festival.

Side is another gift of the Hellenes. As you drive through the town on your way to Motel Turtel, you will see ancient walls, pillars, archways, and fountains flanking the road. And here is the largest ancient theater (seats 25,000) in Asia Minor. People poke through the ruins looking for coins and other antiquities that can be sold or collected, even though this is actually illegal.

The Turtel is a modern hotel with an excellent restaurant. We suspect that when you sit down to lunch in the open-air dining area and look out across the azure water, the sight of the Roman theater arches on the opposite shore will elicit a gasp of delight.

Each of the Turtel's forty-five rooms (ninety beds) is equipped with bath and shower, and each room has a balcony overlooking the Mediterranean. If you want a beautiful beach to yourself, here is one. This hotel is a good place to spend a day or a week, and you are well situated for an easy drive back to Antalya or on to Alayna.

In the village of Manavgat, just two and a half miles out of Side on the way to Alanya, is the Manavgat waterfall, which is truly spectacular scenery. This road to Alanya (Coracesium of old) parallels some fifty miles of elegant beaches. Just park your car and enjoy the sun and surf. Within ten years, Turkey's now un-

The Hotel Turtel is on the Mediterranean coast between Antalya and Side.

spoiled natural beach areas will have to emerge as *the* place to go.

Not too far along the road from Side, is Colaki, the legendary village of left-handed people. You're in the vicinity when you see bottles, all colors and sizes, on the chimneys of the houses. These bottles are not there for decoration or recycling; nothing of the sort. According to local custom, the number of intact bottles indicates the number of marriageable daughters in the house. Broken bottles signify daughters no longer available. If you're single, you might stop and inquire.

About twelve miles this side of Alanya is Incekum Beach and the Incekum Motel, the newest in the area. From the hotel to the water's edge is some 200 yards of fine white sand. The Turks have given it the right name; Incekum means soft, sandy beach.

Since the coast here is open to the Mediterranean, there is a cooling breeze off the impossibly blue water and soft rollers coming in. The water is cooler than along the Aegean, which on hot summer days is a real benefit.

As for the population density of the beach, it is about nil. A most memorable experience is a morning swim, say at about six or seven o'clock, before anyone is awake. The solitude, with the sun coming up over the pines that encircle the beach is a rare scene, and one to remember.

Incekum is just far enough from Alayna to have quiet when you want it, and close enough to have the excitement of the Bazaars and marketplaces when you want that. You have a choice of table d'hôte or à la carte menu either in the 200-seat restaurant or on the open-air terrace. In addition, there is an American bar, discotheque, card and reading rooms, miniature golf course, ping pong, and a children's playground. That last point calls to mind that you may request an extra bed in a double room for $1.50 per night. Doubles cost from $15 to $25 a day with meals.

Half a mile down the road toward Alanya, two modern motels share the same grounds and reception area. The complex is called Motel Aspendos-Yalihan. Together they offer eighty-five balconied rooms with splendid views of the sapphire sea. For about $10, two people can enjoy a clean, attractive room, three good meals, and a number of extras.

For example, for a small fee the motels provide sightseeing tours to Aspendos, Perge, Side, Termessos (the only city in Asia Minor that Alexander the Great was unable to conquer), and Manavgat. There is also a post office, so you can send home packages that may become a burden on your flight, and a Shell service station.

As you drive from the Incekum area to Alanya, keep a sharp eye out for a cliff that juts out from the roadside over the Mediterranean. According to legend, if you see the water below a hole at the base of the cliff, your wish will come true. We recommend this be done only when someone else is driving. Otherwise, the car may well wind up in the sea, quite a distance below.

Alanya, already well known in both Hellenic and Roman times, was captured in the thirteenth century by the Seljuk Sultan Aleddin Keykubad. He had the walls of the old city restored, and built new cisterns, mosques, and ramparts. These magnificent crenelated fortifications are on a promontory some 800 feet above the sea. At the east corner of the walls is the splendid octagonal

Red Tower (Kizil Kule), built in 1225. Nearby are the Seljuk shipyards, which are unique in that ships could be brought inside their protective walls. No trip to Alanya can be complete without a boat ride that will take you close to, or into, the arched entrance.

Anita believes Alanya (and Turkey generally) is a shopper's paradise. There is something for everyone, and the price is right. Jewelry, antique, and coin shops are often combined, and rug and clothing shops abound. One thing you must not miss is the delicious ice cream. Be sure to watch them place a scoop on a cone. The ice cream is so thick that the vendor pinches it off, giving it a dexterous twist with his thumb. Because it is so good, most people take the bowl size, about a half pound! At twenty cents a bowl, this brings back memories of the good old days in the States, when a nickel bought an ice cream cone that was a meal in itself.

Following the main street through Alanya (Atatürk Caddesi, actually state highway 6 and the E-24) for about a half mile will bring you to one of the most posh hotels along the entire Turkish coast.

Motel Alantur attracts many young marrieds as well as single adults who enjoy sports and dancing. Its discotheque resembles the cabin of a jet plane; the walls and ceiling are sheets of silver bubbles, and the floor is a silvery metallic sheet. The lights are orange bubbles. Dana and Andi claim it's the wildest looking disco in all Turkey. In the dark, the white leather furniture reflects the lights, adding to the psychedelic experience.

Because this disco swings until two to three in the morning, the Alantur has done something that many other hotels could well emulate. For the comfort of those who want to sleep, the disco is air-conditioned and soundproofed.

In case you want to take a dip close to your room, a lagoon has been built, with a wooden foot bridge to the beach. There are thatched sunshades and stands, which are used in the evening for serving döner kebab and other delicacies.

Single room reservations may not be honored at the Alantur in high season, and a 30-percent deposit is required with all advance reservations. A double is from $10 to $15 a day with meals.

Driving on from Alanya, the next stop is Anamur, the most

southerly point on this stretch of coast. The next seventy miles of driving are all hairpin curves up and down the mountains skirting the shore. And unexpectedly, miles and miles of banana plantations on the hillsides, down to the water's edge.

But at the end of the tortuous road, as if to greet the worn-out traveler, is the thirty-room Boğsak Motel, just outside of Silifke. At the Boğsak you can swim off the golden sandy beach, drink a cold glass of cherry juice (very refreshing), and spend one or several nights.

Two Kervansaray Mocamps are located on beaches near the Antalya-Alanya and Alanya-Mersin roads. Thirteen miles outside of Alanya, a short distance from the Incekum Motel is Alanya Mocamp, one of the most outstanding. At the other end of the highway, sixteen miles outside of Silifke and a few hundred yards from one of the two castles of Korykos is the Kizkalesi Mocamp, directly at the water's edge.

Silifke, in the province of Mersin, is just thirty-nine miles from the city of Mersin. Although the drive is along the shore, you can park almost anywhere for a swim; few accommodations are available.

Not far beyond Silifke you will pass the Maiden's Castle, on an island several hundred yards off shore. The twelfth-century castle is still intact. Legend has it that the ruler of the area was told his daughter would die from the bite of a snake in her eighteenth year. To prevent this, he had the castle built and housed his daughter there. In her eighteenth year, one of her servants came back from shore with a basket of grapes. Unknown to all, a snake was coiled among the grapes. When the young girl placed her hand in the basket she was bitten and died.

Mersin and Adana, forty miles beyond, are major transportation centers. At Adana, THY has regular flights to Ankara, Istanbul, Izmir and the island of Cyprus. Mersin, a major seaport, offers biweekly crossings to Famagusta (Magusa on Turkish maps), Cyprus. Turkish Maritime Lines cruise ships put in at Mersin several times a week, and passage can be booked for the trip back to Izmir or Istanbul.

The crossing to Famagusta *should* be a magnificent way to

cross the 120 miles of Mediterranean. It should be a relaxing six- to eight-hour crossing, with pleasant dining facilities and lounge areas, and it should be inexpensive. Unfortunately it is none of these.

The Tayfun Shipping Company of Nicosia, Cyprus, operates the tiny ferryboat *Delphinus*, and the Hittite Tourist Agency at Uray Caddesi 15, Mersin, is apparently the only agency that has information on the schedule. It is not to be found in *Car Ferries in the Mediterranean and the Black Sea*, that excellent publication put out by the Automobile Association (London). I suspect they would prefer not to be reminded of it.

The ugly fact is that the *Delphinus* is a dirty little ship that carries six cars and 120 people. For adults, a one-way crossing is approximately $14, children from three to twelve years pay about $7.50, and students with a bona fide I.D. card can buy a ticket for about $12.20. Automobiles go for $29. But remember, only six cars go, so it's got to be an early reservation. The schedule calls for a sixteen-hour crossing, but if the wind should blow up a bit, it's eighteen hours, and rough seas guarantee a twenty- to thirty-hour crossing. All this without provision for food or drinking water (except what you bring yourself) and sanitary facilities that become inoperable and unusable by the third hour at sea. There are no lights on deck and no handrails.

There is no reason why this crossing should not be up to the standards of numerous other car ferries. We offer you this caution so you will know what to expect if you do make this trip. Happily, the Turkish government has at last put a major liner in service on this run, although there is now only one crossing per week.

Food and Drink. Turkish food is unusual and delightful; the Turks have intermingled the cuisines of east and west and have managed to blend the best of both.

Before you get into the main courses, try *mézé*, an incredible variety of hot and cold appetizers. If you've had *tapas* in Spain, you will have an idea of what *mézé* is like. The dishes might include mussels (*midye*) stuffed with a rice mixture, beans cooked in a marinade, yogurt with cucumbers, pickles, *börek* (a filled puff pastry), eggplant salad, and anchovies in oil.

Shish kebab (*şiş kebabi*) is found on menus everywhere. The meat, kebab, is usually lamb (*kuzu*) or goat, broiled on a metal skewer, or shish. Usually pieces of tomato, pepper, and onion are also cooked on the skewer. *Döner kebab*, almost the national dish, is a whole leg of lamb broiled on a vertical rotating spit and then cut into luscious slices.

Shish made with fish or chicken consists of spiced pieces skewered and cooked on hot coals. The fish most often used in Turkey are sea bass, swordfish, *trancha*, and *lagos*. For us, *trancha* is the most delicious; *lagos* is similar but smaller. Both are strikingly white and are found only in Turkish waters.

Biber dolmasi are stuffed green peppers, and *valanci dolma* are stuffed grape leaves. *Mousaka* is a meat and vegetable casserole, and *menemen* is a highly spiced tomato dish covered with fried or scrambled eggs. Although Turkey is not an Arabic country, it is Moslem, and pork is forbidden. Accordingly, ham, bacon, and pork are rarely offered in restaurants and hotels. However, in some international-type hotels, you can get bacon if you request it.

Turkey makes some good red, rosé, and white wines. *Raki*, a native drink flavored with anise, is usually served with food, especially with *mézé*.

Turkish fruit is famous, from the oranges, bananas, and pomegranates of the south to the black cherries of the north. Pastries are very rich and delicious—and don't forget Turkish ice cream, *dondurma*.

CYPRUS

It has been said that Cyprus is a big island but a small country. The wide variety of scenery, splendid beaches, and wealth of archeological and historical treasures renders a quality to its character rarely found elsewhere. Its diversity is such that you can water ski and snow ski on the same day, in the same area.

Cyprus is also the island of Aphrodite, goddess of Love, who legend has it, was born on one of its beaches—Paphos.

With 450 miles of coastline, there are a variety of beaches: some well-developed resorts with modern hotels, others secluded and surrounded by scented pine, cyclamen, and flowering mimosa, while still others are tucked away in tiny harbors guarded by romantic medieval castles.

Cyprus, the third largest island in the Mediterranean, has a population of less than 700,000 Greek and Turkish Cypriots. Its uncrowded condition and melding of two ancient and influential cultures living cheek by jowl, have helped to make Cyprus an exceptional tourist attraction. Unfortunately for Americans, this island has been off their beaten track. The British, on the other hand, have grown so fond of it that many retire there, particularly to the beaches of Kyrenia. More recently, Scandivanians, Israelis,

Belgians, and Germans have been coming in increasing numbers.

The Cypriots don't say stranger or foreigner; they just say *xenos*, which means a guest. *Philoxenia*, which means love for the guests, is not a modern device thought up for purposes of tourism; it is a religious obligation dating back to ancient Greece. Zeus, among his many offices, was regarded as the minister to all travelers, the *xenios* Zeus. A guest arriving anywhere was believed sent by Zeus and consequently was treated with extreme hospitality and respect.

Though Cypriots no longer believe that Zeus sends tourists, the same deep-rooted tradition makes the people of this island as hospitable as their ancestors. Don't be surprised if an unknown passerby salutes you on the street. Be as friendly, return the greeting. And don't be surprised if a shopkeeper offers you a chair and perhaps lemonade or coffee. It's the proper setting for good bargaining, but you don't have to feel that you are obligated to buy. All this just makes life a little more pleasant.

Philoxenia really means that Cyprus is reaching out and welcoming you.

Climate. Until you look at official records, it is difficult to believe that the sun shines 340 days of the year in any country. It does in Cyprus, and there are only two seasons, summer and winter.

Cyprus is one Mediterranean island where swimming is guaranteed all year around. From January to March, the mean sea temperature goes from 61° to 63° F. In April, it rises to 66°, and by September it reaches 80°. During December, the mean sea temperature is 66° F., a good deal higher than in January. Air temperatures parallel this trend; from January to March, the air is about 2° or 3° warmer than the water. And from April to September, the temperature rises sharply and is 5° to 20° warmer than the water. From May through October, the weather is completely predictable: no rain.

Of particular importance is the lack of humidity in summer and the offshore evening breezes that arrive so punctually you can set your watch by them. This happy combination mitigates what

TURKEY

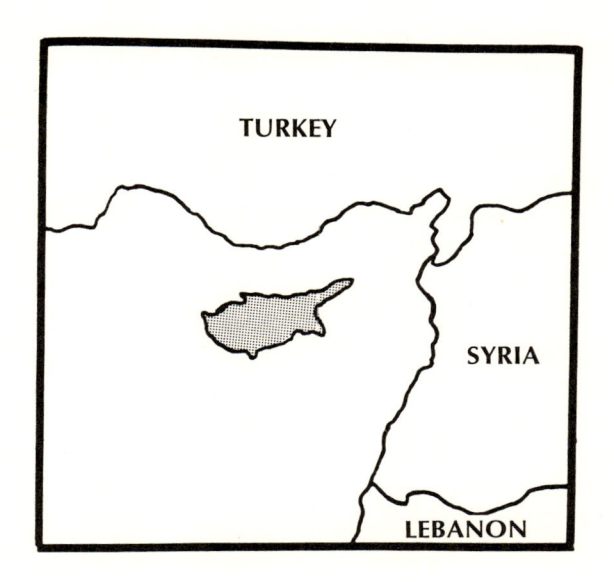

SYRIA

LEBANON

Cape Andreas

Kyrenia

Nicosia

Famagusta

CYPRUS

Larnaca

Paphos   Limassol

would otherwise be unbearable heat. Yet in spite of the heat and the long dry spell, the parched and dusty countryside is dotted with grapefruit, citron trees, grape arbors, and the tallest Russian thistles to be seen anywhere, including the USSR. We've found some to be well over six feet tall!

Because of the warmth and the lack of rain, you can travel light.

Transportation. Cyprus is in the far northeast corner of the Mediterranean, equidistant from Turkey and Syria. This location is responsible for its excellent climate, and it also makes Cyprus easy to get to. Tymbou International Airport, five miles out of Nicosia, the capital city of Cyprus, is less than an hour's flying time from countries in the Middle East and north Africa. Flying time from London, Rome, and Athens is similarly short: four, two and a half, and one and a half hours, respectively.

Nicosia is served by BA (BEA), KLM, El Al, Interflug, Olympic, THY, Alitalia, and a number of other airlines. Consequently, a direct connection from any major city is easy to arrange. The most direct and most numerous flights are via BEA-Cyprus Airways—with the sign of the winged moufflon (a large-horned sheep).

The sea route to Cyprus can be particularly pleasant. Passenger ships and cargo vessels regularly ply between ports in Cyprus—Famagusta, Limassol, and Larnaca—and Italy, Greece, Turkey, and Israel. Detailed information on ports of call, schedules, and prices can be obtained from Zim, Adriatica, Chandris, and Epirotiki lines, for the longer trips.

A new line has begun service between Mersin, Turkey, and Famagusta; Denizyollari, Turkish Maritime Line, has put into service M/F *Yesilada*, a drive-on, drive-off, clean and comfortable car ferry. Unfortunately, it only makes the crossing from Mersin on Monday, returning on Tuesday. On Wednesday, the crossing is made by that foul scow the *Delphinus*—discussed in more detail in the chapter on Turkey.

At both the airport in Nicosia and at the seaport of Famagusta, customs officials are courteous, helpful, and speedy. At both places, taxis are abundant. Most of the drivers will offer to become your guide for the length of your stay. Before giving a fast "no," consider that there are no trains on the island and that although there is bus service to all major towns, you'll be restricted to its schedule. The other alternative is to rent a car and drive yourself. Taxis go all over the island rather reasonably. Trips from Famagusta to Nicosia, Limassol, Larnaca, Kyrenia, and Paphos for the morning or day are a regular service. You'll see taxis parked all over the island waiting for clients. However, it isn't necessary to make a decision on the spot. Stop at several of the many taxi stands and ask about specific trips or daily or weekly hire.

BEACHES

Famagusta. Famagusta, from the Greek name Ammohustos, meaning "buried in sand," is indeed apt. Cyprus' second largest city, which dominates the eastern coast, is surrounded by sandy beaches. Twenty miles of beach stretch from Famagusta south to Cape Greco, and eighty-five miles of beach border the entire length of the panhandle, a narrow finger of land stretching from Famagusta to Cape Andreas.

Fortunately, hotels do not dot the coastline; most of these long stretches of clean, fine sand are still in a primitive state. You can drive out of the city in either direction and park on wide, golden sand or pebbly beaches. For those who want a quiet, "skinny dipping" beach to themselves, it isn't necessary to drive more than a few minutes in either direction.

For those who prefer mingling and meeting people, Varosha's Golden Mile is made to order. Varosha, by the way, is the name given to the modern part of the city; the old quarter is referred to by the Cypriots as Famagusta. The Golden Mile starts at the tip of Eleftheria Street, curves out and around past the yacht club, swings wide past King George's Hotel and the Alasia Center, then runs the full length of Kennedy and Roosevelt Avenues, where twenty deluxe and first-class hotels are clustered. And from there the golden sand just continues on and on, past the hotel belt.

Eight deluxe and eleven first-class "A" hotels are on or near the sand. In fact, Varosha-Famagusta has 34 of Cyprus' 134 hotels

Almost the full sweep of Famagusta's beach can be seen while dining.

around its curving ribbon of beach. Accordingly, accommodations should pose no problem.

The water along the beach is the lightest blue, glass clear, and calm. It's especially great for children and water skiers. (If you crave rollers and swells, try the Paphos district on the southwestern tip of the island.)

Cloudless skies and the hot sun make this an excellent suntanning area. That's what is drawing the Scandinavian and German tourists—that and the fact their marks and kröner go a long way here. This also applies to dollars—Cyprus gives good value for your vacation money.

In Elba we noted that each hotel guest was assigned an umbrella and sun chair. This is not yet done in Famagusta, and it produces some strange behavior. In July and August the sun and sand can become very hot, and a beach umbrella and chair becomes a necessity. Being late sleepers, we didn't get out to the beach before nine or ten o'clock the first few mornings. On the beach we found few people, but the chairs and umbrellas were all taken, "reserved" with towels, rocks, robes, and other paraphernalia. We and others were loathe to remove them. After lunch each day, these marked chairs became filled, so we decided to find out how this occurred.

Shunning the extra hours of sleep, we rose early and kept a vigil from our balcony. Our German and Nordic friends were coming out between six and eight in the morning to "hold" the chairs and umbrellas, then returning to sleep! After nearly a week of this unacceptable behavior, we resolved to put a stop to it.

At midnight, with only the moon to light our way, we slipped down to the beach, removed all lounge cushions and umbrellas to a hiding place, and piled up the metal loungers in odd places. Satisfied with our work, we went to bed, setting the alarm for seven the next morning. And then we watched from our balcony as the same eager ones came down to the beach. The shock proved effective. That afternoon, a new group was able to use the lounges and umbrellas.

This is boating water. All manner of light and heavy craft with motor, sail, or both can be rented for the day or week. Motor boats for water skiing are generally available at each hotel.

Raymond André, the manager of the brand-new, 144-room deluxe Aspelia Hotel, assured us he will attempt to make this a hotel of unequaled service. His managerial record in the Bahamas and Switzerland should make this more than a hope.

In contrast to Yugoslavia, Cyprus has no really big hotels. For example, the largest hotel on the island is the 200-room Ledra, in Nicosia. Famagusta beach has the second largest, the 182-room deluxe Loiziana. But there are over a dozen second- and third-class hotels of five to thirty rooms just off the beach, and north and south of the town. As all beaches are open to the public, there is no difficulty in living in a small hotel some few blocks from the Golden Sands and walking or driving to the beach.

From the Asterias, Aspelia, Cypriana, and several of the other deluxe and first-class hotels along Kennedy Avenue, it's just a short walk into the heart of Varosha. Buses are available, but the walk is short enough so that you can get a good look at homes, shops, and people.

Seven miles north of Famagusta, within easy walking distance of the ruins of ancient Salamis, is the seventy-four-room deluxe Evagoras Hotel in chalet style. If you don't care for high-rise hotels to the left and right and don't mind being a ten-minute drive from town, this could be the beach for you. It's quiet and uncluttered.

A word about Cypriot hotels. The Cyprus Tourist Organization in Nicosia has established five categories, from deluxe to fourth class, with two subdivisions in first class. For each of these a fixed price is published. Except for fluctuations in international currency rates, you know in advance what each category of hotel charges; not a bad idea.

Kyrenia. The district of Kyrenia though the smallest of Cyprus' six districts, has much to offer. Its location on the northern coast ensures a cooler summer and cooler sea than the southern coast, and it gets fewer visitors than Famagusta.

Twenty minutes and fifteen miles from Tynbou airport brings you over the hump of the Kyrenia hills to one of the most breathtaking views on the Mediterranean, a spectacle of snow-capped mountains stretching from St. Hilarion Castle as far as the eye can

Around Kyrenia's harbor are the remnants of defensive works dating back to Byzantine times.

see, with the blue sea below.

Around Kyrenia's small horseshoe-shaped harbor are the remnants of defensive works dating back to Byzantine times. The eastern side of the harbor is dominated by a great square castle that is now used as a beach, swimming pool, and boating club. Southwest of the town, 2200 feet above sea level, is the fairytale castle of St. Hilarion.

Long sparsely inhabited sandy beaches flank the town to the east and west. Six miles east, out Gladstone Avenue, is Pachyammos Beach. Pachyammos in Greek means "thick sand," and the name is appropriate. There are no hotels out this way; accommodations are in Kyrenia proper. It may be possible, however, to rent a room in a private home. There are no channels to assist with this—you must manage it on your own.

As the ride from town to the beach takes ten minutes or less, a hotel in Kyrenia would be the best bet. There are seaside restaurants at Pachyammos, so food and drink are no problem.

To the west of town, in the area of Karavas, is Five Mile Beach. Here too, development has been slow, and the ancient beaches have changed little. But there are several small third- and fourth-class hotels. For example, some hundred yards from the sea is the Klearchos, a twenty-five-room, third-class hotel. All rooms have a balcony, bath, and shower. The Mermaid, a fourth-class accommodation with nineteen rooms overlooks one of the finest sandy bays. As yet, all deluxe and first-class hotels are in Kyrenia itself.

The great thing about these beaches is not only the swimming, but the underwater fishing, snorkeling, and scuba diving. The colorful fish, aquatic plants, shipwrecks, and caverns provide true underwater adventures.

Water skis can be rented and arrangements for towing made at several of the local hotels. All hotels in Kyrenia are open all year and are quiet places, as are the beaches. Few places are more isolated than the long stretches of beach on either side of Kyrenia.

The town itself, a small fishing village, is a blend of old-world charm with the amenities of a modern seaside resort. For so small a town, less than 5000 people, it has a number of good hotels, restaurants, and shops. Along Kyrenia's waterfront, called the Kimon Coast, an extension of Aristides Street, and along the breakwater at the edge of the sea are several fine hotels.

The Catsellis Dome Hotel, Kyrenia's 175-room deluxe hotel, has a most unusual pool right in the Mediterranean. It extends way out offshore, a most unlikely place for a pool. To get to it, guests have to walk across the causeway from the hotel.

Three fine first-class hotels are the Ruby Rock at the end of Konon Street; the Coeur de Lion Marangos, which preserves the memory of Richard the Lionhearted; and the Dorana, the youngest and most up-to-date.

The town has several good restaurants and discos. At Marabou, you can order Cypriot specialties, and Turkish-style *meze* is a regular feature. The dining room overlooks the sea with its yachts, and the castle. Twice weekly, local groups put on a display of folk dancing.

At the corner with the town's only traffic light is Bamboo Dis-

Mare Monte Hotel is six miles west of Kyrenia, on Cyprus' rugged north coast.

cotheque. It boasts the latest equipment, loudest music, and psychedelic lights to match. If you've had all the quiet you can take after a day or two on the beaches, here's the place to shatter it all.

Paphos. Cypriots—Greeks and Turks alike—agree that the district of Paphos, including Paphos itself, Ktima, Polis, and Karavastasi, is probably the most attractive in Cyprus and the least visited by vacationers. Any visitor to Cyprus should spend at least a few days on and around its beaches. Paphos is romantically associated with Aphrodite (Venus), the Goddess of Love and Beauty, who, according to Homer, was born from the soft seafoam, breaking against Petra tou Romiou, the great rocks on the southern coast of the district.

Paphos has an abundance of semi-tropical greenery, exceptionally soft honey-colored sand along its beaches, and clear, clean water. There are no cathedrals, no palaces, discos or boutiques.

The loveliest beach in the area, Coral Bay, is seven miles northwest of the town. It has an idyllic beauty, especially at sunset when everything takes on a pinkish-orange hue, and the beach is deserted except for a few sea birds wheeling and turning in flight. After a few days, the outside world is forgotten.

I suspect this may not be attractive to tourists on a whirlwind tour. More likely, the long, curving, all-but-deserted beaches are for those who want to relax, to get entirely away from the technological work-a-day world—and have the time to do it.

Accommodations in Paphos, though scarce, are adequate, for there is no great influx of tourists at any time of year. In addition to three hotels in the center of town (a first, second, and fourth-class) with a grand total of sixty-seven rooms, it's usually possible to find a private dwelling with a spare room or rooms. Food is abundant and inexpensive at local open-air restaurants, which cater to the local residents. Red mullet, called *barbounia* by the residents, is the best fish and is always fresh. Most of the harbor restaurants serve it grilled or fried. Should you come here, you become part of the town, and language differences are no barrier to friendliness.

Limassol. Possibly you've wondered about carob beans and where they come from. Wonder no more; they come from Cyprus generally, and Limassol in particular. In addition to its carob beans, whose singular aroma is unforgettable, Limassol is the center of the island's wine industry. Is it any wonder, then, that this is the busiest of the island's towns as well as its principal commercial port? But Limassol has also gained the admirable reputation of being the most festive of Cyprus' towns. Hardly a month goes by without the citizens organizing some colorful attraction.

The district of Limassol has long been famous for Mt. Olympus, its popular winter resort. It is in this district that you can water ski and snow ski on the same day. Few places can offer that degree of diversity.

Limassol's best beaches are not along its harbor waterfront. "Ladies Mile," seven miles west of town, is the most attractive beach in the area. It is long, wide, and not at all restricted to the distaff side. So far, no hotels of any consequence have been built out this way. After a short drive or bicycle ride from town, you know you'll have an undeveloped beach, if you prefer that.

If your predilections run to the more sophisticated, try the other end of town. Bordering the sea along 28th of October Street in the direction of Larnaca are several elegant beaches and hotels to match. Two miles from the center of town, on its own stretch of well-cared-for beach, is the showplace of the southeast coast, as well as one of the most outstanding hotels in Cyprus; the 154-room Apollonia Beach Hotel is one of Trust Houses Forte International's most opulent hospices.

The hotel sits on a rise above the beach. From the rear, steps lead a short way down to the sandy beach, where a breakwater that extends out from shore doubles as a sunning and lounging area. It's all very congenial.

For us, the height of the Apollonia's luxury and the mark of its singular distinction rests not in its terraced restaurant, bar, or even the sea views from balconied rooms; for us the laurels go to its American-style toilets, or shall we say sanitary facilities, which are not only lovely to look at, but they work. Unquestionably, the Apollonia has the most beautiful bathrooms in all Cyprus. By comparison with deluxe hotels in other countries, it is quite inexpensive. And because it's not a large place, reservations must be placed early.

A quarter of a mile beyond the Apollonia, amid a dozen acres of glorious greenery, is the Miramare Hotel. Its beach, to the rear of the hotel, has remained undeveloped. A number of large old trees stand almost at the water's edge, and in the heat of summer these offer cooling cover.

The calm, usually flat surf is great for toddlers, which helps to make this a family-type hotel. The Miramare has its own speed boats and water skiing equipment and can provide instruction for the whole family.

These hotels are well located to serve as a base from which larger beaches, such as Ladies Mile, as well as many archeological sites, can be visited at your leisure.

Limassol is ideally located for visiting the Platres Folk Festival. Each year at the end of August and the beginning of September,

Platres, in the foothills of the Troodos mountains, becomes the gathering place for the hill people. In reality it is a friendly rivalry to see which village has the best dancers, singers, marksmen, and artists. The last evening of the week long festivities concludes with the selection of "Miss Platres." The festival is a good opportunity to buy a host of handmade local handicrafts.

Larnaca. Known for its regal palm trees and pink flamingos, which gather by the hundreds on its lakes, Larnaca is an old-world town on the southern coast, half an hour's drive from Nicosia. Its central location makes it an ideal spot from which to explore the rest of the island.

The drive into Larnaca helps set the tone. Athens Street along the harbor has an impressive palm-lined promenade, and extending the length of it is an open-air café-restaurant. Take a brief walk around the promenade or stop for a dish of ice cream under the palms; you will see that people are really enjoying themselves.

Although you have your choice of wide sandy beaches at either

"Main Street," Larnaca.

end of the harbor front, there is only one hotel in town—the Four Lanterns, at the east end. It is a first-class "A" accommodation with only thirty-seven rooms. What it lacks in size it makes up for in character and location. If you want one of these rooms, you must speak up early. And to get the full benefit of the fixed prices, you must stay at least two nights; it's hardly worth the effort to come for less than a week. If you want to jump out of bed and onto the pebbly beach just across the road, this is the place to head for. There are also pensions and private rooms available, for vacationers who wish to live as the townspeople do.

The Kataklysmos Fair and Festival, celebrating the birth of Venus from the waves, is held here annually during June. Folk dancing and singing, fireworks, greasy pole climbing, and other competitive events draw thousands of people to Larnaca's waterfront.

Between Larnaca and Dhekelia, on the road back to Famagusta, are several miles of primitive sandy beach that just long for people. If you're driving around, pull off the road and walk down, the beach is all yours.

Cape Andreas. Eighty-five miles north of Famagusta, at the extreme tip of Cyprus, hard by the Monastery of Apostolos Andreas, is a primitive, soft, white sandy beach, named Paradise Beach. Although the entire coast between Boghaz and Rizokarpaso is uninhabited beach and yours for the basking, the area near the monastery is the most beautiful. All Cypriot monasteries offer free lodging, so if you've a mind to spend a day or two amid marvelous scenery and views—especially dawn and sunset—take advantage of the rooms at the monastery—but don't forget to drop a donation into the church box.

Places of Interest. Cyprus is a festival of ancient cities, temples, Byzantine churches, mosaics, monasteries with fresco paintings, medieval castles, cathedrals, and walled cities. Its ancient Grecian past and the more recent three hundred years of Turkish rule are still very much part of Cyprus. Because there are so many things to see, we have picked only a few highlights, particularly those in

The ruins at Salamis offer a variety of statuesque beauties.

the vicinity of beaches.

At the top of the Panhandle (a very un-Greek or Turkish word to describe the eighty-five-mile index finger of land stretching from Famagusta to Cape Andreas), almost at the edge of the sea is the Apostolos Andreas Monastery. Had you crossed from Mersin, Turkey, to Famagusta you would have seen it to starboard as the ferry rounded the cape. St. Andrew, to whom this is dedicated, was the miracle worker of Cyprus, and the monastery is the Lourdes of this part of the world.

Six miles from Famagusta are the not-so-ruined ruins of Salamis, not to be confused with the small Greek island off Piraeus after which it was named. Tefkros, a hero of the Trojan War, founded Salamis and named it after his home island. It wasn't until 647 A.D. that this immense commercial center was finally abandoned. Baths, theater, gymnasia, and Agora are in a fine state of preservation. During the summer, performances of ancient Greek dramas are held in the original theater.

A walking tour of the old city of Famagusta is definitely in order. Because of the troubles between the Greeks and Turks, Greeks are not permitted to enter the old city.

To the tourist, particularly an American, this presents no problems. Your taxi driver, invariably a Greek, will bring you to the gates of the town and either wait for you or return in an hour or two. He can't go in, but you may move about freely. Be sure to have a Bubble-Up or two. This is by far the best soda pop on the island; we think it's one of the best to be found anywhere. (Bubble-Up isn't sold in Varosha.) Be sure to sample Turkish candy, ice cream, cheese, or a meal if you don't have to rush; try not to rush —remember, you're on vacation.

Thirty minutes from Famagusta, on the southwest outskirts of Larnaca, is the Tekké of Hala Sultan at the upper end of the Salt Lake. The Shrine of Hala Sultan, foster mother of the Prophet Mohammed, is the third most important memorial in the entire Mohammedan world.

Two miles south, at the lower end of Salt Lake in the village of Kiti, is the famous church of Panayia Angelokistos that contains in its central apse a seventh-century mosaic of the Virgin Mary and child with the archangels. This mosaic is considered to be one of the finest examples of Byzantine art anywhere.

Between the village of Episkopi and the Kouris River, about ten miles west of Limassol, are the ruins of the early Bronze Age city of Curium. Mosaics among ruins of a later age tell of the transition from worship of Apollo to Christian worship. In the semicircular theater, built to seat 3500, performances of ancient Greek and Shakespearean dramas, as well as concerts by moonlight, are held regularly from June through September.

Shopping. There is great temptation to shop in Cyprus. The problem is what to choose from the variety of handicrafts and souvenirs. Island specialties are the attractively embroidered bedspreads, pillow cases, curtains, and handbags, which can be found in many novelty shops from about $3 to $65.

Lace from Lefkara, a hill village between Larnaca and Limassol, can compete with handmade work from any country. The intricately designed tableclothes, tea sets, and mats have made the town justly famous.

Cypriots have an ancient tradition of working copper. Many shops carry a variety of engraved, hammered, and enameled copper plates, bowls, and vessels. Silver is another metal that has long been worked here. Bowls, plates, and filigree jewelry, including men's cufflinks, are reasonably priced.

Ceramic pieces in both traditional and contemporary designs can be found in specialty shops. For example, Dolphin Pottery, down the street from the Catsellis Dome Hotel in Kyrenia, has a wide selection of pottery, as well as wrought iron and other metals. Also in Kyrenia is Keramey's pottery factory. Be sure to pop in for a good look at local items.

You would do well to think about purchasing a cold-weather coat or jacket. On the outskirts of Nicosia, past the Bel Cola factory on the old Kyrenia road, is a sheepskin shop. Beha's will take your measurements and cut a coat to your design that you might have even before you leave.

Bear in mind that Cypriots cherish their siesta. Most shops close at least from one to three in the afternoon; others, requiring additional relaxing time, extend this to four. Banks close at noon. So plan your shopping for the early morning and the cool of late afternoon. Anyway, the place to be during the heat of the day is the beach.

A final tip. Keep a few dollars tucked away for the duty-free shop at Tynbou airport. A bottle of Filfar Orange liqueur is hard to come by anywhere else.

Foods and Drink. Perhaps the sayings that civilization begins at the dinner table and that variety is the spice of life had their origins on Cyprus. As a consequence of the long contact with both east and west, its restaurants, taverns, and hotels serve English, French, and other European dishes as well as Cypriot specialties.

Spain has its *tapas* and Italy its *antipasto,* and Cyprus' *meze* can compete favorably with both; it has even more dishes than Indonesian *rijsttafel.* When you order *meze* (*mezedes* or *mezedakia*), be prepared for up to twenty appetizers and highly seasoned aromatic delights. For example, cheeses such as *kaskavali, halloumi,* and *feta* along with tomatoes, olives—green and black, fresh and pickled—sliced artichokes, houmous (ground chick peas, olive oil, garlic, and beetroot), mullet, both red and gray (*barbouni*), shrimps, octopus and squid, chicken and turkey in various sauces, green peppers, *seftolia* (a Cypriot sausage), *koupepia* (vine leaves stuffed with ground meat) and *beccaficos,* a national delicacy.

Following this grand opening comes salad, unusually tasty with fresh coriander, fresh olives, and *feta* cheese, and another side dish—*Taramosalata,* made from fish roe.

Main courses, if you still have room and no will power, can be *mousaka,* made with layers of ground meat, sliced potatoes, eggplant, squash, peppers, and herbs. *Tavas,* another Cypriot specialty, is made with veal, onions, and herbs, and served piping hot in small earthenware bowls.

Souglakia or *kebab* may be chunks of either lamb or pork skewered and grilled slowly over a charcoal fire. Eaten with *pita,* a flat, unleavened bread sprinkled with chopped onion, salt, and pepper, you have a mouth-watering gastronomic gem. Depending on the restaurant or tavern, this can be a meal in itself with the delicious local yogurt.

Another cautionary note. Portions here are man-sized, so consider having a little of each or you'll never make it all the way.

Another tempting dish is *avgolemono,* lemon and egg soup. You'll find lemon in almost everything and at every meal; *patcha,* lamb stew with lemon, and a variety of fish—*synaguda, fangri,* trout, and *viahos*—all with lemon.

Lunch and dinner or even a snack cannot even be contemplated without a sweet and wine or other drink. *Kataifi, baklava,* and *galatopureko* are all rich almond and honey pastries that need grape juice, coffee, tea, or a dry wine to reduce the richness.

For this, ouzo is recommended in small sips. It is a heroic distillation of fermented anise seed that needs no aging to produce its lightning bolts. "Extra-fine" is the strongest of the three types. Good ouzo turns white the moment water is added; you've got to be brave to drink it neat. Watch out for the drink called zivania, especially the pink, cinnamon-flavored variety; it explodes on contact.

Commanderia, the rich sweet dessert wine, is believed to be

the oldest wine known. It is a fine after-dinner drink and makes a good gift or souvenir.

Of course coffee is an integral part of Cypriot life, served sweet and medium, or very strong. Since I am not a coffee drinker, my reaction to Cyprus or Byzantine coffee, as it is often referred to, was that it was strong enough to walk on.

Not to be omitted are the ripe figs, melons, peaches, apricots, grapes, and cherries, which abound in every town and village. The word for it all is *"Kopiaste!"*

ISRAEL

ISRAEL IS NOT grand boulevards and stately mansions; Israel is a feeling. The Promised Land, the Land of the Book. People come to see, walk, touch, and feel. And above all, to wonder. For many people Israel is not just another place to go, not just a place to merely "do."

All along the Mediterranean shore, from the biblical Ashkelon in the south to Achziv, just below the Lebanese border, magnificent beaches are strung out one after the other. The 120 or so miles of this "Sunshine Coast," as the Israelis have dubbed it, include miles of quiet sand, solitude, and peace, as well as popular beaches with friendly people. There are hotels and vacation villages, restaurants, and cafés.

When the sun goes down, the sand turns from gold to purple, and the blue sky turns flaming, colors rarely seen in a sunset. In the evenings, you are close to the bright lights of the cities, should you want entertainment.

Israel's beaches are one of its best-kept secrets. Although quite definitely on the beaten tourist track, relatively few visitors to Israel take advantage of them. Most vacationers flock to the cities to tour the numerous shrines and holy places so precious to

Christians, Moslems, and Jews. As a consequence, the many beaches along the Mediterranean coast are left almost exclusively to the Europeans, who always seem to know where the good beaches are.

It is true that most people would not travel thousands of miles simply to lie on a beach. But because Israel is a relatively small country—two hours of driving time is about sufficient to traverse the country from end to end—the attractive beaches rather than the crowded cities can become your base of operation for excursions and tours to the historic and sacrosanct places. In addition, most Mediterranean beaches are only a short distance from the beaches of the Sea of Galilee, the Dead Sea, and the Red Sea.

Climate. With its warm, sunny summers and mild winters, Israel's climate is for the most part typically Mediterranean. For all intents and purposes it has two seasons: summer from May to October, and winter from November to April.

Away from the coastal plain, in such areas as the Hula Valley near the Lebanese border and Eilat on the Gulf of Eilat, temperatures of 95° to 105° F. are not uncommon in August. On the other hand, all along the coast from Ashkelon to Achziv, temperatures from 65° to 89° F. are the rule in August—the hottest month of the year.

During 1970 and 1971, forty-six rainy days were recorded in the coastal plain, as compared with sixty-one in upper Galilee. Most of the rain fell between October and April; December, January, and February are the wettest months. For the vacationer this means few rainy days to interfere with the well-laid plans.

Transportation. Israel lies on the eastern seaboard of the Mediterranean, in the area where Asia meets Africa and Europe. It is bounded on the north by Lebanon and Syria, on the east by the River Jordan, and on the southwest by the Suez canal and the Gulf of Suez.

Six shipping lines and seventeen airlines operate regular year-round schedules from New York to Israel. Marseilles, Genoa, Naples, Venice, Istanbul, and Limassol, Cyprus, are the main European embarkation ports.

From the United States, Pan American, El Al, the Israeli air-

Inset map

TURKEY

CYPRUS

SYRIA

LEBANON

JORDAN

EGYPT

Main map

Nahariya
Acre
Haifa
Tiberias
Caesarea
Netanya
Tel Aviv
Jerusalem
Ashkelon
Dead Sea
Beersheba

ISRAEL

Eilat

line, and TWA fly directly to Tel Aviv's Lod (Lydda) Airport in approximately ten hours. BA (BEA) has daily non-stop flights from London, as does Alitalia from Rome, KLM from Amsterdam, and Air France from Paris.

It is usually possible to travel one way by air and one way by sea without losing the benefit of round-trip fares. This is worth looking into.

BEACHES

Israel's long and nearly straight coastline can be divided rather easily into three areas: the south, to Tel Aviv; Sharon, or the central coast; and Carmel and northern Galilee.

The wide south, part of "the fertile crescent," includes Gaza, the floral beaches of Ashkelon, the outskirts of modern, well-planned Ashdod, the small town of Nitzanim, and Palmahim, with its Diplomats Beach. These relatively uncrowded beaches draw the vacationer southward.

North of Tel Aviv, the Yarkon River is a natural boundary marking the lower edge of Sharon. Included within it are Herzliya, Netanya, Hadera, and Caesarea, the larger of the seaside towns, as well as such hideaways as Ramat Hasharon (Heights of Sharon), Shefayim, and Michmoret. Through the summer and fall the famous lilies of Sharon dot the sands in this entire area.

Carmel, gradually rising north of Caesarea, becomes a mountain near Haifa. Hanging gardens and houses clinging to the slope of Mount Carmel look down on the very blue Mediterranean and Haifa's tinted sandy beaches. Akko (Acre of Crusader fame), across the Bay of Haifa, as well as Hof Dor, Neveh Yam, Kiryat Yam, Shavei Zion, Nahariya, and Achziv are all part of cool Carmel.

I might say at the outset that the water along the entire Israeli coast is not as placid as in other Mediterranean countries. That the seas can be rough is attested to by the strict safety precautions existing at most beaches. In fact, visitors are asked to swim only at beaches staffed with lifeguards. But the water is clean and refreshing, even invigorating. With the sun as hot as it is, the cool water is indeed a welcome respite.

ISRAEL

Ashkelon to Tel Aviv. The ancient Philistine city and modern Israeli resort of Ashkelon is one of the best swimming and sunning areas along the entire coast. The beach here stretches for miles, as far as the eye can see, and is very wide. Actually I should say beaches, because cliffs separate the huge main beach from a series of smaller, less crowded ones. At several points you are swimming beneath the ruins of Crusaders' fortifications built right into the cliff face overlooking the Mediterranean.

A series of steps leads down from the free parking lot to the fluffy, high-piled sand of the beach. As you walk down the first set of steps and reach the second landing, you will be amazed to see, as big as life, a ship built of concrete. It's actually half a ship, and the bottom is a café-snack bar, very cleverly done. While eating, people can sit facing the sea and get the full view.

The fellow on horseback, in case you're interested, is part of the beach patrol, keeping an eye on anyone who might be swim-

Ashkelon's beach is long, wide, and studded with remembrances of things past.

ming or bathing too far from what the lifeguards deem safe. We liked their concern, since the water is far rougher than we experienced elsewhere in the Mediterranean.

Shell picking is particularly good, especially the small colorful varieties. Dana and Andi, the family equestrians, found horseback riding along a Mediterranean beach "out of sight." The beach is long enough to take a quarter mile at full gallop.

At first glance, you'd easily mistake the Roman columns projecting from the cliffs for a battery of cannon. Ashkelon is full of Roman antiquities; the Crusaders who captured the city centuries later used the Roman pillars as reinforcements for the walls they constructed, and today the pillars are used for fun and games on the beach.

Nearby is another unexpected delight, a green and well-cared-for national park, where the sites of five civilizations have been excavated. You can picnic here, set up a tent or caravan (as trailers are called), search for antiques, or just loll on the grass. Any shards or ancient items you find belong to you.

Accommodations in the area range from the four-star King Saul and the Shulamit Gardens, each with 108 well-decorated comfortable rooms; the venerable bungalow-hotel Dagon with its mini golf course, swimming pool, and reputation for old-world hospitality; to the gay and lively French Village Resort. Although ostensibly for members only, the French village will quickly make you a member for the length of your stay. It helps to speak French, and they are concerned that it maintain an international atmosphere. As a consequence, few Israelis are invited to join.

Ashkelon is a good base from which to take excursions to the Sinai, the Dead Sea, and Eilat, as well as Jerusalem, only forty-five miles away.

Between Ashkelon and Tel Aviv are a number of small hideaway beaches. Just to the north of Ashkelon is Nitzanim; you have to be looking for the signs or you'll miss it. All you need do is drive up, park, and the beach is yours. There should be a lifeguard here, but little else.

Ashdod, a little farther north, is a booming new port city, growing and developing under a master plan that includes a major

Roman ruins, not old cannons, but just as good for cavorting about on the beach at Ashkelon.

Tel Aviv's beach is crowded, and the water is swift and cool.

resort just south of the city. For the present, two hotels near the beach are about all that's available: the three-star Miami and the Galei Ashdod.

At Yavneh and Palmahim, which are on the outskirts of the Tel Aviv area, the beaches are flat and undeveloped, with cool, fast water. They do have lifeguard stations. Beyond Palmahim are the crowded beaches of Tel Aviv, which we do not recommend. We found that on the city beaches there were so many people playing paddle ball that it was unpleasant for those who wanted to relax.

The Sharon. Ten minutes north of Tel Aviv is Herzliya, Israel's most fashionable beach resort, the focal point of Israel's Riviera. They say that in Herzliya you find the biggest cars and the smallest bikinis. Tree-lined lanes shield the villas and bungalows of foreign diplomats, leading industrialists, and highly placed professionals. Its five-star hotels, the Accadia Grand Hotel and the Sharon, cater to a cosmopolitan crowd that has made the gleaming

The Accadia Grand Hotel is at Herzliya, just a few miles north of Tel Aviv.

sands of Herzliya Beach internationally known. The glamour of the area is augmented by the ruins of Apollonia just a short way up the coast.

Fashion and glamour not withstanding, this is a quiet place, quite unlike the general character of Israel. With all its high fashion and "big names," it is informal. The beach is simply lovely, one of the widest and best kept in the country. It is rarely crowded, even on Saturdays, when Israelis generally turn out en masse. Should you want to be close to Tel Aviv, yet away from its clatter, consider Herzliya.

Like most of Israel's beaches, Herzliya is officially opened for swimming and bathing on May 1. From then on, lifeguard stations are manned daily. Prior to May in this part of the world the Mediterranean is just a little too rough for safe swimming; the undertows are strong and swift.

Should you decide to take a swim, the warmth of the air could easily entice you to venture out too far; stay close to shore and be sure someone is available in case help is needed.

"Hill swept by the sea breeze" is the meaning of Shefayim, a beach that is off to itself in the heart of the Sharon. But Shefayim is not the usual beach with nearby hotel; it is a resort run by a kibbutz. The word "kibbutz" means grouping or bringing together, and a kibbutz is a gathering of people who believe in social and economic equality. They are guided by the precept, "From each according to his abilities, to each according to his needs."

But although all kibbutzim are guided by this principle, they are not all the same; each kibbutz has its own character and personality. One difference is the type of industry the kibbutznikim (plural for members of a kibbutz) have adopted as their means of support.

Of Israel's 250 kibbutzim, some twenty-five have opted for recreation and leisure and have gone into the resort business. Of Israel's network of Kibbutz Guest Houses, five are on the coast on or near excellent beaches, or what they've made into excellent beaches.

Obtaining accommodations at a Kibbutz Guest House is a

great way to get more of a "feel" for the country. You also avoid large cities, but are close enough to them for sightseeing.

Before Israel became a state, Shefayim, fifteen minutes north of Herzliya, was a center for illegal immigration, and many Jews fleeing Europe arrived in the Holy Land via the kibbutz. Today, the pioneers of Shefayim have found another use for their favorable seaside location, as an outstanding beach resort where the emphasis is on personal attention. At Shefayim you can really relax on the all but private beach, which is clean and flat and a haven for scuba divers and snorkelers. A full range of sports facilities is provided at no extra charge.

Similarly, you are invited to participate in folklore programs and outings in the Sharon area. At night there are films, dancing, stage plays, and a variety of guest artists. There's hardly a better way of meeting kibbutz people and getting a closeup view of this unique social phenomenon.

The resort includes modern, two-story, multi-unit dwellings, as well as a series of one-level attached bungalows, surrounded by trees, grass, flowers, and shrubs. They obviously have a fantastic gardener—or two. Food is served in a large airy dining room, where members of the kibbutz and guests eat together—except that guests have tablecloths.

Requests for reservations should be addressed to Shefayim Guest House, Post Shefayim, Israel, or to Kibbutz Rest and Guest Houses, 100 Allenby Road, Tel Aviv. These accommodations are not available through travel agents.

Twenty minutes north of Shefayim on the Express Highway, turn left at the traffic signal and drive into a charming little town in the heart of Israel's citrus belt. Take café-lined Herzl Street straight to the shady promenade, park your car, and walk down the steps to the beach. Once there, it will be obvious why Netanya's natural, untampered-with beach has long been a favorite with Israelis. Did you ever sunbathe in powdered brown sugar? Nature gave Netanya a delightful type of sand that few beaches have.

Another built-in attraction is the breeze, which makes sailing ideal. Boats such as Lightnings, Thistles, and a variety of larger types may be rented on the beach. As the surf here is not as heavy as at Ashkelon or Tel Aviv, this is a good place to try out the *haseke*, Israel's own contribution to surfboarding.

This widest beach in all Israel is well protected by lifeguards and provides such amenities as showers and dressing rooms. Recently, a small but adequate café-restaurant of contemporary design has been built on the sand next to the cliffs, so it's no longer necessary to leave the beach for a snack or drink.

For a town of its size, Netanya has an uncommon number of hotels. All thirty-two family-type, government approved, modern, and most important, within easy walking distance of the beach. Three of them—the two-star nine-room Tayelet to the left of the Tourist Information Office, the two-star, twenty-six-room Ruven, and the Ein Hayam—are just in front of the Promenade and overlook the beach.

The largest hotel in town and the only one with five-star rating is the posh Four Seasons. It has only 129 rooms, but very elegant ones. From the post office on Kikar Haatzmaut, the Four Seasons is to the right, the last hotel on the beach at the farthest set of steps to the beach.

Not only is its beach a jewel, but Netanya itself is the center of the diamond-cutting industry. You are welcome to visit the factories and watch the craftsmen at work; and you may even purchase diamonds at unusually low prices through the government's special tax-free program for tourists. Now that's an inducement!

Being in the very center of the Sharon coast, Netanya is only seventeen miles from Caesarea, with its fascinating Roman and Crusader ruins. It's sixty miles from Jerusalem, and half that distance to upper Galilee, so all these areas are within a day's excursion.

In addition to the five Kibbutz Guest Houses along the coast, Israel offers yet another type of facility, the Holiday Village. Of the eight, five are along the Mediterranean coast. The others are in the Eilat and Sharm-e-Sheikh areas far to the south. The French Village (C.E.T.) in Ashkelon is in this category, as are Hof Yarok and Kayit Vishayit in the Sharon, and Hof Dor, Neve-Yam, and Achziv in Carmel and Upper Galilee.

Hof Yarok or Green Beach, just south of Netanya, is a very

new, very modern 150-room bungalow colony that has reached out to beach lovers from France. But here too, all you need do is apply. If your French is rusty this is the place to relearn it.

They've done a great deal with stone and wood here. A deserted, treeless shoreline has been transformed into a series of well-designed, low stone and concrete buildings in subdued earth tones. Trees have been planted (a number already offer shade), flower gardens developed, stone walks and plazas laid. As for sports, they have installed an Olympic-size swimming pool (with warm water for the winter months), courts for volley ball, basketball, and tennis, and a riding stable. Horseback riding along the beach in the late afternoon and at dusk is becoming a favorite pastime.

The bungalows are about a hundred yards from the water, so you can easily pop in at sunrise, sunset, or moonrise. As you may have suspected, Hof Yarok is an active place, frequented by young adults and young marrieds. Of course, it's excellent for children. The wood-paneled central dining room is attractive by any standard; kosher dietary laws are strictly observed.

Another Recreation Village, Kayit Vishayit, is undeniably different from Hof Yarok or any of the others. In 1940, a group of young pioneers settled near the ruins of Caesarea and established Kibbutz Sdot Yam—Field of the Sea. Appreciating the importance and historical value of Caesarea, they built the Museum of Caesarea Antiquities, cultivated the fertile land, and were among the first collective settlements to engage in deep-sea fishing. More recently, the enterprising kibbutznikim have ventured into tourism and established the Kayit Vishayit Company—Beach Resort and Recreation Enterprises. They've decided to share their stretch of golden beach and its echoes from the past with all the visitors they can accommodate in the forty-four bungalows they've built in clusters some fifty yards from the sea.

The kibbutz members, realling their pioneering days, chose a very simple but modern design—inverted right triangles. These small but adequate contemporary buildings are large enough for two cots, with the possibility of adding a third, if the squeeze is necessary. Although these bungalows do not contain sanitary fa-

The enterprising "kibbutzniks" of Sdot Yam offer bungalows on the shore for those seeking a different kind of vacation.

cilities, rooms with full facilities and services are available in the kibbutz proper.

This area of the coast is one of the best for deep-sea diving and sailing, and Kayit provides everything you might need on a "for hire" basis. This can be an excellent place to relax and swim, get to know the kibbutz way of life, and see Israel on a shoestring.

Caesarea. In the early 1950s, a young kibbutznik from Sdot Yam, who was working a section of the beach, lowered the blade of his tractor and struck a large "stone." Scraping away sand and debris, he discovered to his astonishment a full-length statue, which turned out to be a headless Roman. The hunt was on. Since then, archeologists and historians have unearthed and pieced together the 2500-year-old story, and today Caesarea is revealed in all its glory: streets, fortifications, aqueducts, reservoirs, homes, churches, synagogues, hippodrome where Christian-eating lions pleased the crowds, and amphitheater. Everything but the amphitheater has been left as it was found.

Large sections of the great aqueducts, built by the Sixth and Tenth Roman legions under Herod the Great to bring water from fifteen miles away, are intact along the beach. Though it has long ceased carrying water, the aqueduct now offers shade to those who want to sleep on the beach, provides privacy for young lovers, and is a convenient place to change a bathing suit. It's all very natural.

But in spite of its pleasant atmosphere, Caesarea mostly generates controversy. At one extreme are those who would like to see Caesarea as the Israeli Riviera competing with anything in the entire Mediterranean as an exclusive playground for the wealthy. At the opposite pole are those who want it to be a resort with mass appeal, à la Coney Island. Fortunately, for the time being, little has happened to move it one way or another.

The beach front of the tapering aqueduct has become one of the most popular along Israel's coast. Thick, warm sands stretch for four miles, and the finely etched dunes at the base of the aqueduct bring an element of romance to the scene.

For reasons yet unknown, the water at Caesarea is far warmer than elsewhere, and lots of fun and thrills can be had diving in the shallows in search of ancient coins. Treasure hunting is another favorite pastime, because the area was inhabited in turn by Jews, Romans, Crusaders, and Ottoman Turks.

Caesarea's sheltered bay and cove in the area of the old Roman port is ringed with Turkish buildings, including some art galleries and restaurants. Should you be on the beach or in the vicinity when the lunch or dinner bell sounds, try the Straton Restaurant, open every day except Thursday. It has a distinguished international cuisine.

But the town itself has little in the way of hotel accommodations, with the exception of the latest addition to the Dan chain of hotels. The five-star Dan Caesarea, opened in October, 1972, is small, only 110 rooms. Its setting on a small hill overlooking the sea is lovely. A unique feature is the magnificent eighteen-hole golf course adjoining it. This is the only golf course in Israel, and it caused quite a stir. Golf courses seem to be a trademark of capitalism (there are none in the Soviet Union or any other Com-

Caesarea's beach is hard to match—anywhere. The ruins and bikinis satisfy most vacationers.

munist country). To put it next door to the Sdot Yam Kibbutz was too much for some people. But that controversy has been settled; in fact, a member of the kibbutz became the golf pro.

The Carmel. Hof Dor, also known as Tantura, is another of the Recreation Villages, this one at the lower edge of Carmel and the pride of Kibbutz Nachsholim.

Hof Dor is situated just off the express highway between Haifa and Tel Aviv, about a half hour's drive from Haifa or an hour from Tel Aviv. A good location for visits to Caesarea, to the Arab and Drusian villages on Mount Carmel, to Haifa, upper Galilee, and Tiberias.

Best of all, Dor, mentioned in the Book of Joshua, has an extraordinary beach. Offshore is a string of four good-sized islands that give protection even during the worst storms, making this an ideal swimming area the whole year round. Hof Dor is a children's paradise because of the calm and protected water. Also, the kibbutz atmosphere is child-centered. Hof Dor is really for single people, young couples, and families with children. Guests are free to make personal contacts with the kibbutz members.

Unlike some of the other villages, this one is small, having but fifty-eight rooms; it does not hold to dietary laws and is open only from May through October. For reservations, write Hof Dor directly at Hof Harcarmel Mobile Post, Israel, or the Tel Aviv address for Kibbutz Guest Houses, noted earlier.

Ten miles and fifteen minutes north is the beach and guest house of Neveh Yam, just a skip away from the ruins of a thirteenth-century Crusader castle at Atlit.

The lawns surrounding the white multi-unit concrete dwellings extend almost to the sea, and they've managed to grow shade trees near the sand. On the beach itself are showers, sanitary facilities, and a café-snack bar that is quite reminiscent of an American hamburger stand.

This is a good sailing and spear-fishing area, and a good place to work on balancing and maneuvering the *haseke*, with its ten-foot double paddle. The waves give you a fast ride hereabouts. If you've never played *pongy*, here's your chance. *Pongy*, another Israeli concoction, is miniature tennis!

The uninhabited beach continues along to Atlit, and any part of this beach is open to you. Simply find a place you like and become a squatter. One afternoon while doing just that, we came across a group of horseback riders who told us how easy it was to go from town to town via the beaches. Unbroken from north to south, the beaches are a natural trail for those who prefer traveling with a touch of adventure.

Mount Carmel, which means "Vineyard of God," cradles the lovely city of Haifa, a lively place surrounded by beaches and resorts. Beyond the large port of Haifa, take the Jaffa Road to Rothschild Avenue. At the end of Rothschild, you come to Rambam Hospital and, to the rear of it, Hof Hashaket, the Quiet Beach. You have to find the entrance gate and pay a fee of about 50 cents. Few people seem to know why this beach is called quiet. Some believe the water is unusually calm here, others say it is because it's away from traffic. Whatever the reason, this is a good place to sunbathe and swim any day except Saturday, the Israeli Sabbath

Horseback riding on the beach at Atlit is a common sight, especially in the cool of late afternoon.

and day of rest. On Saturday morning, particularly, people go to the beach in droves.

The beach has a concrete walk almost to the water's edge, and just off the walk is an umbrella-shaded open-air café. Scattered around the beach are permanent sun shelters, yours for the basking.

Continuing along the Jaffa Road in the direction of Tel Shikmona will bring you to large, flat Carmel Beach on the outskirts of Haifa. Carmel, for which there is a 50-cent fee, has all the amenities and is protected by a breakwater, which makes swimming a little easier.

If you don't wish to pay a fee for using a beach, walk or drive a bit farther until you come to Free Beach. You'll know you're there when you see the buildings of the army base next to it. Free Beach is clean and inviting, but if it's an unusually hot day you'd best bring something to cover your head. Although it has lifeguards, Free Beach has no sun shelters.

The one thing that detracts from the big city beaches is the

Israeli penchant for paddle ball, a game in which two people hit a small, hard ball back and forth with a wooden paddle. When hundreds do this at one time, the din can be deafening. That's one of the reasons why we don't recommend the beaches at Tel Aviv. The noise is deadly, to say nothing of the tricky running required to get to the water between flying balls.

Haifa, Israel's third largest city, with a population of over 200,000, has fewer hotels than a number of smaller towns. However, it does have one of the largest and finest hotels in the country, the five-star Dan Carmel. The outstanding feature of this distinguished hotel is its breathtaking view. Atop Mt. Carmel, it commands an unobstructed panorama of the entire town, the bay area, and north as far as Lebanon.

The Dan Carmel and the two four-star hotels—the Shulamit, also on Mt. Carmel, and the Zion, on Baerwald Street—advertise that they maintain strict kosher dietary laws. Although these two have less than 100 rooms each, it isn't necessary to make reservations six months in advance. Outside of Tel Aviv and Jerusalem, the pressure for rooms is not so great. I might add that since distances between cities in Israel are short, it is a good idea to find accommodations away from those two cities.

Across Haifa Bay, some sixteen miles north, is the walled city of Acre, Akko to the Israelis, a city of white domes and graceful minarets on the sapphire blue Mediterranean. With the development of Haifa's modern harbor, the large ships have left Akko's waters to the fishermen, whose colorful open boats crowd the old harbor, their nets spread to dry on the pillared khans (inns). The most completely preserved Crusader city in the world, Akko is actually two cities, the old and the new. The enchantment lies with the old, of course, and that's also where the best beach is.

Hof Argaman (Beach of Purple), a delightful beach beginning at Akko's sea wall and continuing past the buildings and grounds of the Nautical College, offers a most unusual atmosphere. The sharp contrast between the bikini-clad modern women and the traditional Arab women, heavily draped from head to toe and sometimes veiled, is a rare sight.

To get there, follow Yehoshafat Street right down to the beach

The old walled city of Acre is glorious testimony to the days of old.

and parking lot. Here too, there is an admission fee of 50 cents. Beyond Hof Argaman is Free Beach, but it is not as clean nor does it have the facilities.

At Hof Argaman, you are just a step from Kapuburj, the tree-lined gate leading to Rehov Salah-a-Din and the heart of the old walled city. Follow this street directly to the dazzling white-domed Mosque of Al Jazzar, take a left, and you'll come to the bazaar. The street is crammed with stalls filled with all manner of things to buy; Arab dresses, grapes, vegetables, cakes and candy, jewelry, embroidery, wall hangings—what a way to go to the beach!

Back for a swim and sun bathing and then another visit to the old city. This time make a point of wandering about the court of Al Jazzar's Mosque. Once behind its walls you're in the magic-carpet land of a thousand and one nights. The only way to capture make-believe is to bring a camera loaded with color film. There is so much to see in the old city that each day can be another adventure into the past. Historians believe that it was from these dazzling white sands that glass was first made, and it was from the snails in the bay that the Phoenicians extracted the crimson or purple dye called Tyrian purple.

Relaxing on a beach and swimming always stirs the thought of something good to eat, and the old city can serve that need. Just outside the Mosque of Al Jazzar are several good restaurants that provide an opportunity to enjoy typical Arabic food.

Above Akko are Shavei Zion with its Kibbutz Guest House; Nahariya, whose sole reason for being is its excellent beach, which for us is reason enough; and Achziv, with a Club Mediterranée, just below the Lebanese border.

Shavei Zion is a small and lovely town set between the brilliant blue sea and the green-blanketed Galilean mountains. From here all of western Galilee becomes an easy excursion. Shavei Zion itself is the site of the oldest church excavated in Israel. Its fine mosaics draw thousands of visitors. The town has a lovely park, but best of all is the beach maintained by the kibbutz.

There are only two places to stay in Shavei Zion: the Dolphine House, a three-star, sixty-four-room hotel, and the Kibbutz Guest House, Beit Chava, which has bungalow accommodations for about ninety people. Both observe the dietary laws.

Nahariya in the heart of upper Galilee is quiet, friendly, and charming. Horse-drawn carriages jangle their way past gardens of oleander and open-air cafés to the esplanade and Galei Galil Beach. The Ga'aton Brook, flanked by stately eucalyptus trees, divides the boulevard in two, as it flows through the center of town to the long, wide, handsome beach.

Nahariya has several municipal beaches and free beaches, but Galei Galil, which charges a fee, is clean and safe, protected both by a breakwater and by experienced lifeguards. The beach also has an Olympic-size swimming pool, a children's pool, cafés, restaurants, and a variety of sports facilities. To the left of the beach is a lush green park, ablaze with flowers. For anyone craving moments of quiet solitude, all you need do is cross Ga'aton Brook.

Sailing, water skiing, and skin diving are the rage here, and the equipment can be hired. Although Nahariya has become popular as a honeymoon resort, all ages can be seen parading on the boulevard and sipping drinks at the cafés. At night, this little town is a beehive of activity, especially in the discos and nightclubs.

There's no space problem here. Nahariya has at least twenty hotels, including the four-star seventy-five-room Carlton, right on the boulevard, a few hundred yards from the beach. With the exception of the twenty-six-room three-star Astar next door to the Carlton, all the hotels observe dietary laws.

North of Nahariya the sandy sunshine coast gives way to small rocky beaches. As a consequence, there are more intimate and secluded spots, a welcome change from the long, flat beaches of the Sharon and south.

The kibbutz of Gesher Haziv selected this site for their guest house, which has become so popular that a new wing with forty-six rooms is under construction. It's a lovely spot on a low hill overlooking the sea. They've done a beautiful job of landscaping, so that dining becomes particularly pleasant as you look out the huge picture windows. The kibbutz has many Canadian and American members; consequently, almost everyone speaks fluent English. The beach is in the shadow of the ancient Achziv ruins. Dive off the rocks and look around in the crystal-clear water for ancient remains, which are yours if you can retrieve them.

A very different sort of holiday is in store just a short distance away at the Club Mediterranée, exclusively for members. The iron gates can be opened only by the guard on the inside and then only on orders from the director. The security is incredible, but so is the Club. The number of people hanging around trying to get in on any pretext, to eat at its sumptuous tables, play on its well-cared-for beach, and use its many facilities attest to its desirability.

Reservations for Club Med may be made through offices of Club Mediterranée, in New York City, or through American Express travel agencies. As in the other Clubs, it helps to speak French here, but it isn't absolutely necessary. Here, too, all ages mingle with no difficulty. This Club is of the South Sea Island variety, with thatched huts and community facilities. It's for those who don't mind roughing it.

From here, all of western Galilee as far as Golan and the Syrian border are open to you. The Sea of Galilee (also called Lake Kinneret and Lake Tiberias) is an easy one-day junket.

It seems to be a fact that the entire coast from Ashkelon to Achziv is one long beach. You only have to choose the type of beach and how far you want to be from the main cities.

Shopping. No trip to Israel could be complete without shopping. From the sophisticated boutiques of Tel Aviv to the chattering, bustling, aromatic bazaars of Jerusalem and Akko, shopping becomes an adventure rather than a chore.

With the "ingathering" of people from almost every country in the world, a melting pot if there ever was one, Israel has brought together talents and skills as disparate as diamond cutting, carpet weaving, and glass blowing. Israel is truly a marketplace, and the time-honored tradition of bargaining has attained the level of an art form. Just about everyone does it, including most shops as well as stalls, flea markets, and the bazaars.

You'll find a variety of copper and ceramic items, silver and Oriental jewelry, religious articles (Christian, Moslem, and Jewish), carpets, furs, and diamonds. Knitwear, sportswear, suede and leather goods from such well-known exporters as Beged-Or, Goltex, and Aled by Iwanir are available at prices substantially lower than in Europe or the States.

Visitors paying with travelers or personal checks are entitled to an additional 15 percent off on shoes, sandals, clothing, jewelry, leather, and carpets. Shops offering this service display a sign on their windows. There is also a 30 percent reduction in the price of leather goods bought in shops but delivered to the airport or pier.

At Lod Airport, and at the Dan Hotel in Tel Aviv, the Accadia in Herzliya, King David in Jerusalem, Dan Carmel in Haifa, and the Ayeleth Hashachar Guest House in upper Galilee, near Safad, Eshkar Duty Free shops can be your best buys. Large selections of watches, cameras, perfumes, and liquors, as well as first-class Israeli products are generally available.

Small diamonds are an Israeli specialty, and there is a flourishing jewelry trade, which caters to a wide range of tastes and pocketbooks. Jewelers work in both European and Oriental styles, creating an extraordinary variety of ornament. East and west have met in Israel with often fascinating and highly original results. Much used in Israeli jewelry is the Eilat stone. Ranging in color from clear turquoise to light green, it lends itself well to gold and silver settings. Ask to see it.

Israeli craftsmen have produced candelabras, serving dishes, coffee sets, crosses, candlesticks, and Torah crowns in silver, black iron, copper, brass, and bronze. Equally attractive are the products of the potter's wheel—indigenous contemporary art forms, free-flowing shapes and angular lines, as well as more simple styles.

The Jerusalem House of Quality at 12 Hebron Road is becoming world famous as an exhibition and sales gallery of top Israeli craftsmen. Visiting hours are Sunday and Thursday from 10 A.M. to 10 P.M. and Friday from 10 A.M. to 1 P.M.

Keep the name Maskit in mind. Maskit's three Handicraft Galleries, in the El Al Building in Tel Aviv, at 6 Nordau Street in Haifa, and in the Hasharon Hotel in Herzliya, are good sources for a full line of Israeli handicrafts.

For distinctive Arabic gifts and souvenirs, *nargilehs* (water pipes), *khaffiyehs* (traditional Arab headdress), and the colorful hand-embroidered dresses unique to the Bedouin women of the Negev may be purchased in a number of shops, or bargained for, even haggled over, in the bazaars.

Compared to the Grand Bazaar in Istanbul, the Arab quarter of Jerusalem is a pleasure to stroll through. There is a calmness, an ease here. The shopkeepers do not jump all over you trying to drag you in, and there are no "steerers" trying to press you into shops. Nor do the children try to sell everything that isn't nailed down.

Some of my most pleasurable moments were just sitting and talking with shopkeepers while Anita, Andi, and Dana tested their bargaining technique against these veterans. I'm sure they didn't win, but we all enjoyed it.

The Arabs in the old city have a patience and hospitality not often found among their cousins in other Mediterranean countries. They seem really to enjoy the tourists, and their calmness can be infectious. It also helps business.

Remember to look for the "Recommended for Tourists" signs of the Ministry of Tourism when shopping, but at the same time, don't overlook the small shops on the side streets. It often pays to shop away from the main thoroughfares.

Remember too, that most shops close at four on Friday afternoon and do not open until sundown on Saturday. Sunday is a normal working day. Israel also practices the Middle Eastern siesta, with shops closed from one to three. So—buy it now!

Food and Drink. As you would expect, Israeli food is not indigenous, but consists of a welter of dishes brought from around the world. The result is that in the major towns you can expect to find Rumanian, Indian, Greek, Turkish, Italian, Chinese, German, Arabic, and Yemenite specialties as well as hamburger and fried chicken.

Often, the décor of the restaurant reflects the owner's native land. Service, on the other hand, reflects the individual as well as the temper of the times, and in this Israel is no exception, except that it is still young. At times the service is good, even excellent, but it can also be poor. Realizing this, the Ministry of Tourism has established schools to train service workers. Time is on their side.

Some dishes that Israel has adopted are hot, spicy Rumanian lamb, kebab fashion, called *batracian*; Hungarian *guvetch*, a goulash of eggplant, squash, sausage, and onions; and *kreplach*, a meat-filled dumpling like Chinese wonton or Italian ravioli. And *kishke*, that Jewish haggis, is not to be excluded, nor Holstein schnitzel—a Wiener schnitzel with a fried egg topped with anchovy.

However, if one dish could be said to be pure Israeli it's *Falafel*, a sort of sandwich. In fact it is a *pitta* stuffed with deep-fried balls of chick peas, tomatoes, coleslaw, sliced green peppers, and an overlay of *tehina*, a sesame-seed paste. *Pitta* is a soft, flat, round Arabic bread. Usually it is cut on the flat side, and the pouch is filled with all kinds of goodies.

Speaking of *pitta*, one of the most luscious, mouth-watering affairs is a *schwama*, a meal in itself. We recommend it in place of a sit-down lunch. The pouch of a pitta is stuffed (literally) with generous cuts of lamb (grilled on a vertical rotisserie), tomatoes, cucumber salad, pickles, peppers, and a dollop of hot sauce. What can you say but wow! They've obviously found the answer to the problem of keeping a sandwich from falling apart.

A *schwama* and a cold drink are really all anyone needs to be comfortably full. We found that a *schwama* and a half could easily replace dinner. At 60 to 65 cents each, that's hard to beat for anyone trying to stretch a buck. In Jerusalem, food stands serving *schwamas* are found around Zion Plaza and Nathan Strauss and King George Streets.

Israelis like to eat; in fact, they overdo it. Catering to this national pastime are hundreds of restaurants throughout the country. This is not meant to be a restaurant guide (of which there are many), but we mention a few places to keep in mind should you be in the vicinity.

In Tel Aviv, try the Sitar Curry House, at 10 Shalom Aleichem Street, some hundred yards west of the El Al Building. It serves exotic but inexpensive Indian dishes; soup, meat curry, vegetables, dessert, and wine cost about $2.50.

In Jerusalem, just a walk from the American Colony Hotel at Nablus Road and St. George Street, toward the old city, is the Arabesque. This is an Arab-Israeli restaurant frequented by few tourists. It is inexpensive and serves typical Arab dishes.

I might add that this area of town is Jerusalem's red-light district, but is not so noted on any tourist maps. Although this most ancient of professions is considered illegal, its continued practice in one of the world's oldest cities must attest to man's inherently contradictory nature.

Up from Herod's Gate, near the post office on Saladin Street is the Golden Chicken, an unusually good Arab restaurant. Here two can eat lamb chops and kebab, grilled chicken, fish, and filet mignon with all the trimmings, Arab-style, including Turkish coffee, for about $4.

In Haifa, two quite different establishments should be sampled. In the center of town at 2 Habankim Street is Bankers Tavern, a gourmet-type restaurant specializing in seafood but ready to prepare many international dishes. In the Mt. Carmel area, at 2 Wedgewood Avenue, there is an interesting and bustling dairy restaurant called Zvika's. It is run by two former paratroopers, friends of Zvika Kestler who had the original idea. In the States we'd call it a pancake house, as the specialty is pancakes, some eight varieties. In addition, it is big on salads, fish, omelets, and blintzes.

Two hotel restaurants, expensive but good, with the type of service all hotels should strive for, are the Accadia Grand Hotel in Herzliya and the Four Seasons in Netanya. Both dining rooms are beautifully decorated and have lovely views of the beach and sea. Both have international cuisine and are open to the public.

Be prepared for Israeli breakfasts. Be prepared for olives, black and green, fresh tomatoes and cucumbers, sliced carrots, green peppers, and cheese! And to wash it all down, *leban* or *eschel*, two yogurtlike drinks that you eat with a spoon. Between seven and ten-thirty every morning the whole country is eating this.

Don't be surprised to find *gaspacho* (sometimes written *gashpacho*) on menus. But it's not the Spanish vegetable soup; in Israel *gaspacho* can be anything from a cold cucumber consommé to a vegetable salad. It's a good idea to ask before ordering.

GOVERNMENT TOURIST OFFICES

Information can be obtained from the offices listed here as well as from your own travel agent.

Portuguese Government Tourist Information Bureau
570 Fifth Avenue, New York, N.Y. 10036

Spanish National Tourist Office
589 Fifth Avenue, New York, N.Y. 10017

French Government Tourist Office
610 Fifth Avenue, New York, N.Y. 10020

Italian Government Travel Office—ENIT
630 Fifth Avenue, New York, N.Y. 10020

Malta Mission to the UN
249 East 35th Street, New York, N.Y. 10016

Yugoslav State Tourist Office
509 Madison Avenue, New York, N.Y. 10022

Turkish Government Tourism and Information Office
500 Fifth Avenue, New York, N.Y. 10036

Consulate General of Cyprus
820 Second Avenue, New York, N.Y. 10017

Israel Government Tourist Office
488 Madison Avenue, New York, N.Y. 10022

Index

Achziv, Israel, 237, 238, 240, 247, 256, 257
Adana, Turkey, 214
Adra, Spain, 58
Agde, France, 89
Aguadulce, Spain, 49, 58
Águilas, Spain, 60, 61
Aiguablava, Spain, 38, 71-72
Aix en Provence, France, 94
Akko, Israel, 240, 254, 256, 258
Alanya, Turkey, 184, 207, 209, 212-213, 214
Albacete, Spain, 40
Albufeira, Portugal, 5, 12, 20-24
Algarve coast (Portugal), 1-33
   accommodations, 5-7
   beaches, 7-28
   climate, 1-2
   food and drink, 30-33
   places of interest, 28-33
   shopping, 29-30
   transportation, 2-4
   See also names of cities and towns
Algeciras, Spain, 49

Alghero, Sardinia, 100
Alicante, Spain, 38
Almansa, Spain, 40, 61
Almeria, Spain, 49, 57, 58, 79
Almuñécar, Spain, 49, 56
Alvor, Portugal, 5
Ampurias, Spain, 73
Anamur, Turkey, 213-214
Ancona, Italy, 155
Ankara, Turkey, 184
Antalya, Turkey, 207, 208, 209
Antequera, Spain, 40
Arcos de la Frontera, Spain, 38, 47
Argelès, France, 89, 90
Arles, France, 82, 92
Armação de Pêra, Portugal, 16-20
Artés, Spain, 40
Arzachena, Sardinia, 115
Ashdod, Israel, 240, 242-243
Ashkelon, Israel, 237, 238, 240, 241-242, 247
Aspendos, Turkey, 210, 212
Atlit, Israel, 252
Avignon, France, 92

Ayamonte, Spain, 4

Badajoz, Spain, 4
Baia Sardinia, 115
Banyuls-sur-Mer, France, 89, 90
Bar, Yugoslavia, 154, 155, 175
Barcelona, Spain, 36, 67, 77, 78, 84
Bari, Italy, 154, 155, 175
Barlavento (Algarve coast), 2
Barumini, Sardinia, 114
Bečići Beach, Yugoslavia, 167
Beja, Portugal, 4
Benicarló, Spain, 40, 65
Benidorm, Spain, 62
Béziers, France, 84, 89
Bilbao, Spain, 78
Biodola, Elba, 122, 129
Blue Grotto (Malta), 146
Bodrum, Turkey, 182, 201-204, 209
Boka Kotorska (Yugoslavia), 164, 165, 177
Bosnia and Hercegovina, 151, 177
Brindisi, Italy, 198
Budva, Yugoslavia, 155, 164, 165, 167, 168, 178

Cabo de Gata (Spain), 58
Cabo de Palos (Spain), 59
Cabo de São Vicente, Portugal, 27-28
Cadaqués, Spain, 75
Cádiz, Spain, 38, 41, 42, 46, 47, 77
Caesarea, Israel, 240, 247, 248, 249-251
Cagliari, Sardinia, 98, 100, 114, 115-116
Cala de Volpe, Sardinia, 104, 105-106
Calahonda, Spain, 57
Caldas, Portugal, 30
Calella de la Costa, Spain, 68
Calpe, Spain, 62-63
Campo de Tenis (Spain), 54
Canet de Mar, Spain, 68
Cap d'Agde, France, 82, 89

Cape Andreas, Cyprus, 221, 231
Cape San Antonio, Spain, 63
Capoliveri, Elba, 128
Caprera (island), 104, 108
Capriccioli, Bay of, 96
Capriccioli, Sardinia, 117
Carcassone, France, 86, 92, 94
Carmel, Israel, 240, 251-258
Carmel Beach, Israel, 253
Carvoeiro, Portugal, 14-16
Casares, Spain, 50-51
Castell de Ferro, Spain, 57
Castellón de la Plana, Spain, 64-65
Cavo, Elba, 120
Cavoli, Elba, 127-128
Cavtat, Yugoslavia, 155, 162, 164
Cesme, Turkey, 195-198
Ceşmealti, Turkey, 189
Cetinje, Yugoslavia, 177-178
Chios (island), 198
Chipiona, Spain, 46, 47-48
Civitavecchia, Italy, 100, 101
Colaki, Turkey, 211
Collioure, France, 89, 90
Comino (island), 131, 132, 133, 136, 138
Cominotto (island), 131
Coral Bay, Cyprus, 227-228
Corquinyoli, El (Spain), 69
Cospicua, Malta, 149
Costa Blanca (Spain), 34, 35-36, 39, 40, 58-64, 80
Costa Brava (Spain), 34-35, 38, 39, 68-75, 79
Costa de la Luz (Spain), 34, 36, 38, 39, 40, 41-49
Costa del Azahar (Spain), 34, 35, 38, 39, 40, 64-66, 80
Costa del Sol (Spain), 34, 36, 38, 39, 49-58, 80
Costa Dorada (Spain), 34, 35, 38, 66-68

INDEX

Costa Smeralda (Sardinia), 96, 98, 102-108, 117
Côte d'Azur (France), 82, 89
Côte Vermeille (France), 89
Curium, ruins of, 233
Cyprus, 214, 217-236
    beaches, 221-231
    climate, 218, 220
    food and drink, 234-236
    places of interest, 231-233
    shopping, 233-234
    transportation, 220-221
    See also names of cities and towns

Dalmatia, 151, 152, 158, 164, 180
Dead Sea, 238, 242
Denia, Spain, 62, 63-64
Denizli, Turkey, 208
Deran Sveti Nikola, Yugoslavia, 175
Didymi, 198, 201
Diplomats Beach, Israel, 240
Dubrovnik, Yugoslavia, 152, 154, 155, 156, 161, 167, 169, 175-176, 178, 179

Eilat, Israel, 238, 242, 247
Elba, 117-130
    beaches, 120-129
    climate, 119
    food and drink, 129-130
    places of interest, 129
    transportation, 119-120
    See also names of cities and towns
El Grao de Castellón, Spain, 64
El Rompido, Spain, 44
El Saler, Spain, 64
Elvas, Portugal, 27
Elviria, Spain, 52
Emerald Coast, *see* Costa Smeralda
Ephesus, 198, 201, 209
Estepona, Spain, 49, 50, 54
Estremoz, Portugal, 5
Évora, Portugal, 4, 27

Famagusta, Cyprus, 214, 220, 221-224, 232-233
Faro, Portugal, 2, 3, 12, 27, 29, 30
Filfla (island), 131
Five Mile Beach, Cyprus, 226
Foça, Turkey, 191-195
Fontanilla, La (Spain), 46
Fornells, Spain, 72
Forte Village complex (Sardinia), 108-113
Fort St. Angelo, Malta, 149
Foxes, Bay of (Sardinia), 98, 102
France, *see* Languedoc-Roussillon coast
Free Beach, Israel, 253, 256
Fuengirola, Spain, 49, 51, 53-54
Fuentebravia, Spain, 47

Ga'Aton Brook (Israel), 257
Galei Galil Beach, Israel, 257
Galilee, 238, 240, 247, 251, 256, 257, 258, 259
Galilee, Sea of, 238, 258
Gandia, Spain, 66
Garrucha, Spain, 59, 60
Ggantija, Gozo, 146
Ghajn Tuffieha, Malta, 138, 145
Ghajn Tuffieha Bay, Malta, 138
Gharb, Gozo, 143, 145
Gibraltar, 49
Gijón, Spain, 39
Golden Bay, Malta, 138
Gozo (island), 131, 133, 136, 138, 142-145, 146
Granada Province (Spain), 55, 57
Grand Harbour, Malta, 149
Green Beach (Hof Yarok), Israel, 247-248
Gruissan, France, 82

Hadera, Israel, 240
Ħaġar Qim, Malta, 146

Haifa, Israel, 240, 251, 252, 254, 259, 262
Hercegovina, see Bosnia and Hercegovina
Herzliya, Israel, 240, 244-245, 259, 262
Hierapolis, Turkey, 208
Hof Argaman, Israel, 254-255
Hof Dor (Tantura), Israel, 240, 247, 251-252
Hof Hashaket, Israel, 252
Hof Yarok, see Green Beach, Israel
Huelva, Spain, 42
Hula Valley, Israel, 238
Hvar, Yugoslavia, 155
Hypogeum (Malta), 145

Incekum Beach, Turkey, 211-212
Iskenderun, Turkey, 209
Is Morus (Sardinia), 112
Israel, 237-262
　beaches, 240-258
　climate, 238
　food and drink, 260-262
　shopping, 258-260
　transportation, 239-240
　See also names of cities and towns
Istanbul, Turkey, 181, 182, 184, 188, 208, 209, 214, 238
Izmir, Turkey, 182, 184-189, 191, 198, 208, 209, 214

Jávea, Spain, 62, 63, 64
Jerez de la Frontera, Spain, 46, 47, 48
Jerusalem, 242, 247, 258, 259, 260, 261, 262

Kamenari, Yugoslavia, 165
Karavas, Cyprus, 226
Karavastasi, Cyprus, 227
Kayit Vishayit, Israel, 247, 248-249
Kiryat Yam, Israel, 240

Kiti, Cyprus, 233
Koločep (island), 158
Korčula, Yugoslavia, 155
Kotor, Yugoslavia, 165-167
Ktima, Cyprus, 227
Kupari, Yugoslavia, 155, 158-159
Kupari Bay, Yugoslavia, 159
Kusadasi, Turkey, 184, 194, 198-201, 209
Kyrenia, Cyprus, 217, 221, 224-227, 234

La Barrosa, Spain, 46
La Escala, Spain, 73
Lagos, Portugal, 6, 7-9
La Granadella, Spain, 63
La Grande Motte, France, 82, 83, 84, 90-92
La Maddalena, 108
Languedoc-Roussillon coast (France), 82-95
　beaches, 86-92
　climate, 84
　places of interest, 92-95
　transportation, 84-85
　See also names of cities and towns
La Puntilla Beach, Spain, 46
Larnaca, Cyprus, 220, 221, 230-231
Las Antillas, Spain, 44
Lefkara, Cyprus, 233-234
L'Embouchure de l'Aude, France, 82
Lepetane, Yugoslavia, 165
Leucate-Barcarès, France, 82, 85-89
Levante Beach, Spain, 62
Limassol, Cyprus, 220, 221, 228-230, 238
Lion, Gulf of, 82
Lisbon, Portugal, 2, 6, 27
Liscia di Vacca, Sardinia, 104
Livorno, Italy, 120
Lloret de Mar, Spain, 68-69
Lokrum (island), 158
Lopud (island), 158

INDEX 269

Loulé, Portugal, 29

Macho Castle (Spain), 65
Maddalena (island), 104, 108
Madrid, Spain, 38, 76, 77, 78, 80, 85
Maiden's Castle (Turkey), 214
Málaga, Spain, 38, 39, 49, 79
Malgrat, Spain, 68
Malta, 131-150
  beaches, 134-143
  climate, 132
  food and drink, 150
  places of interest, 143-150
  transportation, 132-134
  See also names of cities and towns
Manavgat, Turkey, 212
Marbella, Spain, 49, 51-53, 54, 80
Maresme, El (Spain), 67-68
Marfa, Malta, 142, 145
Marina di Camp, Elba, 125-127
Marmaris, Turkey, 204-207, 208, 209
Mar Menor (Spain), 61
Marsalforn, Malta, 145
Marseille, France, 84, 86, 238
Masnóu, Spain, 68
Mazagón, Spain, 42-43
Mazarrón, Spain, 61
Mdina, Malta, 147-149
Medina Sidonia, Spain, 46, 48
Mellieha, Malta, 138
Mellieha Bay, Malta, 137-138, 145
Mersin, Turkey, 207, 209, 214, 215, 220, 232
Mġarr, Gozo, 142, 145
Mġarr, Malta, 142
Michmoret, Israel, 240
Mijas, Spain, 55
Mlini, Yugoslavia, 160-162
Mnjadra, Malta, 146
Moguer, Spain, 46
Mojácar, Spain, 39, 59-61, 76
Monchique, Portugal, 30, 32
Montecristo (island), 125

Monte Gordo, Portugal, 27
Montenegro, 151, 152, 164-175
Montes de Alvor, Portugal, 5
Montpellier, France, 82, 84
Morinj, Yugoslavia, 165
Mostar, Yugoslavia, 176-177
Motril, Spain, 49, 57
Mount Carmel, 251, 252, 254
Murcia Province (Spain), 77

Nahariya, Israel, 240, 256, 257
Narbonne, France, 84, 86, 92
Nebioglu, Turkey, 189
Neretva Gorge (Yugoslavia), 176
Nerja, Spain, 49, 55
Netanya, Israel, 240, 246-247, 262
Neveh Yam, Israel, 240, 247, 252
New Beach, Yugoslavia, 159
Nicosia, Cyprus, 220, 221, 224, 234
Nîmes, France, 84, 92, 95
Nitzanim, Israel, 240, 242
Nuro, Sardinia, 115

Oawra, Malta, 140
Olbia, Sardinia, 100, 115
Olhão, Portugal, 29
Oropesa del Mar, Spain, 65-66
Ortano, Elba, 128-129

Pachyammos Beach, Cyprus, 225
Palau, Sardinia, 108
Palmahim, Israel, 240, 244
Palos de la Frontera, Spain, 42, 46
Pamukkale, Turkey, 208
Paola, Malta, 145-146
Paphos, Cyprus, 217, 221, 223, 227-228
Paradise Bay, Malta, 139-140
Paradise Beach, Cyprus, 231
Patras, Greece, 198
Pelegrin Hills (Yugoslavia), 159
Peñiscola, Spain, 65
Perast, Yugoslavia, 165

INDEX

Perge, Turkey, 209-210, 212
Perpignan, France, 82, 84, 86
Pescara, Italy, 155
Petra tou Romiou (Cyprus), 227
Petrovak, Yugoslavia, 175
Piñar Beach, Spain, 64, 65
Pineda, Spain, 68
Piombino, Italy, 117, 119-120
Piombino Marittima, Italy, 120
Piraeus, Greece, 198
Platres, Cyprus, 229-230
Playa de Herradura, Spain, 55
Playa de Nueva Umbria, Spain, 44
Playa de Perdigón, Spain, 44
Polis, Cyprus, 227
Port Ambonne, France, 89
Portimão, Portugal, 6, 12, 29, 30, 32
Port Lligot, Spain, 75
Porto Azzurro, Elba, 120, 128
Porto Cervo, Sardinia, 104, 105, 107-108, 117
Porto de Pitrizza, Sardinia, 104
Portoferraio, Elba, 119, 120-123, 129
Porto Rotondo, Sardinia, 104
Porto Torres, Sardinia, 101
Portugal, see Algarve coast
Port Vendres, France, 90
Praia da Rocha, Portugal, 5, 6-7, 9-13
Praia de Cabanos, Portugal, 27
Praia dos Três Irmãos, Portugal, 13-14
Priene, 198, 201
Procchio, Elba, 123-125
Provence, France, 94
Puerto de Lumbreras, Spain, 40
Puerto de Mazarrón, Spain, 61
Puerto de Santa Maria, Spain, 46, 47
Punta de la Mona (Spain), 55-56
Punta del Sebo, Spain, 44
Punta d'es Mut (Spain), 71
Punta Umbria, Spain, 44

Quarteira, Portugal, 23-27, 32

Quercy, France, 92
Quinto do Lago (Portugal), 25, 32

Rabat, Gozo, see Victoria, Gozo
Rabat, Malta, 136, 144, 147
Rábida Monastery (Spain), 46
Ramat Hasharon, Israel, 240
Ramla Tal-Bir Bay (Malta), 136-137
Red Sea, 238
Rehov Salah-a-Din, Israel, 256
Rhodes, 204
Risan, Yugoslavia, 165
Roca Grossa (Spain), 68
Romazzino, Sardinia, 104, 106-107
Ronda, Spain, 53
Roquetas de Mar, Spain, 58
Rosas, Spain, 73
Rota, Spain, 46, 47
Rouergue, France, 92

Safad, Israel, 259
S'Agaró, Spain, 70, 71
Sagres, Portugal, 5
Saint-Cyprien-Plage, France, 82, 89-90
St. Julian, Malta, 140-142, 144
St. Pauls Bay, Malta, 140
St. Tropez, France, 89
Salamis, ruins of, 232
Salina Bay, Malta, 140
Salobreña, Spain, 56-57
Salt Lake (Cyprus), 233
Sancti Petri, Spain, 46
San Felíu de Guixols, Spain, 69-70
Sanlúcar de Barrameda, Spain, 47
San Pedro de Alcántara, Spain, 49, 51
San Pol de Mar, Spain, 68
San Roque, Spain, 49
Santa Cristina, Spain, 69
Santa Margherita di Pula, Sardinia, 108-113

INDEX

São Brás de Alportel, Portugal, 5, 29
Sarajevo, Yugoslavia, 177
Sardinia, 96-117
  climate, 98, 100
  Costa Smeralda, 96, 98, 102-108, 117
  food and drink, 116-117
  places of interest, 114-115
  shopping, 115-116
  southern coast, 108-114
  transportation, 100-102
  See also names of cities and towns
Sa Riera, Spain, 73
Sassari, Sardinia, 115
Scutari, Lake (Yugoslavia), 178
Senglea, Malta, 149
Seville, Spain, 4, 27, 38, 46, 77, 78, 79
Shar-e-Sheikh, Israel, 247
Sharon, Israel, 240, 244-249
Shavei Zion, Israel, 240, 256-257
Shefayim, Israel, 240, 245-246
Side, Turkey, 210, 212
Silifke, Turkey, 184, 214
Silves, Portugal, 29
Sinai, 242
Siniscola, Sardinia, 115
Sitges, Spain, 66-67
Sliema, Malta, 140, 141
Slovenska Beach, Yugoslavia, 167
Sotavento (Algarve coast), 2
Spain, 34-81
  accommodations, 38-41
  beaches, 41-75
  coastline areas, 34-36
  food and drink, 78-81
  shopping, 76-78
  transportation, 36, 38
  See also names of cities and towns
Spartaia, Elba, 124
Split, Yugoslavia, 155
Strp, Yugoslavia, 165
Sutomore, Yugoslavia, 175

Sveti Stefan, Yugoslavia, 155, 164, 165, 168-169, 170
Syracuse, Sicily, 133

Ta'Cenc (Gozo), 142-143
Tantura, see Hoff Dor, Israel
Ta'Qali, Malta, 149
Tarifa, Spain, 48, 49
Tarxien, Malta, 146
Tavira, Portugal, 27, 28-29
Tel Aviv, Israel, 240, 244, 254, 258, 259, 261
Termessos, Turkey, 212
Tiberias, Israel, 251
Titograd, Yugoslavia, 178
Torremolinos, Spain, 49, 51, 54, 55
Tossa de Mar, Spain, 69
Turkey, 181-216
  beaches, 188-215
  climate, 182
  food and drink, 215-216
  transportation, 182, 184
  See also names of cities and towns

Ulcinj, Yugoslavia, 155, 170-175, 178

Valdilagrana Beach, Spain, 47
Vale de Lobo (Portugal), 5, 25-26, 32
Valencia, Gulf of, 64
Valencia, Spain, 38, 64, 77, 78
Valetta, Malta, 133, 139, 140, 141, 144, 145, 146, 149
Varosha, Cyprus, 221, 224, 233
Vejer de la Frontera, Spain, 48
Verdala Palace (Malta), 147
Victoria (Rabat), Gozo, 142, 144, 145
Vilamoura (Portugal), 26-27
Vila Real de Santo António, Portugal, 29, 30
Vista de los Angeles (Spain), 59
Vittoriosa, Malta, 149
Vjetrenica (Yugoslavia), 177

Wied-iż-Żurrieq, Malta, 146

Yavneh, Israel, 244
Yugoslavia, 151-180
   beaches, 156-175
   camping, 155-156
   climate, 152, 154
   food and drink, 178-180
   places of interest, 175-178
   transportation, 154-155
   See also names of cities and towns

Żabbar, Malta, 144
Zagreb, Yugoslavia, 154
Zamora, Spain, 40
Zavala, Yugoslavia, 177
Żejtun, Malta, 146
Żurrieq, Malta, 145